Drew's Blues

Drew Page, 1942

Drew's Blues

A Sideman's Life
with the Big Bands

DREW PAGE

Louisiana State University Press / Baton Rouge and London

Copyright © 1980 by Louisiana State University Press
All rights reserved
Manufactured in the United States of America

Designer: Albert Crochet
Typeface: VIP Goudy Old Style
Typesetter: G & S Typesetters, Inc.
Printer and binder: Thomson-Shore, Inc.

LIBRARY OF CONGRESS CATALOGING IN PUBLICATION DATA

Page, Drew, 1905–
  Drew's blues.

  Includes index.
  1. Page, Drew, 1905–   2. Jazz musicians—
United States—Biography. I. Title.
ML419.P35A3   785.42'092'4   [B]   80-12942
ISBN 0-8071-0686-0

*For all the wonderful band leaders, singers,
entertainers, and sideman musicians who
contributed to this book by just being themselves*

Contents

Illustrations following pages 54, 112

Preface

        BECAUSE OF MY fifty-two years as a full-
time musician and because I am one of the few left who could tell
what went on in the jazz and pop music business during that time,
various people have suggested that I write some of my memories.
Responding to their suggestions, I retired temporarily in 1976 to
devote my full attention to the project. I would like to thank my
editor, Judith Bailey, for her meticulous attention to detail during
the production of the book.

    The music business was fun, and though I didn't make a lot of
money (I found I could live cheaper without it) in my years in the
business, I have no regrets. Naturally, I don't have many lumps under the rug, but I have all the little things I need, and I don't need
two of everything. And money couldn't have bought all the fun I
had or as good a wife or better friends. For me, work was a half
century of travel vacation with pay (such as it was). The hard part
was staying alive long enough to start the traveling, for I had a beginning so humble there was no way to go but up.

Drew's Blues

1

I WAS BORN on January 5, 1905, near Mineral Wells, Texas, in a shack out on the east bank of the Brazos River. There were already six in the family—my parents, a brother eighteen months old, and my mother's three teenagers by a former marriage, two girls and a boy.

Because my mother was in ill health, the family had come to Mineral Wells hoping that the water there would be beneficial to her. It wasn't, and in 1907 we moved to Sinton, down near the Gulf Coast. My oldest sister had married, and she stayed in Mineral Wells, so there were six of us on the 425-mile trip. It was a major move back then, especially since we went by covered wagon, there being few railways and no automobiles or airplanes for cross-country travel. The trip took about six weeks and was mostly through near-virgin territory with the roads no more than buggy tracks.

The wagon was not the luxury type one sees in the movies, but was an ordinary farm wagon expanded to the width of bed springs with home-contrived arches for the canvas cover. It wasn't big enough for all of us to sleep in, so the older kids slept on the ground with the other denizens of the Texas brush country. I vaguely remember fighting mosquitoes, spiders, and scorpions and running scared from snakes and wild animals.

Sinton was no better than Mineral Wells for my mother's health, so after staying there a year or so we went to Denison, up near the Oklahoma line. Grandmother Hendricks lived there, and it was my mother's hometown. I was there on my fourth birthday when I got my first pair of pants. Until then I had worn dresses, graduating to flour sacks with holes cut in them for my arms and head. I told my brother Ben, "You can't call me 'Bubber' anymore; I'm a big boy now." We saw Halley's Comet there a year later (1910), and I expect to be one of the few to see it twice, for it's due again in 1986. I have doubts about seeing it a third time, but you can never tell about musicians.

From Denison we moved to Rogers, Arkansas, still in search of magic water for my mother. Pop bought twenty acres of land a little way out of town at Electric Springs, where steel objects held in the spring water for a moment would become magnetized. I became better acquainted with snakes, wild animals, and various other pests while in Arkansas. Also with poverty. Pop worked in town in a cider mill for fifty cents a day, and that pittance wasn't enough to provide us with luxuries, not even shoes. Pop grew a few things that could be put up for the winter, and such wild edibles as huckleberries, blackberries, hazelnuts, walnuts, chinquapins, hickory nuts, and grapes were all over. And we had chickens, a hog every year, and a cow.

Pop piped water to the backyard from a spring up the hill, so we had running water, except when the water in the pipes froze, and we had to melt ice. Pop would get up early in the morning, kill the copperhead snakes and some of the rats in the kitchen, fix his own breakfast, and set out on his long walk to town, about four miles away.

At night after cooking dinner, washing the dishes, giving Ben and me tick-and-chigger inspection (in season), and salving our poison ivy welts, he read storybooks to us and sometimes played the guitar and the french harp (harmonica). I hadn't even known there were instruments to make musical sounds, as the only music I'd heard before was my sisters' singing. These new sounds fascinated me. The tunes stayed in my head and I learned to play them on the french harp. Our other entertainment was looking at pictures in the stereoscope and playing a card game called Authors. Once a neighbor took us to see a picture show in town, and another time a neighbor brought a talking machine—an Edison that played cylinder records as I recall—and played "Preacher and the

Bear" and "Old Time Religion." I was amazed to find that music could be put on a machine and played back.

Another new contraption was the telephone, and Pop had one put in for emergencies. Since we were a mile off the main line along the buggy road, Pop hooked our line to the barbed wire fence that ran along our lane. We were on a party line for the whole countryside, and sometimes all the parties got on at once, and we would play and sing a concert for them. We were invited to per-form at social gatherings, too.

Ben and I went to school for a couple of months one time—until the weather got too cold for us to go barefoot. We rode bare-back on an old nag that somebody had given Pop. But our real school was at our mother's bedside. She was a fairly well-educated woman for that time in that part of the country, and when we finally started formal school again, back in Denison, we went into the third grade and were at the head of the class in all three Rs and in spelling. The bees always ended with Ben and me trying to spell each other down.

It was in 1914 that we returned to Denison because my mother's illness was terminal, and she wanted to die at home. I was nine when she died. She had been too ill in the last two or three years for us to see her much, and I was too young before that to store away many memories of her, but I remember her always admonish-ing us not to lie, cheat, or steal. She instilled in me an assumption of honesty I have never been able to completely overcome, even after I found that there is almost nothing a completely honest per-son can succeed in, since the term *success* has become nearly syn-onymous with money acquired in any way possible.

Pop got a job at the cotton mill and we moved from Grandma Hendricks' house to one of our own, on Armstrong Street. The house had an indoor toilet, a relatively new convenience I hadn't heard about yet. My half sister Sue told me to pull the string that hung from a water tank near the ceiling, and when I did, I came out yelling. I was afraid I had ruined the thing. There was a bath-tub, too, which sure beat the heck out of washtubs.

I hadn't known any other kids before or even seen very many, but our new neighborhood was teeming with boys. (In those days the girls stayed indoors.) Ben and I got acquainted the hard way, since it was the custom to harass new kids in a neighborhood by throwing rocks at them. The newcomers had to prove themselves. In Arkansas our chief daytime activity had been throwing rocks at trees, snakes, and other objects, and compared to the town kids, we were experts. We went down to the railroad tracks and picked up a supply of throwable rocks, and when we were attacked, we counterattacked, making our territory pretty scarce of boys for a while—till their bruises healed. Then we were accepted, and hostilities settled down to "my dad can whip yours." Our games were marbles, mumbly-peg, shinny, and hoop rolling with a stick guide ("hoop and guide"), and at night we played under the flickering arc lights at the corner of our block. In baseball season we went to the games to watch Roger Hornsby and Ray Querry play, peeping through knotholes in the fence or getting admission by turning in foul balls that came over the grandstand. Once we saw Ty Cobb play an exhibition game, and we heard Hornsby's farewell speech before he left the team to play for St. Louis. Ben and I became ardent baseball enthusiasts and vacant-lot players.

Sue had gone to work at Madden's department store, and she had found a beau, Paul, whom she later married. He owned one of the few automobiles in town and took us on a joyride one night. I had seen a car in Rogers once, a chain-drive Scripps-Booth, but this was the first time I'd been in one. Another big event was the arrival of an airplane in town. Having never heard of the airplane (this was only twelve years after Kitty Hawk), I was awestruck.

When Pop organized a band at the mill, I discovered that there were instruments besides the guitar and the french harp. He played the cornet and could also play tuba and string bass, and I learned that he had been a professional musician for a while in his early youth. He later told me that he had played with a traveling chautauqua band and with the Hagenbeck and Wallace Circus band. In those days, some of the industrial companies that had their own bands tried to hire men who could play music. They advertised and got musicians from all parts of the country, so Pop, thus, had about twenty good players in his band. At one of these concerts I found out that music could be written down to be read and played by others. The sounds began to haunt me. I kept hearing in my head the tunes the band had played, and I wanted to learn to play something besides the french harp.

At Christmastime the band gave Pop a new trumpet, so he gave his old cornet to Ben and me. He wrote the C scale on a staff he drew on a piece of cardboard and marked the fingerings for the notes. But he forgot to give us the mouthpiece, and we were too shy to ask him for it. If it hadn't been for that little oversight, I might have become a trumpet player.

The one outsider in Pop's band was a kid neighbor of ours, Herman Dean, a clarinet player. I was fascinated by his clarinet and would hide out near his house to listen to him practice. He must have been pretty good, for he later became the leader of a navy band.

After a couple of years at the mill, Pop quit to become a carpenter. He married again, and we moved to Ada, Oklahoma, where some construction was going on. Sue stayed in Denison, so the family was down to four. Ben and I lost a year in school because Oklahoma had twelve grades and Texas only eleven, and we were not permitted to skip a grade.

Ada was still pretty primitive, and we moved into the worst part of it. We had gas but no electricity, and the only plumbing was a water faucet on the back porch. The powder room was in the alley out back. The water pipe ran above ground under the stilted house, and in freezing weather we had to crawl under and thaw the ice out of it with newspaper torches. We had one coal-oil lamp to light the whole house. Pop's job was six miles out of town in Byng, and since he had to walk, he was gone by five o'clock and didn't get home until seven. He made two dollars a day, six days a week. We kids washed dishes with the old yellow cake soap, tended the garden in season, buried the garbage, and even resoled our own shoes, with a shoe last to brad the nails on the inside. We got a nickel apiece for the picture show on Saturdays.

I got a job for a while delivering the Ada *Evening News* for $1.50 a week. After the country got involved in the war in 1917, the absence of many of the older kids made more jobs available, but most of our jobs were nonpaying. We chopped cotton and later picked it, pulled peanuts, and gathered peach seeds for use in making gas masks. For a while one summer, I made six dollars a week working in a clothes-cleaning shop. I washed the Sunday clothes in gasoline and the work clothes in water, scrubbing them on a board with a stiff brush and cake soap. Since the shop was in the back of a barbershop, I doubled as shoeshine boy.

I had joined the Boy Scouts at age thirteen, and at sixteen, I became the second Eagle Scout in Oklahoma. Ben and I played baseball, too, and when our eighth grade team played the high school team we beat them so badly that five of us replaced five of the varsity team.

By the time I got into high school the war was over but the boys still had to take military training as a precautionary measure. I didn't like being commanded by the big school bullies, who were naturally made drill sergeants, so when I learned that the boys in the school band were exempt from military training, I decided to join up. The only two instruments left to choose from among those the school furnished were a baritone horn and a trombone. I asked for the trombone, but since my first love had been the clarinet I was anxious to get one. Toward the end of the school year the manual training teacher, Dorsey Bradshaw, who was also my scoutmaster, hired me to help him make furniture in the shop after school and on Saturdays. By the end of the year, I was able to make the down payment on a cheap clarinet.

I practiced ten hours a day through the summer and went into the school band in the fall on second-chair clarinet. One of my best friends, Jimmy McCoy, was the solo clarinet player. At that time the bands played legitimate music, such as the *William Tell*, *Poet and the Peasant*, and *Oberon* overtures. Since band music is mostly transcribed orchestra music, in which the clarinets do the work of the violins, some of it is difficult. I played the parts mostly by rote, for I didn't know the fundamental exercises for gaining facility.

Fortunately, though, when a man named Henry Lambert came to Holdenville, a little town near Ada, to organize a national guard band, I enlisted. Lambert had played first-chair clarinet in the

Ringling Brothers Circus band for thirteen years, and I have never found anyone who knew anything about the clarinet that Henry Lambert didn't know. He told me what and how to practice and showed me a few tricks. I drove my family and neighbors crazy for the next two years, blowing that "dadgummed thing," as Pop put it, six or seven hours a day during the week and ten to twelve on Saturdays and Sundays.

I wanted to become a professional musician, but about the only possibilities then were symphony orchestras, concert bands like John Phillip Sousa's, or theater pit orchestras. Dance or jazz bands were just beginning to become part of the music business, and since dances were not allowed in Ada, I had never even heard a dance band.

In the summer of 1923 when I was eighteen, I answered an ad in *Billboard* magazine for oil-field workers who could play band instruments. I was in good physical condition, having been active in sports at school, so I got the job and went to Salt Creek, Wyoming, near Casper. The company band had never gotten started, but my laborer job was still good. I dug ditches with pick and shovel for a while and later helped a cook set up meals for a work crew out near Teapot Dome. I was offered a job playing in the movie house but refused it because I didn't think I was good enough. That was one of my failings—a belief, handed down by my father, that we Pages were never as good as other people.

Since the cook was a homosexual and I wasn't, I quit the job after a few weeks and left to study clarinet under Boh McKofsky at the A & M college in Stillwater, Oklahoma. McKofsky was a fine clarinet teacher, and apparently, his estimation of me was good, too. He put me on solo clarinet in the summer-term band and encouraged me to attend college there and play the chair in the regular band, with its section of thirty-five clarinets. I intended to accept the offer after I finished high school, but things happened to change my mind. (Twenty-five years later, when Boh was head of the music department at Oklahoma University, he was instrumental in getting me an honorary certificate to teach music in Oklahoma schools, though I never used it.)

Back in Ada, I went through my final year of high school, gradu-

ating in 1924. Sometime during that year, I had filled in with a tent
show orchestra and was offered the job permanently. After the
summer at A & M, I had also been getting offers from some other
schools, and an Oklahoma senator offered to recommend me for
appointment to West Point. As an Eagle Scout, I had also been a
candidate to accompany Admiral Byrd on a mission to explore
Antarctica, but I lost out to an Eagle Sea Scout. It was a disappointment at the time. I was anxious to get out of Ada because my
girl friend had jilted me, and as it happened, I heard that a carnival
band playing in Holdenville needed a clarinet player. I took a train
up there, talked with the leader, and got the job. It paid twenty
dollars a week and a berth in the band car; meal tickets for the
commissary were five dollars a week. I didn't stay with the show
very long, though, because my old scoutmaster, Dorsey Bradshaw,
asked me to go along with him to Phoenix, where he had accepted
a teaching job. I felt I couldn't turn him down.

Bradshaw's job was in Glendale, about eleven miles from downtown Phoenix. I inquired around and learned that there was a good
clarinet teacher, Albert Etzweiler, at Union High school in Phoenix. He was a marvelous clarinet player, who had been a student at
the recently founded Curtis Institute in Philadelphia. After my first
lesson, Etzweiler offered me free lessons if I would enroll in the
school as a postgraduate student and play the solo chair in the
band. I accepted, taking courses I had already had back home so I
wouldn't have to spend much time studying subjects other than
music.

Etzweiler got me a job playing in the State Fair concert band for
a couple of weeks, and it was at this time (1924) that I had my first
radio job. I played on the air before I'd even heard a radio broadcast, and I was still playing radio when live broadcasts of music
went out of style.

I started learning piano at the Phoenix Conservatory, and because my teacher there thought I had possibilities, he gave me free
lessons. Since I didn't have a piano, I practiced at the Presbyterian
church where I attended Sunday school and church. Our pastor
was partially blind, and one day while practicing, I was asked to
help him prepare his sermon. Although it was interesting work, it

entailed research and it interfered with my practicing. I must have been fairly good at it, though, for the pastor tried to persuade me to take up the ministry. He was planning to go to Alaska as a missionary and wanted me to go along as his assistant and work into the ministry that way. But I had no desire to be anything but a musician and so declined the invitation.

After I'd been in school about three months, my bicycle was stolen, so I quit school and went to work in a filling station in Phoenix. If I remember correctly, I dropped out without telling Etzweiler. For twenty dollars I bought a 1918 or so Model-T Ford, stripped of everything but a seat and a twenty-gallon gas tank, but in good enough shape to get from Glendale to work and back.

Soon thereafter I read an ad in *Billboard* for musicians for the Dodson's World Fair Shows, the same carnival with the same band leader, Max "Monty" Montgomery, that I had started with before. The show was to open in Port Arthur, Texas. I wrote Monty a letter, and to my surprise, he hired me, even though I had left him without notice the year before. I hadn't known about giving notice, and as I recall, I had even neglected to tell him I was leaving. I joined his twelve-piece band a couple of weeks later. The routine in carnival bands was to play in the parades through town, then concerts at the show grounds, and then to split into three or four groups to ballyhoo the sideshows. Usually the show played one-week stands, occasionally staying longer in the big cities.

It was a dirty job. The lots were dusty, we sweated a lot, and we didn't have a bathroom on the train. I had to rent a hotel room once in a while to clean up in. But our griminess didn't scare the girls away—if we stayed downwind. We didn't have to go after them; they came after us, having some idea that musicians wearing band caps were glamorous. I was too shy to be seduced or to do any seducing myself, but there were plenty of chances for both. The girls around carnivals weren't exactly the elite of the towns, but as I came to find out as I went along, there's always a social bracket just above the one you happen to be stuck in, and the one you're stuck in depends on your income. Twenty dollars a week didn't put me above the lot lice, as the carnival folks called the townsfolk. I had quite a few girl friends along the way, all very nice girls whom I mostly took for matinee movies and popcorn. I was patronizing to a pretty little girl of twelve once, taking her on all the rides and to the sideshows. Her parents had me to dinner a couple of times, and I was treated like a real celebrity.

Our drummer on the show, Max Naylor, who was a sort of unofficial contractor for Sousa's band, offered to get me a job for the next season's tour. Again I didn't think I was good enough. Since Sousa'a band was the big time, I thought he must have the best clarinet players in the world. Max said I could take the last chair if necessary, but I couldn't be persuaded. I had known only one other professional clarinet player—the one I was working with at the time—and I couldn't believe I would compare favorably with the big-timers in Sousa's band.

At Monty's suggestion I bought my first saxophone that summer of 1925, a new silver-plated Martin. I got it in Anderson, Indiana, and played it on the job that night, even though I didn't know all the fingerings, especially of the high notes. Luckily, the notes I didn't know didn't occur in the pieces we played, and Monty told me I'd done all right.

Later that summer Monty asked me to go to Beaumont, Texas, with him after the show closed for the winter to play in his dance band there. I didn't know anything about dance music, though, and had no wish to learn it, so I turned down his offer. I had strained my diaphragm by blowing so hard and had to quit the show anyway. I had been corresponding with Bradshaw, who had spent that summer visiting relatives in North Carolina. He was planning to stop in Ada on his return trip to Arizona, so we arranged for him to pick me up in Jackson, Tennessee, and drop me off in Ada.

Back home, I enrolled in East Central State Teachers College, again taking subjects I had already studied in high school, along with psychology, to give myself more time for music. A doctor in Ada told me that I would never be able to blow the clarinet again, so I continued on piano. Once more I got free lessons. In fact, both of the piano teachers in town offered me free lessons since each of them thought I had talent and wanted to claim me as a pupil. Actually, playing piano was, and still is, one of the black arts to me. I had no particular aptitude for it, but because I practiced a lot, I could and did sometimes play some of the old standard pieces in public. I never learned to sight read on the piano, playing it at the same time, though, and I always wanted to whip anybody who could. There's too much involved compared to reading single notes for the clarinet. But I was able to memorize the notes after going through a piece a couple of times; then I would practice them for days without looking at the music again.

After a few weeks, I defied the doctor's orders and went back to the clarinet and saxophone, learning a few Rudy Wiedoeft solos—he was the saxophonists' idol of the day. At the college I played solo clarinet in the band, and for my credits in practice teaching and twenty dollars a month, I was to direct the Horace Mann orchestra. The offer of pay, made by the dean, the band director, and the assistant band director, had induced me to go to school in the first place, but I never got paid. Each of them passed the buck to the other two when payday came around. Though they did arrange for me to borrow eighty dollars from the student loan funds, that wasn't enough to get by on for the year, so when the money ran out I had to quit.

About that time my father decided to go to Dallas to look for work, and I went along with him. We made the trip in a 1922 Star touring car, the kind with a let-down top with isinglass windows to be fastened on with buckles in bad weather. It got us there minus the top, which was blown off in a breeze along the way. In Dallas, Pop and I stayed with my maternal half brother, who was married and settled there. One day while helping Pop check the help-wanted ads in the paper I ran across a notice that read something like: "Wanted. Hot saxophone player doubling clarinet. Glenn Bell, Chamber of Commerce, Marlin, Texas." I had only a faint idea of what *hot* meant, but I answered the ad anyway and got the job by mail.

Bell fired me after the first rehearsal but asked me to stay on until he could get someone else. It happened that the trumpet player could neither read nor play "hot," and he was fired, too. At least I could read. The new trumpet player, Foy Robertson, a handsome big-city fellow from Ft. Worth, was very good, but he couldn't fake either. Well, Bell ended up keeping both Foy and me, and the two of us decided to have a reading band. Foy taught the trombone player, Doug Burtis, his parts, while I taught the other saxophone player, Virgil "Jelly" Brooks, and the piano player, Virgil Howard, who could also read, taught the banjo player, Coulter Richardson.

This first job of mine in the dance band business was a revelation to me. Having been a country boy all my life, I enjoyed meeting people in the outside world and getting to know some of the big-town musicians. Whereas the so-called legitimate musicians were on the serious side of life, the dance musicians were happy-go-lucky and fun-loving. I began to look at things their way.

2

GLENN BELL called his band Bell's Blue Melody Boys. We played dinner music at noontime in a Marlin hotel for our breakfast, and all of us, except Bell, stayed at a rooming house for three dollars a week each. We played at the Oakland Park pavilion one night a week for a percentage of the take, and on our free nights, Bell booked us in nearby towns, also on percentages.

The hardships we endured on those little out-of-town trips seem incredible now; in 1926 a trip of fifty miles often took longer than one of three hundred in 1980. We drove two Model-T Fords, a touring car and a roadster, whose rear lid had been replaced by a high box built onto the bed to hold the drums. Some of the roads were graveled, but most of them in the Southwest at that time were just dirt or sand. The only pavement was on some approaches to big towns. Although the better roads were two-lane, usually merging into one at bridges, most byways were only one lane, and that was preempted in spots by cows or chickens. When it rained, the central Texas Blacklands mud stuck to the tires like glue. To keep the wheels from getting jammed on the fenders, we would have to get out and scrape them off with sticks, standing in the mud, of course, and often getting soaked to the skin. After two or three days of rain, we would have to scrape the tires every mile or so. Now and then, the cars had to be pushed out of bad places, and sometimes, farmers were waiting with horses or mules and chains to pull cars out for a fee. It could take an entire day to go forty or fifty miles under such conditions, but since we left early enough to accommodate the hazards, we never failed to get to a job. Once, though, after a day of traveling forty miles in the mud, we arrived at the dance hall only to discover that a bridge over a small creek in front of the hall had been washed away. We couldn't cross the gully and neither could the dancers, so the whole thing had to be called off. We got back to Marlin about daybreak.

There weren't enough dances for us to work more than two or three times a week, though, and working on percentage, we barely made living expenses. So we finally had to give up. I have two special memories of Marlin, however: I smoked my first cigarette there and had my first drink—I haven't yet had my last of either.

Bell and I went to Dallas, where he had a friend, Johnny McFall, who was one of the best known band leaders in the Southwest. One day I got the chance to sit in with the band at one of his rehearsals. McFall's musicians were good, but some of them were not fast readers, and one of the saxophone players was having trouble with the introduction to "Sugar Foot Stomp." When Bell told him that I could read anything, McFall invited me to sit in. The part was merely a succession of diminished sevenths in broken chord form, and I played it at first sight. Since it was part of one of the fundamental exercises that Henry Lambert had told me to practice until I could "play the whole page in one breath," I thought nothing of it. I didn't have to read the notes one at a time as McFall's man was trying to do.

After the rehearsal, McFall suggested that we see Jimmy Joy, one of the big-name leaders in that part of the country, about a job in New Mexico. Joy, whose real name was Maloney, and his band were at the Baker Hotel in Dallas, and that night I went with Bell to see him. Friendly and sympathetic, he advised us to contact Al Jarvis, a booker in Lubbock, Texas, adding that if we got the job we could use his name in connection with the band, calling it something like Jimmy Joy's Juniors.

Bell sent Jarvis a telegram, and we were hired. By then our band had scattered, so Bell had to get Brooks back from west Texas and Burtis from Marlin. He hired a trumpet player, Raymond Jasper, and a banjo player, Julius Adams. Bell himself switched to tuba, replacing himself on drums with Raymond "Happy" McGuire, who came in from Abilene. Jarvis picked us up in Dallas in a big Studebaker touring car. Somehow, all nine of us managed to get inside after tying the instruments and suitcases onto the running boards, and we took off for Ruidoso, New Mexico, a 620-mile journey that lasted two days and two nights.

The job gave us room and board at Navajo Lodge for playing two dances a week; for cash we were to book out in the surrounding towns—Roswell, Carlsbad, Tularosa, Alamogordo, Artesia, and Carizozo. Our "room" was an unheated clapboard shack on stilts up the hill from the lodge. There was a hydrant outside the shack for drinking water and laundry, and we used the community privies at the lodge. It was almost like home to me. The dining room was a frame building adjacent to the lodge, and the meals were family, or "pitch to the wind," style. There was a tennis court of sorts and a swimming pool a few hundred yards up Bonita River.

The lodge owners, Bob Boyce and his wife, called us the White Mountain Boys, the lodge being near Sierra Blanca, and had picture postcards of the band made up as advertisements. We booked out about four nights a week, and because we were the only band in the territory, people came from miles around. But despite the good attendance, we weren't making any money. Jarvis would give us fifty cents a day if we asked for it, claiming the rest for expenses, payments on the car, and emergencies like paying off duns from his creditors back home. We were all too young and inexperienced to doubt his assurances that we would get our money "later."

The first time we played at Page Park in Roswell a woman approached one of our boys—a very successful ladies' man—to invite him out to her car. He accepted when we took our intermission and later reported that the woman's husband, who had been sitting in the car listening to the music, explained that he was paralyzed from the waist down and couldn't perform his marital functions. So the wife and "Satyr" had climbed into the back seat, while the husband ignored them. For the rest of the summer, the couple drove up to Ruidoso once a week, the husband waiting in the car while the action went on in the bushes. I realized then that some men willingly allow their wives sex with other men in cases of need, but it was quite a while before I learned that some get their kicks out of it.

There were only about eight permanent guests at the lodge, among them a wealthy woman from Beaumont, Texas, a Mrs. Lowell and her three teenage daughters, Andrea, Arlene, and Elizabeth, called Betty. None of us had any designs on the mother, who was around forty-five and seemed like an old woman to us kids, and the two older daughters weren't anything to get excited over. But Betty, who was fifteen, was pretty and well developed for her age. Most of the band boys were too old for her, but Happy McGuire was eighteen and I was twenty-one, and we vied for her favor. Somehow I won out, or rather, her matchmaking mother chose me as the one to accompany them on little hikes and swimming parties and to sit with them at meals, next to Betty. She told me to call her "Mother," and she would slip money to me once in awhile.

Once she invited me on an outing to El Paso and Juarez. I reminded her that I didn't have any money, but she brushed my protests aside, insisting that I not worry about it. The all-day trip was quite an undertaking—135 miles up and down mountains, on a road that was rocky and sandy. Andrea did the driving, Arlene riding in the front seat with her and Betty between Mother and me in the back. We reached El Paso about eight o'clock in the evening and went across the Rio Grande to Juarez, where we had a round of drinks and dinner. When the waiter brought the check, Mother slipped me the money under the table, squeezing my hand affectionately and patting my leg. On the ride back to Ruidoso that night I grew bold enough to put my arm around Betty and kiss her for the first and only time, while her mother looked on. Since Mother seemed to approve, I began to suspect that I had been chosen as her future son-in-law. A kiss offered and accepted was considered tantamount to being engaged in those days. At any rate, that was all there was to the trip to Mexico—the drink, dinner, and Mother's pitch for Betty. Otherwise it was a trip to somewhere just to say you've been there, as most pleasure trips are.

A few days later Mother came to me with a proposition that confirmed my suspicion. If I would "give up this silly music business," she would send me to the college of my choice to learn real estate, which was the business in which her deceased husband had made his fortune. Being wealthy, she naturally thought there was nothing more to it than that, for the rich assume that power comes automatically with money. By that time, I was pretty fond of Betty and told Mother I would do as she wished. After all, I wasn't really in the music business yet and had no idea where I would go after Ruidoso.

We had only a few more days to go in the summer season when some of the boys challenged Jarvis, and we voted to fire him. He went back to Lubbock, leaving us the car to be returned to him on our way back. To our amazement, playing the remainder of our dates, we made an average of twenty dollars a night per man, which was what Jarvis had been putting in his pocket all summer. That was a lesson to me.

Shortly before we were to leave for home, I wired Johnny McFall for a job on Bell's advice. He told me that McFall had wanted to hire me the day I sat in with his band but hadn't wanted to steal me from Bell. I received a handwritten telegram in reply, which was delivered from Roswell by mail. McFall said he had a job for me, so I told Mother I wanted to try music for a while, and then I'd go back to school.

We left Ruidoso in big style. Everybody was there to see us off, some even wearing black bands on their sleeves. The summer had been fun, not least of all because we had been invited to the ranches of a few of the old-timers who had fought the Lincoln County war with Billy the Kid. Frank Coe, whose brother George had written the first book about Billy, told us the whole story, saying that all the Kid's friends adored him for his prowess but that he could be the "meanest little son of a bitch you ever saw" when he had to be. We were taken on a tour of the town of Lincoln and saw the courthouse the Kid escaped from before they could hang him. And Coe autographed some pictures for me: "Frank B. Coe, pardner of Billy the Kid." Some of the ranchers sent us crates of apples later. They were good people.

3

BELL AND I joined McFall's band as soon as we got back to Dallas. Funny how time drags when you are young and eager for something to happen, but looking back, I realize that, after playing less than six months, I was in one of the best bands on one of the best jobs in the entire Southwest. It was unbelievable. I figured it was pure luck, that I really wasn't good enough for the job—and in this case, that was probably a fortunate attitude, for I continued to practice and study. It's better to beware of feeling "good enough" too soon.

Kidd Springs was in Oak Cliff, across the Trinity River from Dallas. The dime-a-dance pavilion was on the shore of a little lake formed by artesian springs. Although we were expected to play without intermissions, we got off the stand twice a night while different trios from the band played sets of jazz. Since I couldn't fake, my ignorance got me out of a little work every night, but I would have liked being able to join the relief groups. Jelly Brooks had told me once in Ruidoso that to become a jazz player I only needed to take the legitimate stuff I was practicing and put licks behind it, but he didn't tell me how to do it.

The one who finally did explain jazz to me was Lyle "Spud" Murphy, an eighteen-year-old South Dakotan who replaced a saxophonist in the band shortly after I joined McFall. Spud and I were the youngest members (the others were old men of around twenty-six), and we became good friends.

The Kidd Springs job was only for the summer months, and though Johnny usually worked one-nighters in and around Dallas during the winter, that year (1926) he got a job in Nueva Laredo,

Mexico, across the Rio Grande from Laredo, Texas. I was making a decent fifty dollars a week and only paying six dollars a week for room and board, so I had bought a 1924 Model-T Ford coupe. There was barely room for three in the car, but Spud, his wife Loraine, and I shoehorned into it for the trip. Even today with paved roads and better cars the 470 Texas-miles from Dallas to Laredo are a long haul, and since Spud hadn't learned to drive yet, Loraine and I shared the driving. Some twenty-four hours after leaving Dallas, just south of San Antonio, we were smashed from behind when I slowed down at a right-angle turn in the highway. The accident occurred in front of a filling station where a mechanic was on duty, so the driver of the other car give me fifteen dollars for the bent fender and drove away. While the mechanic worked on the car, Loraine, Spud, and I had breakfast in a little cafe next door. The car was ready when we got back about an hour later, and having observed the accident and subsequent negotiations, the mechanic, of course, charged us fifteen dollars. It wasn't until we had reached Laredo about noon the next day and checked into the Bender Hotel, that we discovered that Loraine's bags had been stolen at the garage. Luckily, though, all the other bags and the instruments were there, and it didn't occur to us to try and locate Loraine's things.

Our job was at Nick Buccaro's Bohemian Club a block off Nueva Laredo's main street. The old building with its thick walls had once been Pancho Villa's temporary headquarters, and there were dents in the walls near the door, said to have been made by rifle bullets. The club part of the building was an addition of a concrete floor covered by a flat roof with beams but no ceiling. The outside walls were movable, and in warm weather the club was open-air style, with the bar in the old part of the building.

In back of the bandstand in a room used for storing spare tables and an old upright piano, I began to learn music from Spud. He spent his intermissions back there with the piano, and whenever he had worked out something new, he would take me back with him and say, "See what you think of this." Or he would play something and just look at me and grin. I was always eager to listen; it was like taking private lessons in advanced harmony. The two years of courses in harmony that I'd had in school hadn't gotten beyond the church-hymn structure of three chords.

At night after the job we would go to the room that I shared with one of the boys who had a phonograph. The old phonographs worked on a spring principle like a watch and had to be wound up by a crank on the side, each windup being good for one play of a record. I would work the crank and set the needle back to replay sections of the record for Spud when he was writing down all of the band parts. If he wanted to write off a solo he only had to hear it once. Although he usually did his own arrangements, Spud copied from records sometimes to further his knowledge, often transcribing the solos, especially clarinet solos, in three parts for us to play together. When making his own arrangements, he sometimes wrote the second or third parts first so some of the slow readers could practice while he was writing the other parts. If a trumpet player had trouble playing his part at rehearsal, Spud would stand in front of him and say, "You blow; I'll finger it;" though, of course, that meant he had to finger backwards. And he would do the same with the trombone player, working the slide backwards while the player did the playing.

One day Spud asked me to go with him to the record shop to hear a certain record by the Buffalodians, a popular band of the day. When I said the record was very good, he grinned (he never laughed, just grinned and said "huh huh"), admitting that it was his arrangement. He had sent it to the band some time before without telling anybody.

I didn't want Spud to know how ignorant I was about playing ad lib, but finally I asked him how it was done. The principle, he explained, was to play the notes in the chords of the tune. He wrote down the melody of "Clarinet Marmalade" for me with the names of the chords that went with it and told me to practice playing around in those chords. I knew all the notes in all the chords, so that was simple enough for me—my problem was to put jazz ideas into faking, a skill that would have to come later. I began to notice, though, that most jazz players played "blue" notes that didn't fit the harmonic structure of the tunes, and I was determined that, if I ever became a jazz player, I would play within the chords.

My association with Spud Murphy inspired me more than ever to become a musician, for he was a musical genius. Although he had been a student of Red Nichols' father in Ogden, Utah, along with Red himself, he seemed to know all there is to know about music without having to learn it. There was music in his head. No amount of formal learning can match genius, but since I was no genius, my only hope was to study. I was beginning to grow up a little—not emotionally, but mentally and practically. Assessing myself in a vague way and comparing myself with other reading musicians, I began to see the possibilities of going on to better things if I could learn to play well in a dance band. Reading was no problem. I had been corresponding with my girl friend Betty and her mother since leaving Ruidoso, and at last I had to tell Mother that I couldn't give up music to go to school. As a compromise, I was to take a correspondence course in real estate. After looking over the first lessons, though, I threw them away. I couldn't get interested in real estate; in fact, I couldn't get interested in anything but music.

It had never occurred to me that Mother might have had her own designs on me, but now Glenn Bell posed that possibility, speculating that she had really wanted me to romance *her* back in Ruidoso. When I thought about it, his observation seemed logical, and I knew Bell had been around. Consequently, a distrust of people's intentions began forming in my mind.

Most of the population of Laredo was Mexican-American and I enjoyed trying out my high school Spanish on folks. They laughed good-naturedly at my conversational attempts and seemed to appreciate my efforts to adapt. The Mexicans were friendly and happy-go-lucky, and I liked them, though I quickly learned that according to their code of social ethics their girls were off limits to us.

The only Anglo girls who could be considered eligible were a manicurist at the barbershop, her girl friend who was visiting from Sinton, and a cashier in a hotel restaurant. I was one of only two unmarried men in the band, and the other guy was down on women because he'd been jilted back in Dallas. I wasn't interested either because I thought I had a girl already, but the cashier, who was the oldest (thirty-two) but also the prettiest, would have been my choice. The other boys thought she was too old, which left the manicurist and her friend, both in their early twenties. Two of the philandering married men, Johnny McFall and his brother Binks, got them. I began to feel disillusioned with both the men and the women. I could see that, if I set my sights on any particular girl, I would have even more competition from the married men than from the single ones, since, having nothing to lose but a roll in the hay, they tended to come on stronger.

In 1926, movie theaters still used live music—a pianist, an organist, or even a pit band. One theater in Laredo had a five-piece band, and when I saw *The Big Parade* there, I was impressed by the clarinet player, who was just a kid. I went backstage to meet him, benevolently thinking that I might pass on to him some of my knowledge of the clarinet. The kid, nineteen-year-old Jesus Caballero, spoke as little English as I did Spanish, but we managed to get through to each other, and I invited him to my room to play duets the next afternoon. Caballero had never seen any of my music before, so he was sight-reading all the way. I started with the easy duets, and as I progressed to the hard ones, it turned out that he was showing *me* something—namely that I wasn't as good as I thought I was. Some of the passages were so hard I'd practiced them for weeks before I could play them, but Caballero was playing them all as if he had them memorized, never missing a note.

A lot of orchestra pieces are written in keys with two or more sharps, which are easier for violins. To compensate, clarinets are built in two different pitches, one a half tone lower than the other (B-flat and A). If a clarinet player doesn't have an A clarinet, he has to play those parts a halftone lower on his B-flat instrument. So after our session I asked Caballero if he could have played all of that if it had been written for the A clarinet. He just shrugged and said, "Same thing." Years later, a musician in Dallas summed up Caballero's reading ability: "Just draw a staff through the fly specks on the wall, and he'll play them." He was another genius I was to be associated with for many years.

We had been in Laredo about three months when McFall accepted a job offer back in Dallas, even though it was to start immediately and wouldn't allow us time to work out a two-week notice at the Bohemian Club. All of us were to take our instruments home, so we could sneak out of Laredo right after work—all but Spud Murphy. McFall never explained why, but he wanted to leave Spud and Loraine behind. However, since Spud was my particular friend, and I didn't think it was right, I warned him. He and Loraine packed their things and were ready to leave with us.

I left first, taking Gus Manhart, our lead saxophone player, with me. After driving the rest of that night, all the next day, and half the next night, my old Model T stalled. We were fifteen miles from the next town and farther from the last one, but I tried pushing the car for several miles, anyway, before giving up and walking the rest of the way to get the part that Gus said we needed. Being averse to physical activity, he slept while I was gone. It was well into the next morning by the time I got the part and walked back to the car, never thinking that I might ask the mechanic to drive me back. Gus, well-rested, drove us to our rendezvous point in Dallas, where we found a telegram saying, "Come back to Laredo!" So we took the train back, leaving my Ford with my half brother.

The band had been playing for three nights without us. We learned that one of the girls had tipped Buccaro off, and he had sent the sheriff's men after the band, catching them a few miles up the road at Catulla.

The first night back on the job I had some pains in my chest which grew worse the next night, despite the salve that Loraine rubbed on. So I went to a doctor and found that I had a double hernia, having strained myself pushing the car.

By then it was Christmastime, and some of the wives, including the McFalls', came down from Dallas to stay until March, the duration of the band's engagement. So Johnny's girl went back to Sinton, and Binks's girl, Lola the manicurist, decided to come after me. She was very pretty and the most charming girl I had known, vivacious and fun-loving. Before Binks took up with her I had gotten manicures while having my hair cut, just to carry on with her a bit, but I had considered her way out of my league. Now I was reluctant to be second choice, and I was shy to boot, but she was determined. One night she came across the river to the club, which she had never done before, waited till we got off work, then took me by the arm and held on. My suspicion that she was just being defiant made me even more reluctant to go with her, but in fact, she had me hooked. That was the first time I had been actively pursued by a girl, and I didn't know how to escape without hurting her feelings. In those days shacking up was against the law and considered morally wrong. Besides, I had an aversion to taking up where Binks had left off, but my aversion wasn't strong enough to resist Lola's advances. I went along with her, thinking I was merely helping her get even with Binks and feeling bad about it.

We got along wonderfully. We just fell in "crazy" with each other, and naturally, I thought I was in love, though I didn't dare express my thoughts to her or to anyone else. It was my first affair. She wanted to give me money and to buy me things she thought I couldn't afford, but it was against my principles to accept things from women. I wondered, anyway, where she was getting the extra money she wanted to spend on me. One means, according to Johnny, was blackmail. He told me, as a sort of warning, that she was blackmailing her Sinton friend for having gone to bed with him, and though it was none of my business, it made me a little leery of her attentions to me.

Our band was very popular in Laredo with everybody but some of the cops, whose animosity we first encountered in a cafe one night after work. We were all sitting at the counter with several different conversations going on at once, being fairly boisterous, I must admit, though stopping short, I thought, of disturbing the peace. The two plainclothesmen standing at the end of the counter thought differently; they pulled their guns on us and ordered us to leave. We found out later that some time before a musician had gotten the daughter of one of those officers pregnant and then left town. So we were being hassled for his indiscretion. Those two cops kept a close watch on us for the rest of our stay in Laredo and once even came across the border to watch us and follow us around, though they had no authority there. We were careful not to let them incite us to anything rash. Later we heard that one of them killed a man and was tried and convicted of murder.

There were other bits of intrigue going on, too. Liquor could not legally be brought into Laredo from the Mexican side, but instead of arresting those caught trying to smuggle a bottle back, officials on the Mexican side of the bridge merely fined them two dollars a bottle on the spot. Our cars were seldom searched unless we had bought some to bring back, and then the officers usually didn't have to *search* the car. They would just reach in and take the bottle from where it had been hidden. Apparently, identification of the car, its passengers, and the place of concealment had been phoned in by the person selling the liquor. One of our boys, Carl Shamburger, thought it would be smart to smuggle a dozen miniature bottles instead of one big one. He ended up paying twenty-four dollars instead of two, though, because the men at the bridge knew where every one of them was.

One night we were invited by one of the club's waiters to a party celebrating the coming birth of a baby—eight or nine months hence, as it turned out. It was a pretty wild scene. There was plenty of booze, beer, and food, and we did a great job of making it all scarce. The chicken—cooked whole, entrails and all—didn't look very appetizing to me, nor did the rattlesnake steaks, but I went for the enchiladas, chili, and hot tamales. I got fairly chummy with one of the Mexican guests as the evening wore on. Eventually, he offered to sell me his ten-year-old daughter's virginity for fifty dollars—a common transaction in those days it seemed. I declined.

The party ended too late for us to cross the bridge, which closed at twelve, so we had to fool around on the Mexican side of the river until things opened up again at six. Already a little tipsy, we started making the rounds of the all-night joints, stopping first at a whorehouse reputed to have a come-on porno show in the lobby. We saw the show for a peso each (then about forty-eight cents), and though the price of additional favors was also only a peso, we didn't go farther than the lobby. After that, we split up. Gus Manhart and I stopped at a joint where a knife fight was going on. Since we didn't particularly care for knife fights, we retreated to my Ford, encouraged by a volley of beer bottles. At the next place, where the weapons were pistols instead of knives, we didn't wait around to see if the mexican standoff erupted into further action. When we found only a fistfight in progress at our next stop, we figured, correctly, that it must be where the elite hung out. The other boys in the band had discovered some Mexican musicians there, who, when things had gotten good and sociable, invited us to their country club. The club was a thatched roof supported by bamboo poles and covering a patch of desert dust without walls. Some of the Mexican musicians entertained us, and I remember being fascinated by the trombone player, who got a beautiful vibrato without moving the slide. I learned that such a vibrato is produced in the throat by thinking "ya-ya-ya-ya."

The February 22 holiday was celebrated by both the Americans and the Mexicans. For several days, while the festivities went on, the band had to work from eight in the morning until four the following morning, with few breaks, except for meals. Our longest break came when Buccaro gave us tickets for the bullfights, since the club wouldn't be doing much business then. I thought it was inhumane to kill animals for sport, but I went along anyway just to say I'd seen a bullfight. Big deal.

Back at the club, one of the trumpet players discovered the felt hat he played into for effects was missing. We found it in the storeroom soggy with whiskey. Apparently, the hat had served to strain cheap booze so it could be sold as good stuff at the bar. The only effects from all that work were a few collapses, from which we all recuperated in a few days. We didn't get any extra pay because, as we later found out, McFall had neglected to pass our shares of the overtime pay on to us.

There was a gap of several weeks from the time our contract with Buccaro ended in March until Kidd Springs opened for the summer, so McFall booked the band for a month at the Plaza Hotel in San Antonio. During those four weeks, Lola called from Laredo almost every day wanting to come up, but I refused to let her join me. I was sensitive because the boys were kidding me about getting hooked on a whore, and I was afraid of getting in trouble with the law besides. Nevertheless, Lola was one of the best persons I knew along the way. I'm grateful to her for arousing my curiosity about women's motives toward men. She was honest about her free living, refusing to lie her way into men's hearts with honeyed words, only to abandon them, leaving them to wonder why. She taught me to recognize the whorish, vulturous tendencies in certain types of women—from the married ones, willing to pay for the sex they want with gifts, to the single ones seeking security in the form of money. Being able to spot such traits has kept me out of a lot of trouble over the years. Even though I sometimes got involved with opportunistic women, I did it with my eyes open.

Our rooms in the little Bluebonnet Hotel in San Antonio overlooked the deck of the Gunter Hotel where Doc Ross's band was playing, and there I heard Jack Teagarden for the first time. He was only twenty, but we had all heard of him. Young musicians have always been eager to meet their peers and delighted to meet their superiors, whether superior in talent or in reputation. The Southwest was an unlikely place to find other musicians, though, for the action, especially in recording, was back East in those days. Still, I had met Ack Kavish and King Jackson in Laredo, which was even farther off the beaten track than San Antonio. They had been down the street at the Texas Inn with Jack Kane's band from Minnesota. I also chanced on a few transients, like Red Ballard and Joe Bishop, who sat in on tuba for a few days with our band. Shortly thereafter, in collaboration with Gordon Jenkins, Bishop wrote the popular standard "Blue Prelude."

Back in Dallas after the San Antonio job, there were lots more opportunities to meet well-known musicians. Boyd Senter, the most famous clarinet player of the day (on C clarinet), was there on a tour plugging some product or other; Vernon "Brownie" Brown was with a name band at the Baker Hotel; Larry "Slim" Conley, the trombonist composer of "Cottage for Sale," and originator of the jug tone, was with a band at the Adolphus Hotel; and Bob McCracken was at the Park Inn, a joint between Dallas and Ft. Worth. Matty Matlock drifted through from somewhere on his way to somewhere else.

We spent four months at Kidd Springs, returning to Laredo in September of 1927 with a slightly different band. McFall had made some changes during the summer: Spud Murphy left, Bernie Dillon came on, and Curtis Hurt replaced one of the trumpet players. Although we had never corresponded, Lola and I renewed our affair, seeing each other often at her place or mine.

Bernie Dillon had brought his beautiful and charming wife

along. When Gus Manhart, whether intentionally or just playing around a little, paid some attention to her, Bernie accused him of being on the make. One day, when I was visiting Gus's roommate, Bernie, carrying a gun, came looking for Gus, but somehow Gus had gotten wind of the situation and stayed away. He didn't show up for work that night but instead packed up and headed back north. His car was found later burned up somewhere along the way. We never saw him again, but once, "Ripley's Believe It or Not" reported that Gus had landed a plane (he had been an army pilot) on high tension wires without being harmed.

McFall needed a replacement for Gus, but there wasn't time to send to Dallas or even to San Antonio for one, so I told him about Jesus Caballero. McFall let me call him to fill in just for the night but hired him to stay on permanently after Caballero played the whole book without a mistake. The kid wore his wavy hair long and combed out at the sides, looking more like a gandy dancer on the railroad than a musician. So McFall suggested that he get a more stylish haircut. The next night when he came to work, he was so slicked up we hardly recognized him. Slick-haired kids were known as "jelly beans," so we promptly dubbed him Jelly, the only name he was known by after that. Jelly and I were often roommates during the next several years and we became the closest of friends. He could already read and write English when he joined the band, so with some tutoring on my part, he was soon speaking fluently.

Johnny McFall seemed to have a talent for doing the wrong things in Laredo. This time we left Nick Buccaro a little before Christmastime for "something better" in Monterrey, Mexico. There was no highway between Laredo and Monterrey then, so we traveled by train. That was the train on which I was amazed to find a Mexican skinning a goat that he had strung from the ceiling of the men's room. Another Mexican, who had been caught trying to sneak across the river to the American side the night before we left, was being returned to Mexico on that train also. In Monterrey the next morning, we heard the volley of shots when the firing squad executed him.

At first Monterrey was fine. We played two nights a week at the Terpsichorean Club, a swanky joint for the city's elite, and were supposed to book the other nights elsewhere. As it turned out, though, there weren't any elsewheres. We managed to book ourselves out only once—in Saltillo, a mountain town that could be reached only by pack mule or train. We chose the train. All I remember about the town was that the horse pulling our cab slipped on the ice and fell, nearly overturning us.

In Monterrey we had prestige, though. One day some Carta Blanca officials took us for a tour of their brewery. There must have been millions of gallons of the good stuff in tanks, and plenty of it in smaller containers for immediate use. After consuming a considerable quantity of beer, we tried to escape, walking down the dusty lane toward town. The Mexicans kidnapped us, took us back, and kept us there a few hours more before allowing us to float out at last.

Once when we played a concert in the local music store, billed as "Johnny McFall, the Paul Whiteman of the South," I got a little too friendly with a girl in the audience—I put my arm around her shoulder while I was talking to her, assuming because of her light complexion and good English that she was from the States. I found out later that she wasn't when I heard that a certain Mexican was looking for the *hijo de cabrio* (literally, "son of a goat," but equivalent in English to "son of a bitch"), who had put an arm around his sister at the music store. Knowing the hands-off policy down there, I was a little apprehensive. Actually, the threat had been simply a matter of observing local protocol. When I met the Mexican, at an informal get-together, he explained that he and his sister had been educated in American universities. He merely laughed when he found out I was the culprit.

After two weeks at the club, the manager decided that he couldn't afford us, so we were out of a job. At first, McFall agreed to play the club once more, on New Year's Eve, even though that left us unemployed for several days. He had second thoughts, though, deciding that it would be better for us to return to Laredo and then go on to Dallas. We couldn't leave, though, because the manager wouldn't let us get our instruments from the club until after the New Year's Eve party. McFall immediately and conveniently found a ten-dollar bill fluttering along the walk in front of the hotel and he took off for Laredo, saying he would see us later in Dallas. I discovered later that he had raised more money when he got to Laredo by hocking the burnished-gold baritone saxophone that I had left with Buccaro at the club. I never got the sax or the hock money back.

Since all of us were broke, we began to run up our hotel bills, eating at the hotel restaurant and even charging our laundry to our bills. We were in hock pretty deep considering that we had only one night's work to depend on. When the hotel clerk came to the room, where we loafed together, to settle the account, one of our fun-loving boys thought he'd solve the problem by tearing up the bills and throwing them out the window. The clerk was furious. That was the first time I witnessed a Mexican tirade. He carried on for a full minute without seeming to take a breath, accompanying the speech with appropriate gestures. We were all laughing, and when he finally paused, exhausted, we asked Jelly what he'd said. Jelly, who couldn't speak English well enough yet to interpret, gave us the Mexican shrug and replied, "He says *no*." I don't know why we weren't arrested. Jelly may have smoothed it over with the hotel manager later, but at any rate, we managed to stay out of jail.

We spent our leisure time eating, trying to read the newspaper, *El Sol*, and playing billiards at the club. But the club members turned cool toward us after one of the boys ripped the felt on one of the tables. We thought one of the members, a banker, was still sympathetic, though, when he offered to take us out one night to a roaring joint somewhere in the country to entertain us. He ordered rounds of drinks as fast as we could swallow them, but since we weren't fast drinkers, we were there for quite a while before we built up to our capacities. Suddenly, we noticed that our banker had disappeared, leaving us with an unpaid bar bill and, since we had come in a cab, no way to get back to the hotel. Quite a jam to be in in a foreign country. Luckily, Tom Herron had some hidey-hole money we didn't know about, a twenty-dollar gold piece, which, with Jelly's ten-dollar piece, bailed us out. (We were paid in gold in Mexico.) The bar prices weren't high, nor was the taxi fare, so we made it back to our hotel in good style. I guess the club, or at least the banker, got even for that slashed felt.

I hadn't been especially worried about getting back to Laredo, partly because I didn't have the sense or experience to realize what a mess we had gotten into, but also because Lola had been calling me every day, wanting to come down, and I knew that in a pinch she would have bailed the whole bunch of us out. When New Year's Eve finally came, we made enough money to get ourselves out of hock at the hotel and back to Laredo. From there, we migrated up to Dallas, even though we didn't have jobs. At that time of year, there isn't much going on in the music business anywhere, and all the sensible musicians have already latched on to what few bread-and-butter jobs there are for the winter. Only a few lucky ones could expect to work through Lent. McFall was temporarily on our blacklist, but he didn't have a job for us anyway. We got an unexpected break, though, that at least earned us some experience, while putting off starvation for a few days.

4

WORD ABOUT OUR band had gotten back East, and the Music Corporation of America (MCA) was interested in hiring us. McFall had been leery of their propositions because they wanted to put the band under a big-name leader, and he was afraid he would eventually be eased out. MCA, which had been formed only a short time before, consisted mainly of Jules Stein and Billy Goodheart, who had both played in bands around the Midwest during the twenties. Stein had spoken to McFall when he went to hear the band at Kidd Springs the summer before.

Don Howard, who was now our unofficial mentor, got in touch with MCA and found their offer still open. We were to go as an organized band under Ted FioRito to the Kenmore Hotel in Albany, New York. Incredibly, after only sixteen months in the dance band business, I was going into the big time. Of course, that may seem like a long time when, nowadays, kids start at the top and work their way down.

The trip was such a disaster that the Laredo fiascos looked good in comparison. Goodheart met us in St. Louis, accompanying us to New York City, where we arrived in great style, feeling sure we had it made. After a day and night in New York, we went on to Albany. We had set up the band for a get-acquainted rehearsal and were all in place when FioRito came in. "All right, gentlemen," he said, "let's get it over with."

"Good," we said. "Where's the music?"

"Where's the *music*!" Ted exploded. "Don't you have a library?"

We didn't, of course. Naïvely, we had assumed that Ted would have his own library, while Ted and MCA had naturally expected us to have one. We managed to stumble through the first night without music, relying on the faking by our soloists. Ted featured himself at the piano on his own songs, to take up some of the slack, playing his new waltz, "Laugh, Clown, Laugh," more than once. The next day, he went back to New York. We were stranded again, our big job having lasted one night. As in Mexico, we southerners even had a hard time understanding the language spoken in New York, but this time Caballero couldn't help us out.

I got a chance the following night to sub for a saxophonist in Phil Romono's band, which was playing at the Ten Eyck Hotel. Split up, the ten dollars I made gave each of us a dollar to eat on. The next day MCA brought us back to New York, where we rehearsed a stage show for two or three days, but since nothing happened with the act, MCA decided to send us back to Dallas. They paid our fares and gave us ten dollars apiece for expenses, later billing us for the whole thing—a debt some of the boys had to pay the next time they worked for MCA.

We were disappointed but glad to have a way home. So after spending the night in the hotel, we checked out early the next morning to take the train to Dallas. Our failure was complete when we realized that Curtis Hurt had left his trumpet on the entrance steps to the hotel where we had waited for the cabs. We wouldn't leave without him, so we all went back and, of course, missed our train. For a wonder, the trumpet was still there, but since there wasn't another through train to Dallas that day, we were forced to spend another night in New York, using up nearly all of our travel allowances.

I bought provisions for the two-day trip from one of the "news butches," who came through the cars selling newspapers and goodies at very inflated prices. I had a sandwich to eat on the first half of the journey, from New York to St. Louis, and a little cup of pork and beans from there to Dallas. The last bean, consumed along about Little Rock, was the best.

Hungry and tired, we reached Dallas about noon and, to make things worse, stepped out into a real "blue norther." With no money for cabs, or even streetcar fare, we had to shanks' mare it, some of us carrying horns and suitcases, from the Union Station to the Pittman Hotel, eighteen blocks away.

The Pittman was a little three-story trap near downtown Dallas. The hotel restaurant was run by a lady whose son, Bill "Slim" Brookins, used to sing with our band and others around Dallas from time to time. (He eventually made it into the name bands of the day, but at that time, he was down and out like the rest of us.) Charitable and partial to the likes of us, Mrs. Brookins let us eat on the cuff in her restaurant. She was known throughout the territory for her kindness and was so beloved by musicians that everyone I ever knew made a point of paying her, eventually.

The hotel itself was a well-known haven for musicians out of work. The four-dollar-a-week rent was also cuffable when necessary, but even in periods of affluence many musicians gravitated back to the Pittman because it seemed like home. Then too, it was conveniently located within easy walking distance of the union and of Durward "Gotch" Cline's music store where musicians hung out in the daytime.

Many outsiders frequented the Pittman Hotel, too—nonpaying guests who liked the carefree life of musicians. Clyde Barrow sat in on many of our bull sessions, as did the Hamilton brothers, Raymond and Floyd, who later belonged to Clyde's gang for a while. The Hamilton brothers were operating a cleaning-pressing place up on Harwood Street a couple of blocks away, but Clyde never hinted at his occupation, though he was peddling a little grass and bootleg booze on the side. Smoking or possessing grass wasn't against the law in Texas then. Clyde and others made its purchase more convenient, but it could be bought at a number of places, costing as little as two dollars for a full shoe box of untrimmed stuff. The guys would manicure it in their rooms, crushing the leaves through a wire screen—usually borrowed from one of the hotel windows, frame and all. For a little more money, around three dollars for a cigarette carton full, it could be purchased already manicured. The grass Louis Armstrong was caught with in California, where it wasn't legal, was a goodwill gift from our gang at the Pittman.

We had patched up our differences with Johnny McFall, but we had to do something until Kidd Springs opened again. Curtis Hurt and I got a job for room and board at the Hilton Hotel in Waco with Sonny Clapp, who was riding high on his popularity as composer of "Girl of My Dreams." We were supposed to book out for cash money, but since Guy "Cuz" Draper of Waco had the whole territory sewed up, Sonny gave up after a couple of weeks, putting us out of work again.

Our drummer, Roger Boyd (later coveted by many of the big-name leaders, including Louis Armstrong), and our guitarist, Raby Cummings, had recently come down from Seminole, Oklahoma, where they had been working with Jack Teagarden and Sid Arodin. (Sid was the famous New Orleans clarinet player who composed a ballad-style clarinet solo, which some of us clarinetists played before it was published. The tune had no lyrics yet, and Sid called it, simply and affectionately, "Lazy Nigger." Later, in collaboration with Hoagy Carmichael, the solo became "Lazy River." Sid got only eight hundred dollars of all the money that song made, according to a newspaper report when he died.) Boyd and Cummings were friends of Brooks Pruitt, the piano player in Guy Draper's band. Since Draper was not a musician himself—just a booker and a good businessman (later Johnny McFall got him the job as manager of Kidd Springs)—whoever happened to be the most capable musician was designated the band's leader. At that time it was Pruitt. So when Sonny Clapp gave up, Pruitt, who had been hanging out with us at the Hilton, got Hurt, Boyd, and me on with Draper's band.

Since Waco is surrounded by the same mud-and-sand country as Marlin, the hazards of out-of-town trips were about the same as they had been when, at the start of my career, I was traveling with Glenn Bell. Draper had better transportation, but his eight-passenger Cadillac (counting the two jump seats) was unheated, and the weather was cold. We did what we could to keep warm, wearing overcoats, hats, and earmuffs and covering ourselves with blankets, but nothing kept our feet warm. We would stop once in a while to stamp some of the cold out.

Brooks Pruitt, a tall, handsome, blue-eyed blond, was already a legend in the lore of musicians. He was an excellent pianist and an unwhipped fighter. Having been the light heavyweight champion of his fleet in the navy, he had never been beaten in a fight in civilian life. Although he was usually easygoing and humorous, Pruitt delighted in disproving any insinuation that musicians were sissies.

I wasn't aware that Pruitt resented me until one night when we played Brady, Texas. It had been a hard trip, and Pruitt had had a few drinks of bootleg. After work, when he had run out of booze, money, and patience—in that order—he came to my room at the hotel.

"You got any money?"

"Just a couple of bucks," I said.

"I'll take it," he said, holding out his hand.

"But Pruitt, that's all I've got for room rent and breakfast," I protested.

Grabbing a handful of my shirt, he lifted me up on my toes. "Goddamn it, give me the money."

I gave it to him and he left. "What's the matter with *him?*" I asked Roger Boyd, who had watched the whole scene.

"He seems to think you put him down."

"About what?"

"His reading ability."

Thinking back, I remembered a remark I'd made one night when Pruitt had come to the Hilton, and we were talking about arranging: "I would make an arrangement but I'm afraid you guys couldn't read it." I had only meant that my handwriting was illegible, but evidently, Pruitt had misunderstood. It was a real faux pas, but the next day after I had explained to Pruitt, he and I squared things, so there was no harm done.

Lola showed up in Waco, of all places. She was on her way, with her mother and brother, to join her stepfather in Brownwood, where he was involved in the bootlegging business. While they stayed in Waco for a few days, probably to hustle a little money, Lola and I renewed our little affair.

When Paul Whiteman came to Waco, his band stayed at the hotel where we were playing once a week. Hanging around the

lobby one day, we met some of Whiteman's men, including Fran-
kie Trumbauer and Bix Beiderbecke, as they were leaving to play
an afternoon concert. They invited us to the concert, and as we
walked in, Bix saw us from the wings and blew the musicians'
greeting, a five-note phrase of Ta-ta-Ta-Ta-Ta. We all knew that
the lyrics, though they were never sung, were "You're a horse's ass."
Coming from Bix, that crazy but fond greeting was a real kick for us
kids. That night after the evening concert, we joined Bix for a few
drinks. We all enjoyed ourselves so well that the next morning it
was a case of the blind leading the blind, when as Raby Cummings
put it, we "poured" Bix onto the train.

When the band broke up during a lull in Draper's bookings, I got
a job through my old friend Jelly Brooks in Breckenridge with Harry Harrison's Texans. Warren Doyle "Smitty" Smith, who became
well known when he played with the Bob Crosby band, was playing with the Texans then, along with Jack Free, Jimmy Thornhill,
Raymond McLeod, Freddy Woolridge, Jelly Brooks, and John Haynie Gilliland. It was just a survival job, too, playing one-nighters
around that part of western Texas. We didn't make much money,
but it was fun. Once, I remember, Smitty had set his trombone
down behind the car and then forgotten to load it with the other
instruments. Harrison backed out over it and ruined it. That night
at the Moberly Hotel in Cisco (Conrad Hilton's first hotel), Smitty
played a borrowed trombone—until intermission, when a chan-
delier fell on the chair where he'd laid that horn. He finished the
job on saxophone.

I was broke as usual when I left Harrison, so I went back to the
Pittman in Dallas. Lola called me there; somehow she had found
out where I was. Her mother and brother had gone on to Brownwood by that time, but she had stayed in Waco. Since she was
ready to join them, she sent me gas money, and I drove her to her
old man's place. I got along just fine with her old man. He gave me
a pint of bootleg booze that was so bad I couldn't drink much of it.
I wasn't much of a boozer anyway, but I drank a little of the stuff,
sitting in the kitchen with him, and after a while, he said, "Y'all's
room is upstairs." Real family hospitality.

Lola had a ten-dollar gold piece and a little "business to take care of," so the next day we drove up to Abilene. Lola thought nothing of checking into a hotel with me, but I was uneasy. When the hotel desk clerk turned out to be my old friend Happy McGuire of Ruidoso days, I was embarrassed but relieved. He'd never turn me over to the law. Lola left for a while, I suppose to contact some booze distributors. Since she didn't come back with any money, I don't think she was hustling. That little gold piece was her entire fortune, but ten dollars in those days was a pretty respectable amount of money—about equal to a week's pay, in fact.

Back in Dallas, I accepted a job offer to play in an eleven-man pit band in Beaumont, cuing silent movies and, on weekends, playing vaudeville. I got some good experience there when I got tired of switching clarinets and began transposing instead, so that I could play the parts written in A on my B-flat clarinet. I also had a chance to renew my acquaintance with Betty, my old girl friend, and her Mother. I spent a few nights at their house. Mother still wanted me to quit the music business, but I continued to put her off. I was beginning to feel I wasn't good enough for them anyway. Their money and social standing were more impressive in Beaumont than in Ruidoso, where everybody was roughing it. But I was always one to let the girls do the breaking up, so I just sat back, waiting for the romance to end. The job took so much of my time, anyway, that I couldn't have gone out with Betty if I had wanted to. We played from one o'clock until about eleven, seven days a week.

Beaumont had only one club that used a band. Since I'd heard a lot about that band's leader, the trumpet player Vic Insirilo, one night I went to hear him. In front of the small jazz-style band stood Vic Insirilo and, next to him, a skinny little kid playing trumpet. His style of playing—little as I knew about styles in those days— reminded me of Beiderbecke's. Curious about such a little kid playing along with experienced professionals, I asked about him. The boy was Harry James, just turned thirteen.

It was 1928. Although they hadn't yet been introduced, sound pictures were beginning to seem likely. So the theater let the band go and switched to organ. Vaudeville died out, too. The job had lasted me for three months, though, and since it was about time for Kidd Springs to open again, I went back with McFall.

That summer I met Hix Blewett, a new saxophonist with McFall's band, who became a best friend. In fact, he later was to introduce me to my future wife.

After Kidd Springs, it was back to Laredo again and the same old routine. We were the talk of the town, the law was still eyeing us, and Lola was there. I got the "Dear John" I'd expected from Betty. The fact is that some girls are attracted by the so-called glamour of musicians and their way of life, but once they've hooked such a guy, they immediately want him to quit the business and "go to work" like a good boy. Then, dissatisfied with a humdrum life, they start shopping around for someone more exciting. With Lola it was different. She didn't make such demands, and since we had never expressed any affection in words, there was no resentment when we drifted apart a few years later. I have fond memories of her. As for the others, it's good that I was jilted by the phonies, because I found a girl at last who could accept me as I was without trying to change me.

After Laredo and before Kidd Springs, I joined a band that Brooks Pruitt had put together for a job on "Chancre Alley" in Seminole. It was there that Pruitt got into the only one of his knuckle-busters that lasted more than one or two blows—his. I'd seen Pruitt slap a big SMU football player clear across Ackard Street in Dallas one night, but this time, he was handicapped by being tanglefoot drunk.

When Pruitt, Boyd, Cummings, and I had walked up from the job to the hotel that night, we found the door to the lobby locked. Even though the hotel was one of the best in town, it was still a dump, the floor of the lobby covered with linoleum and the front door, a wooden frame around glass. We could see a big black man with a bucket of water and a mop going over the floor with soap suds. Pruitt rattled the thumb latch on the door, but the man waved him away. Big and muscular, that guy must have outweighed Pruitt by fifty pounds, but size never bothered Pruitt. He kept rattling the latch and began kicking the bottom of the door. The man stopped mopping and came to the door. "You'll have to wait a minute. Floor's wet. Ain't no rooms here anyway."

"We live here," Pruitt said. "Open the goddamn door or I'll kick it open."

The man didn't look pleased, but he shrugged and unlocked the door. When he did, Pruitt came through it like a Texas storm. On his first swing, he slipped, almost falling on the soapy floor, so by the time he had recovered his balance, the man was ready for him, and the fight was on. They slid around the floor for a little while, neither of them able to land a good blow, until the black man grabbed a galvanized metal pitcher from the clerk's desk and came at Pruitt with it. That was the end of the fight, for Pruitt, his sense of fairness offended, wrested that pitcher away from the man and brought it down on the back of his head, putting a dent in the pitcher to match the black man's head. The fellow just sat down on the stairs, holding his head in his hands and mumbling "Crazy man, crazy," while Boyd and Cummings took the exhausted Pruitt upstairs and put him to bed.

Seminole, an oil boomtown, was one of the few places left in the Southwest where musicians could find work. It was a hotbed of jazz, where most of the best musicians in the territory played. While we were there Charlie Teagarden, Jack's thirteen-year-old brother, was playing down the street from us. Musicians could practice on the job at some of the places without fear of the band leader's whip, so the really good ones loved to play there. That was how they got to be good. I guess most of us wanted to play well enough to get into a big-name band, so that we could slack off.

Raby Cummings used to tell a story about Joe Harris, the great trombone player from Sedalia, Missouri. When Joe came to Seminole he was about as famous with his followers as Jack Teagarden was with his, but neither had heard the other play. Jack's group was playing in a room with a small bandstand. Pruitt was at the piano, which was off to one side, its back turned to the customers, and Raby was playing guitar. As he tells it, "When Joe walked in, Jack was playing a chorus. Joe stood by the piano and listened. When Jack finished his chorus, Joe put his head in his arms on the piano and cried. 'I didn't think anybody could play better than me,' he said." According to Raby, the two became friends, spending time together fooling around with their horns in their hotel rooms. Later on, when Jack left a job, Joe would often take his place.

Jack Purvis, the legendary trumpet player, one of the forerunners of the high-note artists, joined the band the summer of 1929. He later made a name for himself with a recording called "Mental Strain at Dawn." Purvis was pretty much of a screwball. He wasn't with McFall for long before having to flee the law. Eventually, he wound up in the Texas State Prison, directing the prison band that used to broadcast from there. Some time later he was reported to be living in a tree on some Pacific island and then to be working as a chef in a West Coast restaurant. I saw him again in Chicago in 1936.

Hix Blewett, who was back with the band that summer, and I were always eyeing the girls who danced by, and commenting to each other about them. We liked to make two or three tentative dates and decide later, though some of the girls did their own deciding. One night when a particularly attractive girl danced by, I side-mouthed to Blewett between a couple of half notes, "See that young brunet there?"

"Yeah," between the next two half notes.

"I'm going to marry her. Do you know her?" As it happened Hix had made a date with her sister that night. So that's how I met Margaret McClure, the girl I married a few months later. Hix called her Marge because Margaret was too much of a mouthful. She wasn't yet sixteen. We went to afternoon movies and things like that for the rest of the summer until I left the band in August.

I was meeting more musicians than ever before and beginning to feel like a pro. Toward the end of July, I got a telegram from Glenn Hughes, affectionately known as "Gotch," a trombone player from Ada whom I had known in school and, more recently, had seen in Seminole. The band he was with had been picked up by MCA and put under the direction of Jack Crawford, the "Clown Prince of Jazz." Gotch was offering me the lead alto spot with the band. (I had been playing lead for quite a while around Texas.) I accepted the job. The salary was to be eighty dollars a week, about tops in those days. It was the big time.

5

IT SEEMS TO ME that during different periods of my life the character, Drew Page, was a different person, almost someone else, and that I am looking back abstractly on those other selfs. That's the way I feel about the nine months I spent with Jack Crawford in 1929 and 1930. I have pictures to remind me that this other fellow I remember was really me.

Perhaps it's the variety of my experiences, none seeming to relate to the others, that has given my life its discontinuity. Some musicians stayed with one band for thirty years, repeating their one year of experience thirty times, but I didn't want that. I have been in just about every city and town in the U.S., as well as plenty of the villages—some of them only wide places in the road—besides working in Canada, Mexico, Cuba, Puerto Rico, Jamaica, and Greenland. The fact is, I have never had a home base, even though I lived in Dallas, Chicago, Los Angeles, and Las Vegas for varying lengths of time. There were so many other places that jobs took me. It was always working travel—the fun we had was just a fringe benefit—and it was an education. Frank Sinatra says he went to cross-country college, which expresses it very well. The road is an excellent place to learn some things about life and people—even things you wished you hadn't learned.

Jack Crawford's band was playing at Crystal Beach in Canada, across from Buffalo, when I joined him. That first night I suppose I expected the same sort of thing that most of the big bands of the time were playing—dinner music, just loud enough to disguise the slurping and smacking but still soft enough to permit talking business or seduction. I had never heard any other kind of big band. So when the band hit the first number, I was a little shocked. They played loud and lively, what we called rompin'–stompin' style. It was the kind of music that the swing bands would later take up, the only difference being that their brass players would develop more range on their instruments.

Since Hilly Edelstein, Crawford's arranger, was a clarinetist, there was a lot of clarinet work in my book. Of course, Crawford was pleased that I played the book without a mistake, but he was also a little miffed because he couldn't stump me. He kept pulling out arrangements with clarinet parts he hoped would be too hard. Some leaders want the musician to play everything right—expect it, in fact—yet are jealous of the good performer. I have known a few leaders who would try to trip up a musician just for the pleasure of bawling him out.

Gotch had recommended me because I could read, though, and after all, the parts were pretty simple compared to the clarinet work in circus and carnival bands or theater pit bands. Perhaps, Crawford thought them difficult because he wasn't a clarinetist, but having no idea that the parts were considered tough, I was a little miffed that Crawford doubted my ability to play them.

I spent thirty-five weeks working with Crawford mostly on one-nighters, although we had longer stays in some of the big cities. We went from New York to Miami (and back), from Grand Rapids, Michigan, to Seattle, and from Seattle to Los Angeles, covering thirty-two states and the District of Columbia in the process.

Since roads still weren't very good, we traveled by train on that tour—the one exception being our boat trip to Miami and back. The trains weren't all that pleasant in those days. The only cooling system was an open window, through which came soot and cinders and, when the air was heavy, smoke from the coal-powered engine. Wearing white shirts, ties, suits, and dress shoes because we had no casual clothes in those days, we were extremely vulnerable to soot and cinders, dust and rain. Staying presentable-looking was a real problem. The train traveler usually wound up with a polka-dot shirt and red eyes.

Some cars had potbellied stoves aboard to provide heat in the winter, but they were of little help. One stove, at the end of the car and usually unattended, couldn't provide much heat. Besides, somehow they always seemed to be in the car ahead of us or the one behind—never in the car where we were riding. So we wore overcoats, thrusting our hands into the opposite sleeves, shivering and cursing.

Nowadays, bands usually travel two hundred miles or more between one-nighters. No one wants to book a band only to find that his clientele is easily able to drive down to hear the band play either the day before or the day after. In those days, though, since bad roads and undependable cars kept people close to home, we didn't have to travel as far. Still, our trips took longer. Even then, train travel, although more tolerable than going by car through mud and sand, took more time because of the indirect routes we had to take. It was inevitable that we'd change trains once a day, and frequently we changed two or three times. There was much less train-changing in the wide-open West, but most of Crawford's one-nighters were in the East. Usually, changing trains meant that each man, carrying his own instruments and baggage, would have to walk fifty yards or more, go up a long flight of steps, cross an overpass, go down another flight of steps, and walk another fifty yards to the next boarding place. After that, there was usually a long wait, which we spent inside on wooden benches that might have been designed by Torquemada to torture the heretics. The separating arms in the benches were carefully spaced to prevent the traveler from lying down and stretching out.

Oftentimes, when the train to the next destination left in the early morning just after we had played a job, the inconveniences were compounded by darkness. Then, because we'd left in the middle of the night, we would arrive early and be forced to sit in the lobby of our next hotel for a couple of hours, waiting for check-in time.

After the two weeks in Crystal Beach where I had joined the band, while we were playing at the Steel Pier in Atlantic City, I heard John Philip Sousa's band. Mr. Sousa, seventy-five at the time, had come out of retirement to play one last concert. The pick-up band he was conducting wasn't very impressive, so I had no regrets about having turned down my chance to play with the band four years before.

We had fans in Atlantic City. One night, after the job one of those fans invited me to a party in her apartment down the board-walk. I was a little apprehensive, having never attended a party as a "celebrity," so I stopped in at a nearby speakeasy to have a couple of beers. The "ether beer" (near beer with a drop of ether added) was pretty potent stuff for a nondrinker to handle.

The distance to the apartment was somewhat increased by the fact that I was perambulating from side to side of the sixty-foot-wide boardwalk like a one-legged spider. By the time I finally arrived at the party, it was in full swing. I was urged to join in the consumption of what was left of the bootleg booze because, the hostess said, I was way behind.

I had assumed that the charming young woman who had invited me to the party was to be my date for the occasion. She had no such idea, however, and rejected all of my clumsy attempts to corner her. I gave up my pursuit, and we settled into light conversation, eventually drifting out onto a little balcony that overlooked the boardwalk and the ocean. She told me that her name was Doris and that she and her sister had just come down from Scranton for the week end. Then, putting her hand on my arm, she said, "I like you but I can't do anything about it." It seems she was married—and to a musician at that. I told her that I had principles too, especially when another musician's wife was involved. Still, we fooled around a little before I told her I'd better be going.

"Not quite yet," she said. "Lou—that's my sister—is waiting for you."

"Which one is she?" I asked, peering into the room where the other guests were carrying on. "Just curious, you know."

"Oh, she's not there," Doris said. "She had a little too much a little too soon. You haven't seen her. She's asleep."

"Does she know about this?"

"Well, she knows about the idea of it."

"What does she think of the idea?"

"She's all for it." She giggled. "I used to do it for her when she was married and I wasn't."

I was beginning to learn that there are all kinds.

After we left Atlantic City, I wrote to Doris for a while, in care of the restaurant where she was cashier. A few weeks later when we played Scranton, I went to her house to have a midnight snack with her and her husband. After the snack and an hour or so of visiting, I said it was time for me to go, but to my surprise, Doris said, "Lou is waiting for you in the bedroom."

Since Lou didn't turn the lights on, I've never known what she looked like. I suppose she didn't know what I looked like either.

There was to be a trip to Europe after Atlantic City—a prospect that made me feel pretty important—but Crawford gave us two weeks off, instead, when the trip didn't materialize. Having no desire to return to Dallas, which I'd left only a few weeks before, I decided to spend the time with Charles "Chuck" Franzen, our banjo and guitar player, at his home in Wisconsin.

I had written Raby Cummings and the Pittman gang for some grass, mostly for the boys in the band who liked to smoke it. I had tried it a few times but didn't like the effects. The fact is, after one drag of the stuff I couldn't find my butt with both hands, much less play my horns. Nevertheless, I carried a stick of grass around with me, thinking I'd try it again.

On the way to Chuck's house in Wisconsin, when I found myself with a couple of hours to kill between trains in Chicago, I took one drag on the stick I was carrying and went to get my first look at Chicago's loop. That was the last of my grass-smoking. All the noise, especially that of the els, was so terrifying that I threw the rest of the stick away. I just wasn't cut out to be a smoker, although I later learned to tolerate a little booze.

Chuck's German-American mother was a marvelous cook, who loaded the table three times a day. If I tried to get away before eating enough to suit them, Chuck and his brother would capture me and drag me back to the table. I gained thirteen pounds in ten days.

After that little vacation, we played one-nighters for a while, headquartering in Pottsville, Pennsylvania. One night when we didn't have to work, we went to hear the Casa Loma Band, which was playing in Pottsville and staying at our hotel. Having never heard of the Casa Loma Band, we were happily surprised. Although they lacked our band's loose swing, they played with a machinelike precision that was quite impressive.

Some of us became visiting friends around the hotel with some of the Casa Loma boys, like Billy Rausch, Gene Gifford, Pat Davis, Kenny Sargent, Howard (Joe the Horse) Hall, and Hank Biagini, the leader. The band hadn't yet hit, so they were surviving on "draw" money—probably a couple of bucks a day. One night Horse went out for a sandwich. When he got back, he asked if anybody wanted a sandwich and then started pulling out sandwiches from everywhere. Horse was big and he had on an overcoat that was big even for him. There were thirty-five sandwiches stashed in that coat.

"How come?" one of the boys asked. "Where did you get them?"

"At the cafe."

"Where did you get the money?"

"I didn't have any money. I swiped them."

A couple of years later when the Casa Loma Band had become a big hit, the Pittman Gang in Dallas, which I had rejoined by that time, sent the band a stick of grass for each member—with his name on it. Since we didn't know whether all the boys indulged or not, we didn't take any chances.

I got to New York with Crawford's band around the middle of December. New York seemed a different place since I wasn't broke this time. I heard Louis Armstrong at the Palace Theater and Coleman Hawkins, a good but then unknown tenor sax player, who was at the Roseland Ballroom with Fletcher Henderson. Henderson's band was the real start of the swing era. Milt Shaw's band, featuring Ray McKinley on drums, was playing alternate sets from the other side of the hall to provide continuous music.

One night we played a double date at the Astor Hotel with Rudy Vallee, who was at the height of his popularity. The much publicized affair had attracted quite a crowd. Rudy was late, so his band played for a while without him, alternating with our band. When he finally did appear, he was brought to the bandstand in a glass cage—a precaution not solely inspired by vanity. There was a real danger that he might be injured by that mob of his fans, all of them eager to touch him.

Naturally, Rudy, the public's idol of the day, was the big attraction, although his band, evidently a pick-up band of New York musicians, was nothing to get excited about. After Rudy left—again via glass cage—the crowd, attracted by our rip-roaring style and enthusiasm, mobbed our band. Before the night was over, there were girls all over the bandstand and one in every guy's lap—except the bass player's. Since he had to play standing up, his girl could only dance with him as he played.

The day after Christmas we left New York on the *Algonquin* for a four-week engagement in Miami Beach. Thanks to Mother Sill's seasick pills, I made it through the two-and-a-half-day journey without getting sick, but no one else escaped. I saw Gotch leaning over the rail one day, along about Cape Hatteras where the sea is rough. "What's the matter, Gotch, you got a weak stomach?" I asked, trying to put him on a bit.

"Hell no," said Gotch, "can't you see I'm puttin' it as far as the rest of 'em?"

The boat was loaded with a swarm of young women headed for Florida vacations. I got acquainted with a couple of them. Helen was married to the manager of a famous swimming star and was on her way to meet her husband, on tour with the swimmer in Miami. She invited me to call on her when we got there. The other girl, Bobby, was a rough kid from Brooklyn. We got along fine despite the language barrier—she spoke Brooklynese; I spoke Texarkihoman. The only trouble was that she liked to beat on me. Since she was a muscular girl, who could hit hard, she had my deltoids black and blue by the time we got to Miami. All the while, she wouldn't let me touch her.

I discovered that being in the big time is no protection against fiascoes when we got to Miami Beach and learned that Carter's Million Dollar Pier, where we were to play, was still being built and was nowhere near completion. Apparently, when a band is booked on a job well in advance, and something happens in the meantime to foul things up—a place has discontinued using bands or isn't ready to open yet—the booking agents send the band anyway, hoping to collect the money from the operators on a play-or-pay contract. That's what Crawford's agent had done to him. We weren't paid until much later, but we spent four weeks there, playing afternoon concerts on the beach as a gesture of fulfilling our contract.

One day Eddie Condon, Red McKenzie, and Gordon Means came to hear us play. As a result, Gotch Hughes and Eph Kelly of our band got together with them for a jam session. Red, who had a group called the Mound City Blueblowers, was a virtuoso on the comb—that is, an ordinary pocket comb with a piece of tissue paper over it, which, when placed against the lips as the player hums, has a sound like the more sophisticated kazoo. Red had a genius for finding the right notes to hum on jazz choruses. Condon played the guitar, and Means kept time wth a pair of whisk brooms on Kelly's tenor case. Means had become famous as a suitcase player since he couldn't carry his drums around to jam sessions. We wound up the session drinking from a jug of bootleg.

A few months later, Red came out with the most sensational jazz record of the time—"One Hour" with "Hello Lola" on the flip side—featuring Red, Coleman Hawkins, and Pee Wee Russell. It was the record that made Hawkins famous.

Bobby, the girl from Brooklyn, came over every day from Miami to see me at the concerts, pursuing me persistently in spite of a good deal of reluctance on my part. I tried to avoid her, but she wouldn't give up, tagging along with me to my room every day only to use me as a punching bag for a while and then take a cab back to Miami. Although I didn't dislike her, I had no money to take her around, and I didn't like being punched. So I finally told her to get lost. She cried a bit but said she would leave me alone.

The next day, though, she was at the concert again. While I was playing, she reached into my pocket, taking my hotel key, and ran away. When I got back to my room, she wanted me to take my toothbrush and go home with her. Since I couldn't argue her out of it, I went, but even though I presumed that the toothbrush meant an overnight stay, I still wasn't after her as a roll in the hay. I was just curious about what she would do after we got to her place.

This time when she started punching me, I warned her that, if she didn't stop it, I might hit her back. The warnings seemed to inspire her to harder blows, so I carried out my threat, hitting her on the arm so hard that she slammed against the wall and slid down to a sitting position on the floor.

She bounced up immediately and began tearing her clothes off, starting at the neck and ripping down, and then ran into the bathroom, coming out a moment later completely naked. "That's what I've been trying to get you to do all the time, you dummy," she said, diving onto the bed.

Helen, the married woman, had been to see me a few times, too. Nowadays, no one seems to care, but in those days adultery was still considered wrong. So when I went to her apartment one day just to pay my respects, and she asked me to stay around for a while, explaining that her husband wouldn't be back until late that night, I wasn't interested. I must say, though, after meeting her husband, I could understand why she had wanted to commit adultery.

After our four weeks in Miami Beach, we were on the road again. We took the *Sequoia* to New York, and after a job there, played one-nighters along with a couple of fortnighters for the next eight weeks. Once we played in Washington, D.C., for a party of politicians, whose guests were the stars of *Showboat*. Some of them came up to sing with us, including Paul Robeson, who sang "Old Man River." In Chicago we played a double date with Wayne King at the Aragon Ballroom. I met Wayne and also Burke Bivens, the third-saxophone player who later wrote "Josephine." ("Josephine" was originally two separate compositions, "Joe" and "Josephine," written for three clarinets in the key of D-flat. I played them in Chicago a few years later before they were put together and published under one title.) Archie Bleyer, then the foremost writer of stocks—printed arrangements—and later a scorer for Hollywood pictures, visited the wings one night.

One of our stops, Wilson, North Carolina, turned out to be a wild place. The former wife of another famous band leader met us at the station leading a party of fans that presented us with a five-gallon milk can full of moonshine as a goodwill gesture. There were parties every night. Pete Peterson, our bass player, got stoned one night and married a girl he had met there. The only other time he ever saw her was a few weeks later when we played in Atlantic City.

At the double date we played with Jan Garber in Philadelphia, our session wound up with Jan, a small man, riding 320-pound Jack Crawford's back around the stage while Jack played his soprano saxophone. No one seemed to have heard of professional jealousy in those days.

Ira Wright, our lead trumpet player, was my roommate. I had nicknamed him "Jazz" because he used some "jazzy" expressions—meaning less sophisticated than the current ones—and because he played the jazz trumpet solos in our band. Jazz had gone to a jam session one night in Pittsburg, and the next day was raving about a trumpet player he had jammed with, Roy Eldridge. Jazz told me what had happened.

"What's your name?" Roy had asked after the session.

"Ira Wright, but all the boys call me Jazz."

"All right," Roy had said. "you be Big Jazz and I'll be Little Jazz."

So, according to Ira, I was indirectly responsible for nicknaming Roy Eldridge.

Marge and I had been corresponding, so the next time the band got a vacation, I went to Dallas to marry her. We did get married, too, in Durant, Oklahoma, (to avoid the three-day waiting period required in Texas) with Jelly Caballero as best man, but the whole thing nearly fell through. When I got to Dallas, Marge was quarantined in a cousin's apartment where there was a case of scarlet fever. Two days before I was to leave, I finally succeeded in smuggling her out of the house. We got by the law all right but then had a little trouble ditching a would-be suitor. That boy followed us for quite a while before Jimmy Thornhill, who had volunteered to take us in his car, could lose him. Later, we learned that the boy had killed himself over Marge's marriage.

There was no time for a honeymoon. We spent the following night in the White Plaza Hotel, and I left the next day for Grand Rapids, Michigan. Our only wedding present was from Curtis Hurt—a baby bottle with a nipple. (We still have it.) Marge and I didn't see each other again until I left the band two months later.

We worked our way to Seattle, playing one-nighters. I could hardly believe the publicity buildup we got in Seattle. There were full-page ads in the papers, with pictures, and the whole story about the band. Although Crawford deserved it, we wondered how Seattle had heard about us since we hadn't cut any records or made any radio broadcasts. Swing bands hadn't caught on yet. In fact, the term *swing* wasn't even used until the early thirties, by Don Albert's band in Texas. Nevertheless, Jack Crawford's was a swing band, and although people liked the band when they heard it, we hadn't gotten the exposure to become really popular. I guess that's why the ads billed us as "Direct from Atlantic City"—everybody had heard of Atlantic City.

We played at a hotel owned by a woman reputed to have earned a fortune in Alaska as a whorehouse madam. Every night she was in the ballroom, making a pest of herself and telling Crawford what kind of music to play. One night Crawford sprinkled itch powder over her back to get rid of her. Another night she fell into the saxophone section, bending a few horns out of shape.

She took a liking to me, probably because she found out that I was writing for the band. She claimed to be a songwriter herself. One day she persuaded me to come to her hotel room to look over her songs. She was showing them to me when her husband came in and pointed a gun at me. Since I had left Texas, I'd grown unaccustomed to such situations, but I remembered enough to be very polite while explaining my honorable intentions. He let me go, making it clear that I had better never return, and I took his advice.

Then I ran into another social problem. A young woman at the dance one night was after me, and although I managed to ease away from her, the next day she came to my room. She was stubborn and I wasn't all that unromantic, but finally I persuaded her to leave. After the job the next night, Gotch told me there was a guy outside waiting for me with a gun. "What for?" I asked. "I haven't done anything."

"He thinks you have. He thinks you are after his girl."

Oh, I thought, the girl who had come to my room. The boys bodyguarded me out of the joint that night, and the offended lover decided to cool it, so for the second time in Seattle, I escaped being shot. It's a good feeling not to be shot once in a while when there are so many chances that you will be.

Fred Solomon, the owner of the Jungle Club, where we were to play in Los Angeles, arranged an incredible welcome for us. A ten-piece band was waiting for us at Union station along with the press and their photographers. When our train arrived, we were posed on the observation platform at the end of the last car and then paraded through downtown in a doubledeck bus, with the ballyhoo band on the top deck, playing "It's a Hot Time in the Old Town Tonight" and other appropriate pieces. The Los Angeles papers had two-page ads, which, as in Seattle, placed heavy emphasis on our being direct from Atlantic City. Of course back in Atlantic City we would probably have been billed as "direct from Los Angeles." Even now, musicians usually find it easier to get a job by writing or calling a friend in a distant city. I've known some mediocre musicians who made careers out of answering ads, working out their dismissal notices, and going on to the next job, obtained the same way.

Crawford didn't want any married men in his band although he was living with a girl, who had sung with us for a while, and he was rumored to be married to her. Peterson had kept his marriage secret, but I told Crawford about mine, making him pretty unhappy with me. I had told him several times that I might leave the band, and that was, after all, the very thing he was trying to avoid with his ban against married men. Crawford and I agreed that I would leave after the Los Angeles engagement so he could avoid the expense of bringing Ira Wright's brother out from Baltimore to replace me.

Although offered a few jobs in Los Angeles, I wanted to get

home to Marge. It never occurred to me to stay in Los Angeles and send for her. That probably would have been better, for the Depression had set in after the market crash a few months before and work was scarce. Since I had been making good money, I hadn't yet realized that the bottom had dropped out of everything.

My brother Ben, Mother, and me.
Mineral Wells, 1906. She instilled
in me an assumption of honesty.

My father (third from left, back row) and the cotton mill band he directed
in Denison in 1915. He had been a professional musician for a while in his
early youth.

When I learned that the boys in the school band were exempt from military training, I decided to join up. I'm on first-chair clarinet here with the Ada High School Band in 1924.

Harry Bennett

The National Guard 112th Cavalry Band. I'm the first clarinetist to the right of the telephone pole. When Henry Lambert came to Holdenville to organize a national

With Dodson's World Fair Shows
in 1925. The routine was to play
in the parades through town, then
concerts at the show grounds, and
then, in smaller groups, we'd
ballyhoo the sideshows.

Bell's Blue Melody Boys at the Arlington Hotel in Marlin, Texas, 1926.
Jelly Brooks, me, Coulter Richardson, Virgil Howard, Foy Robertson,
Glenn Bell, and Doug Burtis. This first job of mine in the dance band
business was a revelation to me.

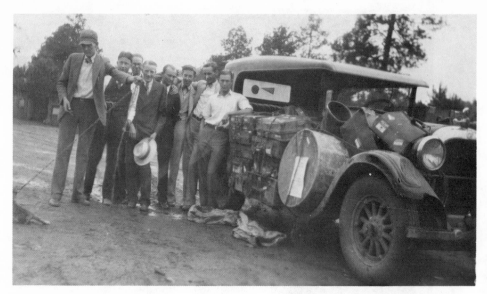

On the road with the White Mountain Boys: Raymond Jasper (with our bobcat mascot), Virgil Howard, Jelly Brooks, Happy McGuire, Glenn Bell, Julius Adams, Doug Burtis, and me. We played two nights a week at the Navajo Lodge for room and board and booked out in the area for cash.

Johnny McFall's Honey Boys when we played Nick Buccaro's Bohemian Club in Nueva Laredo, 1926. Back row: Glenn Bell, Johnny McFall, and Don Howard. Front row: a sub trumpeter, Abe Chesney, Tom Herron, Binks McFall, Spud Murphy, me, and Tincy Horton.

The one who finally did explain jazz to me, Lyle "Spud" Murphy, holding my baritone.

H. Bennett

At Kidd Springs in 1927 with a slightly different band. Standing: Johnny McFall. Back row: Abe Chesney, Curtis Hurt, Tom Herron, Glenn Bell, and Binks McFall. Front row: me, Bernie Dillon, Jelly Caballero, Don Howard, and Tincy Horton.

Fred Solomon arranged an incredible welcome for us when we arrived in L.A. in 1930. We posed on the observation platform at the end of the last car: Pete Peterson, Tim Landfear, Gotch Hughes, me, Ira Wright, Eph Kelly, Eddie Belcher, Les Cripe, Chuck Franzen, and Buck Kelly. In front: Jack Crawford shakes hands with Sonny Brooks.

J. C. Milligan

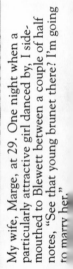

My wife, Marge, at 29. One night when a particularly attractive girl danced by, I side-mouthed to Blewett between a couple of half notes, "See that young brunet there? I'm going to marry her."

Then we paraded through downtown in a doubledeck bus with the ballyhoo band on top, playing "It's a Hot Time in the Old Town Tonight." Our band stands in front of the bus: Taft Schreiber, Les Cripe, Chuck Franzen, Ira Wright, Eph Kelly, me, Jack Crawford, Gotch Hughes, Eddie Belcher, Tim Landfear, Pete Peterson, Buck Kelly, and Fred Solomon, our host.

J. C. Milligan

Fats Obenir (left) with his band in Galveston, 1931. I'm third from the left, Tommy Gonsoulin is fifth from the left, and Irving Verret is at far right. Gonsoulin and Verret were Louisiana boys in Texas territory. *Maurer*

Sitting: me, Margaret Kraft, and the Saturday night drummer. Standing: Glynn Harris, the Saturday night guitarist, Walter Esser, and A. Von Buel-witz. We played noon and dinner sessions on a balcony behind false palm trees, and on Saturday nights, augmented by guitar and drums, we played in the ballroom. *Eckler*

The Majestic Theater in Dallas decided to try vaudeville again in 1932. Curtis Hurt (lower right) and I (upper left) worked in the pit band.

Corny pose at the Limehouse in Chicago, 1937: Jimmy Green and Frank Norton, the trumpet player, sitting on the edge of the bandstand; Mel Henke at the piano and Bob Fuelgraf on drums—both poised to strike; and me, reared back, clarinet pointing to the sky. *Seymour Rudolph*

The Harry James band on the Steel Pier in Atlantic City, 1939. Front row: Ralph Hawkins, Truett Jones, Connie Haines, Harry James, Frank Sinatra, Dave Matthews, and Jack Palmer. Middle row: Jack Schaeffer, Thurman Teague, me, Russ Brown, Claude Bowen, and Red Kent. Back row: Claude Lakey, Jack Gardner, and Bill Luther.

Central Studios

6

AN OLD TRAVEL ad describes the bus of 1930 as a plush coach with reclining seats, vanity mirrors, and a hot water heater—"really something." The fact is, it had to be really something to even make the trips in those days.

Roads, although a little wider than they had been six years before when I'd gone from Oklahoma to Phoenix, were still unpaved. On the desert west of Phoenix, I saw the remains of the first highway in Arizona, which had been made of a single row of railroad ties laid edge to edge on the desert sand. Even traveling on a road like that stirred up so much dust that half the desert land seemed to be up in the air. Barreling along at thirty miles an hour, the bus could usually stay ahead of its own dust, especially going against the wind. When the bus and the wind were going in the same direction at the same speed, though, the synchronized speeds left us with nothing but our own second-hand air to breathe.

The bus's engine would overheat regularly, just as car engines did. We would stop at a service station, and while the attendant was adding water and hosing down the engine, he would give us directions to the next town. Asking directions was an absolute necessity, too, for the highway was so circuitous that, if we had made a wrong turn, we could have wound up back in Los Angeles.

I had become acquainted with my seatmate on the bus, a woman of about forty, and had indulged in a few sporadic bits of conversation with her. That is, she took care of the talking, and I did the listening, nodding occasionally just to keep things lively while counting the saguaros and joshuas. She was trying her best to start up a romance every time we'd stop to eat. I tried to avoid her, especially off the bus.

It was while we were having lunch in El Paso that she suggested in a loud whisper that we spend the night there together and, the following day, cross the border to Juarez. When I refused, she made an offer to foot the whole bill. Since I didn't look broke, I figured she was trying to "mother" me and made a more vociferous refusal.

All the while, I had been looking around. From the eatery's window I could see an airplane parked near the bus. It was only the second one I had seen at close range. My woman friend told me it was a passenger plane, but she didn't know where it was headed. "Go ask," she said.

At the ticket desk I found out that the plane was flying to Dallas.

"Can I get on it?"

"Sure. That's what it's for. It's a new thing. You can transfer to it if you'd like."

"I'd like," I said.

It would have taken about two more days to get to Dallas by bus and only about six hours by plane. I was bus-weary, eager to get home, and anxious to excuse myself from my woman friend. Besides, it seemed a much more adventurous way to go.

The little plane had five passenger seats and on the arm of each was a paper-cup vomitory, a thoughtful consideration. Those old crates couldn't get above the ground winds, so they bobbed up and down and sometimes sideways at a sickening speed. Luckily, though, I didn't have to use my paper cup.

Texans were still fighting the Civil War at that time. Some of the Dallas musicians frowned on me for having consorted with northerners thereby deserting the "Cause" and converting to damyankeeism. Then too, there seemed to be some prejudice in Dallas in favor of Masons. On top of that, there were a favored few, the established musicians, who had all of the "ins" and weren't about to accept the young ones in their oligarchy. In spite of all of my shortcomings, though, I managed to get a job right away, in Galveston, down south of Houston on an island in the Gulf of Mexico. I still had no idea what the Depression was going to mean, and since I felt like a big shot, I had been so loose with my few bucks that we were nearly broke by the time Marge and I got to Galveston. We had just enough to get by on until payday.

Some of us stayed in a little apartment house downtown, which was frequented by musicians. Every day around noon I awoke to the tapping of feet upstairs—Eddie "Snoozer" Quinn was playing his guitar. I had been hearing about Snoozer Quinn since I'd started in the business. He could do things that most modern guitarists would think impossible. Snoozer could play solo passages with one hand as well as he could with two. He had a favorite trick of playing a solo with one hand while lighting a cigarette with the other. Paul Whiteman had hired him as a special soloist and taken him on his tours, but Snoozer had recently quit him and come back to home territory, saying that Whiteman had worn him out taking him around to parties and other off-hour affairs. Snoozer was a retiring sort of person, who lived with his guitar, carrying it around with him wherever he went. He would play it whenever he had a spare moment. Some nights we sat out on a pier, listening to him play until sunup.

The payday I had been counting on never came. We played in the joint for a week before it folded and the operator disappeared. We had to get back to Dallas or starve, whichever came first.

The band leader, Happy King, had an auto (as they were still called), a secondhand one, of course, for no musician could afford to pay $400 for a new one. Even the down payment on a jalopy was usually only within reach for the leaders. "Buy a car and become a leader" was the saying.

So Marge and I rode back to Dallas with King and three other band members. The three Houstoners from the eight-man band had already gone back to Houston. Besides the six of us, the car was also packed with our instruments—one a bass fiddle—and our baggage. After a day and a half of sweat, cramps, and hunger, we chugged and sputtered into Dallas, broke and out of work. Marge and I went to stay with one of her aunts. Actually, that disaster was mild compared to some of those that followed.

Raby Cummings booked a job for a six-piece band in Oklahoma City. He had hired Charles Lavere Johnson by telephone before we left and took Curtis Hurt, Roger Boyd, Jesse James, and me with him. Marge and I rode in the rumble seat of Roger's Model A.

When we arrived in Oklahoma City, we found that the joint, which was in the oil fields on the outskirts of town, wasn't ready to open yet. It was just a pine floor enclosed by a half wall, topped by chicken wire to keep out crashers. We spent our afternoons for several days putting a finish on the floor by dragging bales of hay over corn meal with Marge and Loraine, Spud Murphy's ex-wife who was now married to Raby, sitting on the bales to add weight.

Raby arranged for us to eat on the cuff at a little cafe downtown, which was owned by his cousin, who had the jake leg from drinking jamaica ginger and was, in turn, getting his supplies on the cuff. We got rooms in a run-down hotel with community bathrooms.

The piano that Lavere had to play was so out of tune that he had to compensate by playing the regular key with his right hand while playing a half tone higher in the bass. It wasn't easy, but Lavere is a musical genius.

We didn't have to put up with that piano for long because the joint folded after three or four days. Raby was a good talker but he couldn't get anywhere with the boss, so for finishing the floor, playing the job, and picking up a bucket of toenails every night after the dance, we were zeroed. Consequently, so were Raby's cousin and the hotel. I could have been making a salary in Laredo with Don Howard, but I had turned down the job. I guess I was slow to learn that loyalty is for losers. My father, who was working in Oklahoma City at the time, lent me twenty dollars and I financed the trip back to Dallas for the seven of us.

Right away, Earl Hatch, the fine percussionist and keyboard player who composed "What's the Reason I'm Not Pleasin' You," hired me for a band he was forming to play the Texas Hotel in Ft. Worth. Marge and I stayed with one of her aunts there until I got a week's pay. For playing noon sessions in the lobby of the hotel and dances in the mezzanine ballroom at night, we got thirty dollars a week. Earl was playing piano, accordion, xylophone, and vibes. He taught his brother Bud, who was staying at the hotel for a while, how to play bass and hired him for the band.

After the Texas Hotel job we had one more engagement, at the

Saint Anthony Hotel in San Antonio for four weeks, before the band broke up. Marge, pregnant by then, went to stay with her brother, who was managing W. L. Moody's guest ranch at Junction, Texas, and his wife, while I went back to Dallas to look for another job. After about a month of jobbing around, I was able to rent an apartment and send Marge bus fare to join me.

Roger Boyd called me from Mobile, Alabama, to join a band there, but I didn't want to leave Marge alone while she was pregnant. When Roger got back he told me about an incident on the trip out. At a roadside eatery somewhere in Louisiana he was to pick up a trumpet player who was going to join the band. "I was there on time," said Roger, "but there was nobody in the joint but the counter man and a little kid playing the marble machine. I waited and waited but nobody showed up.

"Finally, I got worried. I had been drinking coffee till I was drunk on the stuff. The counter man saw that I was gettin' fidgety, and he asked me if I was waiting for somebody. I said, 'Yeah, I'm supposed to pick up a trumpet player here. His name is Harry James. You know him?'

"The guy said, 'Sure. That's him over there playing the marble machine.'

"'Oh come on,' I said. 'That little skinny kid?'"

Roger was worried about joining a band that would use a puny little kid like that on first trumpet. He was thinking that, maybe, he should have stayed home. "But man," he said, "was I surprised when we got there and heard him play! Page, you wouldn't believe it! He does everything possible on the horn and half that ain't."

That was the beginning of Harry's fame with the big boys around Texas. The word got around.

I had had to turn down a job with Hank Biagini's Casa Loma band, again because of Marge's pregnancy. Although he was playing the Adolphus Hotel in Dallas, I knew that Hank's was a traveling band that would be leaving soon. I couldn't go on the road again while Marge was expecting.

A couple of weeks later, though, Gotch Hughes asked me to come to San Antonio, where the band was playing the Plaza Hotel, to sub for the lead alto player, Ernani "Noni" Bernardi

(Hank Biagini's nephew). There were several Dallas musicians in the band—Wray Sherrill (an alumnus of Johnny McFall's band) on guitar and vocals, Pete Noriego on first trumpet, "Rats" Hill on second alto sax, Gus Gilbert on second trumpet—besides Eph Kelly on tenor sax, and Bob Zurke on piano.

Returning to Dallas, I got a call from Johnny McFall to go to Laredo again, replacing Don Howard, who had played out his contract. When we went down there in November, I couldn't take Marge with me, but I sent for her after I got settled.

I was apprehensive about running into Lola again since I had heard a few of the stories about her. She had reportedly become a whorehouse madam by that time.

Somehow, she found out that I was back and where I was staying, but when she called me, I told her that I couldn't see her anymore, that I was married now. I knew that just talking with another woman was grounds, if not for divorce, at least for a colossal argument. I never saw or heard from her again. Lola was not adverse to conning people out of money, but she never conned anybody with love. I have a special affection for people who are honest about their emotions since I've run into quite a few who operated the other way—on phony love.

Jesse James played trombone with the band in Laredo. He had brought his wife, Jewell, with him, and when Marge came down, we got an apartment for two couples. I would ride to work with Jesse in his Chevrolet coupe. He was generally a quiet, lovable guy, but he sometimes got carried away with his drinking.

One night when he had been drinking, a couple of the boys wanted to go "whorehopping"—making the rounds of the whorehouses just to interview the girls with no intention of buying their wares. Jesse, in a vulnerable state of alcoholic magnanimity, was easily persuaded to take them. I didn't want to go, so I rode the running board as far as International Bridge and walked the rest of the way home.

Just after I got home and into bed, I heard a crash out on the street. Later one of the boys woke me up to tell me that Jesse had run into a pole in front of the apartment building. Francis "Dozy" Cruz, our lead sax player, was in the hospital, and Jesse was in jail.

I went to see Dozy first. His knee cap had been severed in the accident. The parts had to be drawn back together, and it was a long time before Dozy could walk again. He left the band and quit the music business temporarily.

Jesse was in an alcoholic stupor when I went to see him at the jail that night, but except for some glass cuts on his face and forehead, he was uninjured. He was in no condition to understand the bawling out I gave him. There was nothing I could do to get him out of jail, and having just seen Dozy, I didn't really care. I was glad that I had ducked out of the trip that night.

Marge developed some pregnancy trouble, so we decided to return to Dallas. Marge and Jewell James, who was pregnant, too, although her doctor was telling her she had a tumor, drove the Chevrolet back. I took a bus later, and Jesse stayed on with McFall till the job ended.

Frank Williams, an out-of-town leader, who had, I think, come down from Oklahoma University, hired me for lead alto. We played at Lake Worth, near Ft. Worth, for two weeks and went from there to Medicine Park in Oklahoma.

I happened to hear Joe Gill's band—probably the best band that had come to Texas—on a broadcast from Dallas. The band had originated in St. Louis. Gordon Jenkins was doing the arrangements, and I found myself wishing that I could play with a band like that again.

While I was back in Dallas jobbing around for a few weeks, our first daughter was born. Marge named her Margie Drew after both of us. Then, Jimmy McMannus, who had joined Joe Gill's band, called me, asking me to join the band in Galveston. I thought I had it made again, so, sending Marge and the baby to stay with my half sister in Denison, I went to Galveston.

I walked right into another fiasco. The sax player I was to replace had decided to stay on with the band. McMannus didn't have the authority to hire me, but Gill was supposed to release the saxophonist, so he told me to hang around. I hung around for three weeks.

Two of my old friends were out of work in Galveston, too, Truett Jones and Carl Shamburger. Carl played guitar and saxophone, and also sang. He must have been influenced by exposure to the large population of black people in his hometown, Marshall, Texas, for he had the black man's touch in his singing. Carl put more feeling into a song than any other singer I've heard.

We met Sam Maceo, the reputed ruler of Galveston at that time, who took a liking to Shamburger's singing and began taking us on tours of the whorehouses to entertain the girls. I would accompany Carl on clarinet. His songs made those girls cry, some of them leaving the reception parlor for a while to adjust their emotions before returning for more. Their special favorites were "Was It a Dream" and "Love for Sale."

Finally, Joe Gill suspended the saxophone player for two weeks. It was only fair since he had told McMannus to send for me. I worked the two weeks and went back to Dallas.

Raby Cummings managed to talk the manager of radio station WRR into using a staff band. For six dollars a week, each, our nine-man band played for an hour at noon, an hour at dinnertime, and a half-hour rehearsal before each show. We played thirty short numbers per show, with spot announcement interspersed. Raymond McLeod and Warren Smith, both of whom I knew from the days with Harrison's Texans, were playing with that band, too.

Along with the radio job, Raby booked an afternoon session for five of us in a downtown drugstore, next to Neiman-Marcus. We played up on a balcony, the confectionary section for the kids who could afford cokes, for two hours a day, six days a week. We weren't paid in cash though—only a credit of five dollars in merchandise. Clois "Cubby" Teagarden was with us playing drums on his first professional job. I used the opportunity to experiment, beginning to ad lib in a vague, amateurish way.

The ideas and principles of good jazz filtered down to me from years of working with and listening to good jazz men. I learned that, paradoxically, it's necessary to practice playing ad lib to become any good at it. Those intricate little phrases that jazz soloists seem to produce effortlessly can't well up from inside the performer unless they are familiar to him, unless he has played them before. However, the performer doesn't "think" after he or she becomes proficient. Lots of practice relieves the musician of the need to think; he can play automatically, as if in a trance. Some performers go into a sort of self-hypnosis, afterward having no recollection of what they have just played. I once heard Harry James answer a trumpet player who had asked how he thought of all those things to play. Harry's answer explained the whole thing: "I don't think," he said. "If I did, I couldn't play them."

Good jazz musicians have stored all sorts of phrases in their heads—phrases that they have encountered somewhere before. Exercise books are full of useful passages that can be incorporated in jazz phrases. An unlimited technique on the instrument is what makes it possible to utilize them. Red Nichols, for example, went through the whole of *Arban's Method for Trumpet*—a big thick book—marking every melodic passage that might be used as a jazz "lick" by itself or be combined with part of another. After a lot of practice, those parts of phrases do the combining on their own. Classical music, is, likewise, full of usable phrases. In fact, some classical pieces become jazz when a little jazz interpretation is added to them.

During the twenties, a spate of books came on the market at fifty cents each, containing jazz licks and "breaks". (*Breaks* are the music the soloist plays when the band stops for two or more measures to let him show off.) Those licks and breaks were supposed to be memorized and used wherever they might fit. It was a crude method, but until that time it had been thought that jazz could not be written at all. The books were probably useful to some novices.

Some musicians copied licks from other players, especially from recordings of big-name players, or they got together to exchange licks. Naturally, we were all influenced by others, if only unconsciously. We absorbed the style of the times. I don't believe any of the old masters of improvisation, like Bach for instance, would have been able to sit in with a jazz band or play a jazz solo without having heard jazz before.

As Jelly Brooks had suggested, I began to practice "putting licks behind that stuff." I could tell by the notes in a passage what chord it would fit in. I had not yet heard that Red Nichols had done it, but I went through the books looking for passages and phrases to use as licks. After some time, the parts of phrases began coming together. If anyone had asked me what style I played, I would probably have said *Lazarus*. (That's the clarinetists' bible.)

The only clarinet solos I copied from records were two by Frank Teschemacher, just to analyze what he was doing. One clarinet player, Merle Turner, from Arkansas City, Kansas, made a record once, not realizing until he heard the playback, that his solo was the same, almost note-for-note, as Benny Goodman's on his recording of the tune some time before. I always figured that imitators can't beat the creative artists at their own games anyway.

By the time I had finished the job with Raby Cummings, I was playing a little jazz—enough to get a name for it around the home territory. I had the fundamentals that players who just pick up a horn and start blowing don't have, and success depends on a good foundation. A player who is a master of technique can play emotionally, too—as Billy Butterfield, Jack Teagarden, Charlie Teagarden, Harry James, Coleman Hawkins, and others—or turn around and play with technical perfection. But a musician operating purely on feel is limited. Some of the old stars, famous for their emotional styles, have become legendary, even mythical, despite the fact that they were only mediocre musicians.

Getting known on the air led to night jobs. Playing on percentage, we sometimes earned as much as a dollar a night, but usually much less. One night at a watermelon garden, we got paid in a five-cent slice of watermelon, but the slice was a quarter of a melon—and not the kind of melon you see in stores nowadays, which we call Texas grapes. Although the official record size of a watermelon is 197 pounds, I have seen melons weighing 220 pounds or more displayed for sale. The average size of the watermelons that night was about 45 pounds. Our five-cent slices were just average size, but who could eat a slice of watermelon four feet long anyway?

We did better financially after we got a job at White Rock Lake playing in an open air joint called Lakeside Pavilion, making up to twenty dollars a night until cold weather closed the place for the winter. Cubby was replaced by Jack Free, another of Harrison's Texans, and Bud Hatch took his second professional job as our bass player.

When the pavilion closed, Warren Smith and Henry Laib, our piano player, went to work with Lawrence Welk's five-piece band at the Baker Hotel. Welk had come to Texas from South Dakota and picked up some Texas boys, including Jelly Brooks. Those three friends of mine tried to get me on the band, but Welk wouldn't hire me. He told me later in Chicago that my friends had talked me up so big he was afraid he would have to pay me more money.

Wesley "Freckles" Barry, the erstwhile movie star, came through with a band made up mostly of Texans. My friend, Stanley Hall, who was managing the band personnel, hired me, and I joined the band at the Washington Hotel in Shreveport, Louisiana. After a few one-nighters, we went to the Rice Hotel in Houston for four weeks.

While in Houston I met John "Peck" Kelley, who was playing the Rathskeller in the Rice. Since Barry's band ate at the hotel, I listened to Peck every day at noon and at dinnertime. One day he had a little jam session at his house. Pete Peterson from Jack Crawford's band and Carl Shamburger were there. While Carl was singing, Peck's black housemaid came out of the kitchen, looked at Shamburger for a moment, and then said, "Lordy! I thought that was Mister Armstrong singing."

Wesley's band broke up after the Houston job, so I went back to Dallas, broke as usual. Marge got us free lodging with an aunt again, and I got a job in the staff band at KRLD radio station, which broadcast from the Adolphus Hotel. We only had to play one session a day instead of the two we had played at WRR for the same dollar a day. Marge's aunt lived near the fairgrounds, about two miles from downtown. Lacking streetcar fare, I left the house around six o'clock every morning to walk to the job. There was no place at KRLD to leave instruments, so I carried my saxophone, my clarinet, and the stand for them back and forth every day. I got to know many of the people in that part of town, for they had to walk to work, too. The depression was really being felt. Shanty Morrell was the band leader, but about the only leadership he offered was to tell us, "Play it . . . well, like the big boys do." It was a good thing we knew what he meant, because he didn't seem to.

After a few weeks of that chore, I got a job in a club band again, in Galveston with Frank "Fats" Obenir. We played for the Maceo people at a place called Virginia Inn. Obenir was on drums, Irvin Verret on trombone, Tommy Gonsoulin on trumpet, Dozy Cruz, Cooper Stoughton, and I on saxes, and Henry Laib on piano. We had a local man named Guttwald to play bass with us.

Obenir, who had been Joe Gill's drummer, and I ran into Gill one night. He wanted both of us to come back with his band, although he didn't have a job at the time. We declined the offer. I was still pretty angry about the first time I'd worked with him. Peck Kelley had been with Gill for a while then, and Harry James was on first trumpet.

Vernon Brown, who was with Gill at the time, told me some forty years later how Harry had come to join the band. He and some young friends had come to hear the band and the friends pestered Gill to let Harry sit in, praising him enthusiastically. Gill turned to the band saying something like "All right, let's take care of the little smart asses." He let Harry sit in but called the hardest number in the book for trumpet. Brown said it started on high D, double "f" (or double forte, meaning very loud). Nevertheless, Harry "tore up the joint," playing the part better than it had ever been played before. Gill hired him.

There is a legend that jazz started with a Negro playing his piccolo in a bucket, the word jazz being derived from the abbreviation of a player's name—Jas. for James. That's only one version of how jazz originated. No one knows for certain how it started, but the legends agree that it began in Louisiana with Dixieland jazz. Texas, however, is not part of Dixie, and Texas jazz is a different sort of music from Dixieland. Irvin Verret and Tommy Gonsoulin, from Bogalusa, Louisiana, were Dixieland players, while the rest of us played Texas style, a difference about analogous to the soft Negro-influenced southern drawl, compared to the harsher inflection, influenced by the Mexicans. There has always been a friendly rivalry between Louisiana and Texas musicians, but sometimes personality conflicts change it to something less amiable.

I got my first inkling of the rivalry one night when Cooper Stoughton, a flighty sort of kid, took offense at something Tommy

Gonsoulin had said and challenged him to a knuckle-buster. Neither of them could have fought the gnats off the other's behind, even if he could have landed a blow, which neither of them did. But Irvin Verret was rooting for Gonsoulin while we Texans just naturally rooted for Stoughton. That fight ended in a draw but it made me realize that there was, indeed, a rivalry between the Louisiana and Texas musicans, which, I found out later, some took pretty seriously, even bitterly. As for me—I wound up a fast friend of both Verret and Gonsoulin.

The job with Obenir lasted for four weeks; then it was back to Dallas again. I got a call to join Roy Diven's band at the Natatorium, known as the Nat, in Amarillo, and there, I first met Thurman Teague. Although Thurm was a guitar player, Roy had told him that, if he could play bass, he could have a job. So Thurm took his guitar to a hock shop and made a trade for a bass fiddle. Since he had grown up next door to Bob Casey, a fine bass player, in Illinois, he knew the fundamental fingering and was able to begin as a good bass player without practice.

Soon after getting to Amarillo, I was offered a job as a legitimate clarinetist in a little concert group at Hot Springs, Arkansas. Glynn Harris, the man who had recommended me, warned me that most of the music would be written for the A clarinet, to be transposed on the B-flat instrument. I had done quite a bit of that in the theater in Beaumont but was rusty on it. Since the job in Hot Springs wouldn't begin until October, about three months away, I practiced transposition three or four hours every day for those three months.

It happened that Diven closed at the Nat at about the same time I was to go to Hot Springs. After three months at a steady salary of twenty dollars a week, Marge and I were pretty well off. We had paid five dollars a week for a whole upstairs apartment, and our grocery bill had been around five dollars a week, including goodies for Margie Drew. Even after splurging on new clothes and other luxuries, we had saved about forty dollars. We were in high cotton.

Since buses and trains were routed through Dallas, a long way south, even though Hot Springs was due east of us, we answered an ad in the newspaper for passengers to Hot Springs. The old man we went with managed to get us there eventually, and we had a few dollars left after the trip. We set ourselves up in an apartment for four dollars a week. Since the job in Hot Springs was to pay thirty a week, we had nothing to worry about. It seemed that I was back in the big time again. Everything was fine.

The concert group was under the name of Margaret Kraft, a very fine legitimate pianist, and led by the violin player, A. Von Buelwitz. Both he and the cellist, Walter Esser, had been with the Chicago Symphony Orchestra. Glynn Harris played trumpet with the group, and I was on clarinet. We played noon and dinner sessions on a balcony, behind false palm trees so the audience couldn't see us. On Saturday nights, augmented by a guitar and drums, we played upstairs in the ballroom. The cello player doubled on saxophone, so we had two saxes and a trumpet to carry the load of God-knows-what dance music. It must have been pretty bad, but our patrons were mostly old people who didn't know the difference. They could barely make it to the dance floor anyway. (Hot Springs is a health resort, and in those days it was patronized mostly by unhealthy rich people and gangsters on sabbatical.)

The music that Margaret called out to play was routine to her, but having never seen it before, I was transposing at sight. I did all right on most of it, but there were a few things that I had to take home and practice—like "Dark Eyes," which ran all over the clarinet in the key of F-sharp, and "Calloirhoe Suite," both of them scored for the A clarinet. There is a solo for clarinet in "Calloirhoe Suite" that is the nemesis of all clarinetists. Von Buelwitz always played the passage because it was supposed that an ordinary clarinet player couldn't play it. I was an ordinary clarinet player, having never even heard of "Calloirhoe Suite" before, but the idea that they thought I couldn't play that solo rankled. I took the part home and practiced on that passage for hours every day until I finally mastered it. Still, the violin player always played it and I laid out. When our contract was up, another group came in. The new group's leader was standing behind me while we played our last concert. Margaret called "Calloirhoe Suite," and when the clarinet passage came up, I played it right along with the violinist, just for the benefit of the replacement leader. He patted me on the shoulder and said, "You are the first clarinet player I ever heard play that."

That job lasted until January. Toward the end of the contract I had gotten word from Warren Smith that I could work with Lloyd Snyder in Liberal, Kansas. Any job was good in those days of the depression, this one especially so because Smitty would be there. He was my idol among trombone players, and in those days, he had the whole Southwest "treed" as well.

We had saved a few dollars in Hot Springs, so I decided to buy a car for the trip to Liberal. I paid sixty-five dollars for a 1925 Buick sedan, which I found in a repair garage. The garage man threw in a set of license plates, taken from another car, for free. Licenses weren't as important then.

We cut across the country on county roads and through cow pastures—sand or dust or mud all the way. Liberal was only a few miles away when rain forced us to stop for the night in Perryton, Texas, up in the Panhandle. The top of the old car was leaking on all of us, especially Margie Drew in the back seat. We arrived in Liberal about ten o'clock the next morning. Snyder had waited for me as long as he could before leaving at nine for Sante Fe, New Mexico, to play the governor's ball.

7

LLOYD SNYDER had the best little band in the territory: Smitty on trombone, doubling trumpet and saxophone; George Yadon on tenor sax; Scott Seely on piano; Mickey Tracy on trumpet, doubling violin (and playing jazz on it); Mike Dixon on drums; Les Neaal and I on alto saxophones, Neaal doubling violin and I doubling flugelhorn; Thurman Teague on bass; and Lloyd Snyder himself on violin and trombone. We were a wild and swinging group, playing a combination of jazz and dinner music. It was that band, with some personnel changes, that Buddy Rogers picked up when he became a band leader. But even though it was a good band and we had fun, we played everything on percentage, and since times were bad, we barely made expenses.

Snyder suspended action for a while, so the band scattered. I took Seely, Yadon, Tracy, Smith, and Teague back to Dallas in the old Buick, along with Smitty's wife and their son, Gary, who was three days younger than Margie Drew. We were all about equally well heeled—I had about three dollars—so we brought cheese and crackers along. In Amarillo we stopped at a hotel dining room that charged two bits for all you could eat, children free. The single boys splurged a quarter apiece, but Smitty and I sent our wives and kids in while we waited in the car. We dined on what Marge and Eula Mae (Smitty's wife) were able to skim from the table.

A price war was holding gasoline down to eight cents a gallon, and I had my own tire repair kit and a hand pump for the usual flats. To repair a tire it was necessary to release the clamps holding the rim together, thus breaking the rim and allowing the tire to be removed. That wasn't too difficult, but it was hard to get the rim back together. So, despite our lack of funds, whenever there was a filling station in sight, we'd roll the tire down and let them fix it. Filling stations didn't travel with us, though. We were lucky a time or two, but the trip to Dallas was a thirty-six-hour, four-flat trip.

There were no jobs to be had in Dallas until I finally got an offer from Roy Diven and took Smitty with me. Diven was working out his notice at the Nat in Amarillo, but he had also booked a job in Albuquerque, New Mexico.

The night before we were to leave for Albuquerque, the temperature dropped spectacularly, from seventy-six at midafternoon to ten below the next morning. Marge and I woke up to find a foot-high pile of snow beneath our bedroom window and a frozen car. Smitty and I used newspaper torches to thaw it out. There was a crude heater under the floor between the front and the back seats, covered by an iron grate. To turn it on we had to crawl under the car and open the vent with a wrench. Then, since there was no way to control it, after it got red-hot, someone had to crawl under the car again to turn it off.

In Albuquerque, Smitty's family and mine moved into a private home for five dollars a week each, room and board. I can't recall the name of the woman who owned the house, but her daughter's name was Mary. She was a student at the university across the street and engaged to Harry Hickox, the band leader whom we were following on this job, and who was following us back in Amarillo. They later married and moved to Hollywood, where he became a movie actor and Mary had her own radio program.

We weren't able to work for long before Diven had to lay off some of the band. Since he played trombone and saxophone himself, Smitty and I were the logical people to cut, so we volunteered to leave. We paid Mary's mother for the last week of room and board, but as we were about to take off, she called us back. Handing us the money, she said, "You kids are going to need this. Take it and send it to me later." We still remember that kindness.

President Roosevelt had just declared the national "bank holiday" when we arrived in Amarillo—not that we had any banked money to worry about. Since the flow of money just about stopped, though, the best we could do was a job with a local group in a restaurant that paid us five dollars a week in food. Nelson Grimes, the tenor sax player in the group, wanted to take a lesson from me, so I gave him a few pointers on the bandstand during a break. He tried to give me thirty-five cents, but I refused to take it. He persisted, but I still refused. Finally, he laid the quarter and the dime on the piano keyboard, and when I tried to pick them up to give them back to him, I knocked them down a crack between the keys into the bottom of the piano. Just when it doesn't seem possible that things could get worse, they do. Nevertheless, after a few days we played a dance job somewhere, making enough to get us out of town and back to Dallas.

A friend I'd met in Hot Springs, Bedford Brown, got me a job there at the Kings Hotel, playing dinner music for rooms and five dollars a week. The room deal didn't include wives, so I had to rent an apartment—for four dollars a week, which left a dollar to eat on. We ate up most of the popcorn in town the first week. I was rolling our own cigarettes with Bull Durham.

We were supposed to book dances for extra money, but dance jobs were scarce. I remember playing only two. One was in Pine Bluff. The other was for a CCC camp up in the mountains. Since the camp was for men only and there were no dancing "dates" to be had around there, the entire female attendance was one whore from Hot Springs. Several fights broke out over who was to dance with her next, but nobody was hurt—except possibly the whore, later.

Not only was I unable to make ends meet, but I didn't even have the price of a ticket to hear Duke Ellington's band when he played a one-nighter in our hotel. I felt I had to get out of Hot Springs. Then, somehow, I landed a job in Little Rock with a five-piece local group. The band was playing in a restaurant downtown for meals—unfortunately not including meals for wives—and in a joint a little way out of town at night. I stayed with that job for exactly one day and one night.

Arriving in Little Rock just before noon, I found the restaurant where the band played for the lunch hour and parked the car in front. While I played the noon session, the girls stayed in the car because I had no money for lunch. I had my earned lunch on the break. I explained my embarrassing insolvency to the leader, and he lent me fifty cents to buy lunch for Marge and Margie Drew. That was plenty in that part of the country during the Depression. In some places you could get a breakfast of ham or bacon and eggs with all the trimmings—slices of tomatoes, a big slice of onion, and a quarter of a cucumber pickle—and toast and coffee for fifteen cents. In this case, Marge was able to buy lunch for thirty-five cents and a quart of milk for four cents and still have money to spare.

The owner of the nightclub furnished rooms for the band members, and this time, I got a room for myself and the girls. He also gave us a meal at dinnertime. The owner seemed like an elderly man to us kids, though I imagine he was about forty-five. He took an immediate fancy to Margie Drew, carrying her or leading her around by the hand most of the night.

The bandstand, raised about four feet off the ground, was enclosed by a spear-headed wrought-iron fence, also about four feet high. We got onto the stand by means of stairs on one side that led to a gate on the stand. A musician couldn't have fallen off the stand no matter how drunk he might have been, nor could he have stepped over it. To have hurdled it, landing on the floor eight feet below, counting the fence, would have been disastrous.

We played a set of forty-five minutes, and when we took a break, I headed for the gate to leave the bandstand. The leader called me back. "We stay on the stand," he said. "We don't get off till intermission."

"How come?" I wanted to know. "This isn't a dime-a-dance joint."

"We're locked in," he explained. "We get off once a night."

I went to the gate and found it padlocked. I realized then what the fence was for. There was no way to get off the stand. I went back to the leader. "I've never been in jail before," I said. "What's the charge? What are we in for?"

"The old man's crazy," the leader said. "We have to go along with his fool ideas. It's better than to risk getting shot."

"I don't have to go along with it," I said. "He can take his joint and stuff it." But there was nothing I could do about it. I caught Marge's eye, beckoned her over, and explained the situation, advising her to watch out for the baby. "I'll see you at intermission," I told her. "See what you can find out about this guy and this joint. Looks like we'll have to get out of here."

Marge had been sitting at the waitresses' table all evening, getting acquainted with some of the girls. One of them told her plenty, and when the boss unlocked the gate to let us off for intermission, she filled me in. It seems that the boss had just been released from an insane asylum in the custody of his brother, a wealthy local politician, who had set him up in the nightclub to isolate him from public view. He was said to be pretty peculiar. Sometimes he shot his pistol into the ceiling; he charged his waitresses and kitchen help five dollars for breaking a glass or a dish; he set traps in the hallways and stairways leading to the rooms above where some of his employees stayed. The traps, strings attached to empty tin cans, would set up a racket if someone ran into one of them, and he would come out shooting. The most disturbing news, though, was that one of the offenses for which he'd been committed was child molesting.

Our waitress friend advised us to get away from there. She didn't stay at the club, but instead, had an apartment downtown where she said we could hide out for the night if we could get away. We accepted her invitation, and she gave us her address, explaining how to get there. She was quitting the job, too, she said.

As soon as things had quieted down, we began our escape. Our room was in the back end of the club, downstairs, but the ground sloped away back there, and the windows were about six feet above the ground. I went out the window first, dropping to the ground. Marge passed our bags and my instruments down to me, and I put them in the car. Then she passed Margie Drew down. I stood her on the ground and told her to be quiet. Marge came out the window and I eased her down.

The car was parked around the corner from the club, just off the highway. It was cold that night, so I had a little trouble starting the car. When some lights came on in the club, we knew our escape had been discovered, but at last I got the car started and gunned it out of there. We had gone about a mile or so when we saw that a car was chasing us. I sped up, managing to stay ahead of our pursuer. When we got into town, I began trying to lose him, going all over Little Rock, turning this way and that through side streets, and switching off the lights at times. Finally, I succeeded. We sat still for a while to make sure of it, and when it looked safe to move on, I found the Western Union office and wired my half brother for ten dollars. Then we went to the waitress' apartment. She made breakfast for us and we stayed there until around noon when I called Western Union and learned that my money had arrived. I left town without stopping to collect my pay for the night's work or to pay back the fifty cents I owed the band leader.

8

THINGS WERE STILL bad in Dallas, as they were everywhere else at that time, but a musician could almost always find something to get by on. The ordinary worker had it harder than we did when he was laid off. The advent of radio and sound pictures had just about killed live entertainment. Most of the theaters in the country had abandoned vaudeville, while pit bands were a thing of the past. Vaudeville was eventually to be revived, developing into floor shows, lounge acts, and stage shows, but that didn't do musicians any good at that time. Still, about the time I got back to Dallas from the Little Rock episode, the Majestic Theater decided to try vaudeville again. Jack Stanley, a would-be conductor whom I'd never heard of, had some sort of connection with the theater's manager and, therefore, had the contract for the band.

I went to Stanley's house one day for a rehearsal about the time that Harry James blew into town. He was playing lead trumpet for the rehearsal, and Jelly Caballero was on lead saxophone and clarinet. This was the first time I met Harry, as well as the first time I heard him play in a big band.

One of the numbers we played was a stock "special" on an original composition called "Onivas," which was its composer's name, Savino, spelled backwards. Not designed for amateurs, the number moved so fast and with such varied progressions that we never seemed to play the same note twice. I was a pretty good reader, and there were some other pretty good readers in the band, too, including Curtis Hurt. One by one, though, each of us got stumped and dropped out—even the rhythm section—but Harry and Jelly kept going. They didn't stop until they ran out of notes. That was the fastest two-man band I've ever heard. In all the years I was associated with Harry James and Jelly Caballero, I never heard either of them make a mistake, even on a first reading or when they were improvising. It's a shame that they never worked together.

Stanley started on the job a few weeks later, but he didn't hire any of us who had been at that first rehearsal. In the meantime, most of us had gone on to other jobs: Harry James went to work for Ligon Smith at the Baker hotel; I was jobbing around with Durward Cline and playing a radio station. Since Stanley, an inexperienced conductor, had picked a bunch of inexperienced kids for the theater job, things didn't go well. He lost the job and was replaced by Jeff Holcomb, a real old pro.

Jeff terminated some of the incompetent players and hired Pete Noriego on first trumpet, Curtis Hurt on second trumpet, and me. Before that, the theater jobs had mostly been held by elderly so-called legitimate players, who had no idea of how to interpret jazz. By that time, what theaters needed was new musicians who could play the popular stuff. There were some exceptions, though. The young drummers and piano players generally had no experience playing shows because they had only played ballrooms. For vaudeville shows, drummers had to know how to play all kinds of cues and make sound effects, besides keeping time. Piano players had to know how and when to improvise fill-ins and vamps. Jeff had one of the best drummers, Hank Miller, and one of the best piano players, Bill Heim, in the whole territory.

String players were not used in ballroom bands, so our string section was made up of legits too, but all of the wind players were experienced jazz men, besides being good readers. The seventeen-piece band, or orchestra, consisted of seven strings, four brass, three reeds, piano, bass, and drums. It was a powerful outfit, and according to most of the acts we played, the best on the whole vaudeville circuit. Many of the acts were big names of the day. I remember Kate Smith, Cab Calloway and his band, Amos and Andy (Freeman Gosden and Charles Correll), Frank Libuse, Babe Egan's Redheads (an all-girl band), the Pat Rooney dancing act, and Gil Lamb.

We had another all-girl band once, whose name I can't remember. The girls invited some of us younger guys to one of their rooms after work one night. Curtis Hurt and I were the only ones who accepted the invitation. I had to walk a couple of blocks to pick up my car, so by the time I got to the room the party, augmented by bootleg booze, was in full swing.

I had parked in a limited-time zone, intending simply to drop by to pay my respects. Curtis and the girls urged me to move my car and then come back to the party. I had no sooner moved the car and walked back to the hotel, when I noticed a little commotion going on. I went in to ask the night clerk what was happening. "There's been a raid," he said. "Some party upstairs got a little loud and I called the cops."

The next day at the theater, Curtis came in just before curtain time. He hadn't shaved or changed clothes. "I just got out of jail," he explained.

That theater job paid thirty-six dollars a week. Suddenly, I acquired quite a few friends, many of them looking for loans. I even got requests from friends who had moved far away. I myself have always shied away from friends who were luckier than I, for fear they might think I was after something. This sudden popularity of mine was mild, though, compared to what would come later as I got better jobs. Usually, though, those in the really good jobs are pursued more for their social status than for their money. Even those who make it to the top in spite of a lack of ability are sought after. It's their prestige that counts, not their musical ability.

After about three months, the theater finally gave up the ghost. I had already closed the last house in the Southwest that used a pit band to play for silent pictures, and now I closed the last vaudeville house.

I went back with Lloyd Snyder, in Liberal, Kansas. This time, when the slack summer season came, he booked a job in Colorado at the Flying Horse Inn on top of Lookout Mountain. There was a joint down the road, though, that got most of the business. (Skeets Herfurt was playing there.) Since we were playing on percentage, we weren't making any money at all.

The manager furnished us with cabins. Marge and I shared one with Smitty and Eula Mae. The cabin, two rooms with beds, had no plumbing, so we had to walk a quarter of a mile to a spring, bringing back our water in buckets. We could have eaten in the club if we'd had money to pay for meals. Instead, we cooked over a fire outdoors—next to Buffalo Bill's grave. Cooking our own food, we could fill up on eggs or hamburger meat for about fifteen cents.

Some of us went along with Snyder one day to Denver, where he was going to hock his wife's diamond ring. On the way back we turned off at Golden to tour the Coors brewery, guided by Adolph Coors himself. Booze and beer had just been legalized again, so the first bottle of beer I had had since Laredo was a Coors.

We struggled along on a job for about two weeks before giving up and going back to Liberal. Besides the Smiths and my own family, Yadon, Tracy, and John Haynie Gilliland (the great tuba player from the Harrison's Texans days) were sharing my car. With the bags and horns roped and strapped all over the car, the only way to get into it was through the front door on the right side. After we were all shoehorned into the car, we started down the mountain— with no gasoline. Snyder had borrowed my gas for the trip to Denver and hadn't gotten around to replacing it.

The mountain road, a two-lane switchback, was steep; the last couple of miles was on an 11-percent grade. Some guy up on the mountain advised me not to go down in low gear as I had intended because, he said, coasting with the motor off would fill the engine with carbon. So I used the brakes all the way down. We made it to the first filling station just in time. The brakes were on fire. The station attendant met us with a water hose and put the fire out.

When we stopped in Denver, Snyder heard of a job in Greeley. He contacted the ballroom operator there, who told him that the job was open, but that we would have to have a battle of bands with the other group to see who got the job. The other band was Andy Kirk and his Twelve Clouds of Joy.

Andy Kirk's band was from Kansas City, so we had never heard of it, though later, of course, it became famous. Some of the members then were Ben Webster, Ben Thigpen, Sr., and Mary Lou Williams. Their band played first, and we saw right away that we didn't have a chance against them. Still, you can't always tell what the people will like—witness the host of no-talent outfits that have made it big. So Snyder decided that our only chance was to play our hotel style. It was pretty embarrassing to us. There were two bandstands, on opposite sides of the hall. Kirk's band would play a set; then we would play one. The battle went on pretty lopsidedly. They outdid us on everything, including the ballads. Finally, Smitty and I suggested that we play our jazz since we weren't doing any good otherwise, and Snyder agreed. Kirk's men started coming over to our stand to listen then. Ben Webster said to me, "Man, how do you get that subtone?"

"I don't know," I said. "The same as you do, I suppose. You get a subtone, too."

Ben looked surprised. "Oh, do I?"

I went to a jam session at their house the next day. In those days, blacks had no civil rights to speak of, especially in the South and West, so Kirk's band had rented a house in the colored section of town. Ben Webster, Mary Lou, Thigpen, and I jammed for a while, and later I drove one of the boys in the band to Ft. Collins to pick up some grass. There was nothing wrong in that since it still wasn't against the law, although Marge was a little upset at me for coming home late. It had been a great day for me. I never ran into Mary Lou or any of the men again, but for many years Webster and I sent "hello" to each other by other musicians.

We didn't get the job, of course, but we did get paid for the night we had worked. Back in Liberal we played one-nighters sporadically. It was the wind-and-dust time of year at the beginning of the Dust Bowl era, and we ran into some bad storms. On the way to Dodge City one day, we could see a wall of dust approaching. Once inside it we couldn't see even the hood of the car. Since the car's lights barely pierced the dust, I had to stop. We sat on the highway for an hour or longer. Fortunately, no other cars could move either, so nobody ran into us.

When the air had cleared sufficiently we started on our way again. Then the rain came, even thicker than the dust had been, and by then it was also getting dark. We had to stop and wait until the rain let up because, again, I couldn't see to drive. The rain had turned the unpaved road into a swamp by the time we could see well enough to go on. We proceeded in the mud, sliding into Dodge City at midnight—too late to play the job. The operator was furious, naturally, and we were lucky not to wind up on boot hill. There are some there for lesser offenses.

After more one-nighters, most of them like the one in Dodge City, Snyder booked the band at the Nat in Amarillo for a week before the band broke up again. Radio had evolved from a novelty into *the* means of entertainment and advertising, and we were booked to play a thirty-minute sustaining program from the Nat. It was a big deal, aimed at drawing people to the ballroom.

The broadcast was scheduled for the first dance session. Snyder called us together and gave us specific instructions: "Don't anybody take a drink," he said. "We have to do our best on this show." That was all right with us. There were no drinkers in the band, and it was too early for anybody to be drinking anyway.

We set up and were ready to play, but Snyder was no where to be found. At one minute to air time Seely was prepared to give the kickoff without him. Just as he raised his hand to get our attention, though, Snyder came running up. He watched for the radio man's cue, raised his arms, gave us the downbeat, and fell flat on his back off the bandstand onto the dance floor. He was loaded.

I must say for Snyder that he was a wonderful guy to work for, and I had never before seen him drunk.

I went back to Dallas from there, taking John Haynie Gilliland, Smitty's family, and mine. Somehow we kept surviving.

9

WARREN SMITH and I got our chance to leave the Southwest in 1934. Scott Seely wrote, asking us to join a band that was organizing in Champaign, Illinois, and headed for Chicago.

We left Dallas in November, taking Henry Erwin with us, since Seely had asked us to bring a trumpet player. In the old Buick were seven people—three musicians, two wives, and two kids—and all their worldly possessions. We had a total of about sixty dollars in the kitty and no worries. I can't remember that any musician was ever worried about anything, even in those desperate years of the Great Depression. We had never heard of "the power of positive thinking" or any of the similar flapdoodle put out since. So we didn't even have *that* to worry about. This was merely a new adventure.

The band—composed of Scott Seely, piano; Lloyd Johnson, bass; Paul Donovan, drums; Mickey Tracy, trumpet; Riley Smith, tenor sax; Marvin Mytar, alto sax and leader; and Smitty, Erwin, and me—got together in a rehearsal hall at the University of Illinois in Urbana. Our booker was "Mac" McConkey, who was just starting his agency. He had booked the band for the Madera Ballroom in Hammond, Indiana, just outside of Chicago, but before the job opened, we had to play a few one-nighters. We checked in at the Jackson Park Plaza, a combination hotel and apartment house on the south side of Chicago near Sixty-third and Stoney Island.

At first, we traveled in a big Lincoln, owned and driven by Mytar's father, pulling a trailer for the instruments. The weather was cold and there was lots of snow and ice on the roads. Once, the car broke down at six o'clock in the evening about forty miles outside of Columbia, Missouri, where we were to play at the university. We sat on the highway for three hours, waiting for some kind of help. Finally, the driver of a big truck stopped. Since he was deadheading, he offered to take us all on to Columbia. We transferred the instruments to the empty van and climbed in. It was even colder in that big metal van than it had been in the car. Ten sets of teeth rattled up to the dance hall just before midnight, and we were hungry besides.

The kids hadn't waited for us to start the party. They were having a different kind of ball. Some of them were loaded, and there was quite a bit of sexual activity going on. They didn't seem to care whether the band got there or not. In fact, it's possible that our arrival put the damper on that party.

Mytar managed to rent a bus of sorts, so we could finish the one-nighter tour in a little more comfort. Our only casualty was Lloyd Johnson's bass fiddle. It had to ride on top of the bus, and one night it didn't clear the door into the basement parking lot of a hotel in Davenport, Iowa. Its replacement was crushed when the bus backed over it. The third fiddle's neck was broken when it fell off the bus. But Lloyd's only reaction to each of these catastrophes was the single word, "drat".

We opened at the Madera Ballroom around the middle of December but were canceled after the first week because the place wasn't doing any business. The elder Mytar came up from Springfield, and he and Marv had a meeting with us in their room at the hotel. They gave us a couple of bucks apiece, and the next morning they were gone, taking Henry Erwin with them to work for Mytar in his window-cleaning business. I found myself embarking on my big city career the hard way—broke and stranded in a hotel too fancy for my pocketbook, not knowing a soul in the whole city of Chicago. Besides that, the area was having its coldest spell and worst snowstorm in probably a thousand years. When the sun finally came out one day, Smitty wanted to know what that big shiny ball was up there.

Our family and the Smiths shared a two-bedroom apartment, and Seely and Tracy ate with us. We pooled our money for meals, managing to feed the whole crew for about twenty-five cents a meal, partly thanks to some friends in the hotel who worked in a grocery store and brought us a few things, especially milk for the kids.

One day Riley Smith, who had been around Chicago before and knew a few people, came up with work for five of us. The job was at a club in Cicero called the Hi-Ho, which was Capone family headquarters. Our bosses would be Ralph "Bottles" Capone, Claude Maddox, and Murray "The Camel" Humphreys. Riley Smith graciously bowed out of the job, turning it over to me, while he went back to Lincoln, Nebraska.

None of us—Seely, Donovan, Tracy, Warren Smith, or me—had a hankering to be leader, but we decided that Tracy and I would be leaders in name. We called ourselves the Tracy-Page Band. Tracy would have nothing to do with running the band, though, so it was up to me. I didn't like the responsibility, but no one else wanted the job. The main work was talking to the bosses, and the topic to be discussed with them was our pay. We were supposed to be paid twenty dollars a week, but those guys were allergic to putting out money. The best we could get was only enough for a bare subsistence after the apartment rent was paid. We had taken the job without transferring our union cards to the Chicago local because we didn't have the necessary five dollars each. The bosses told us not to worry about it; they would take care of the union. They probably did, too, for we never heard anything from them. But because we didn't have the union's protection, there was nothing we could do to make them pay us.

The old Buick had started all right after being frozen and buried in the snow for a couple of weeks but the second night it began to conk out on the way to work. I left it at a garage and was never able to get it out again. Riley Smith had told us how to use the public transportation system to get to work: "You take the el to the loop, transfer to one going west, stay on it to the end of the line, and transfer to a streetcar. You go to the end of the streetcar line and take a dog sled the rest of the way." That's about the way it was, too. We seemed to spend more time commuting than we did working, and we worked "from can to can't," as the saying went, which meant from nine to four or five the next morning.

One night the law came in—four federal agents. One of them stationed himself at the entrance doorway, another at the doorway leading to the kitchen, while the other two approached a door at the back of the club where a lookout sat on a stool, keeping constant vigil through a peep slit in the door. They came out with Claude Maddox.

The next day's newspapers had a picture of Maddox on the front page. He had been taken on suspicion of being the man disguised as a policeman, who had mowed down seven members of Bugs Moran's north-side gang in what was called the St. Valentine's Day Massacre. He was also being questioned as a suspect in the kidnapping of the Bremmer boy in Minnesota. But nothing came of the suspicions. Maddox was back at work that night. Everything seemed to have been smoothed over, and he was not bothered further. Another man, arrested on suspicion in the kidnapping, had fingered Maddox without any proof of his participation in either incident.

Some good write-ups in the local Cicero paper and in a little nightlife publication began to attract some musicians and music buffs to the joint. One of these, a band follower named Joe Ford from Waco, Texas, who knew Smitty and me from down there, brought a friend to see us one night. It was Pat Buttram, the boy from Alabama who later became a movie actor and comedian. He had just come to town. Ford told us later that night that, during a football broadcast, the announcer had become incapacitated in some way, so Pat had taken over the microphone to finish the broadcast. He had gotten so many encouraging comments on his performance that he had decided to become a comedian. Some of us went to Ford and Buttram's room after work that night to listen to some of Buttram's material. After the ensuing drinking session, I spent the night on the floor of their room.

Those were the days of singing waitresses, waiters, and sometimes bartenders. At the Hi-Ho it was waitresses, one of whom was a beautiful and voluptuous brunet named Margo. She was married to a drummer Smitty had known back in Texas. The drummer, one of the handsomest guys I had ever seen, worked around the corner from the Hi-Ho at a joint called the Palomino. He came in one night to wait for his wife to get off work. The bosses didn't like that, so they ordered him to leave. That morning when Margo got home, she found that he had been badly beaten. When we saw him a couple of weeks later, his face was still a mess and some of his teeth were missing.

Another time I was sitting at the bar when a man came in to collect a bill from the bakery. The bosses ordered him out. Then I saw a man take a piece of lead pipe from under the bar, and wrapping it in a napkin, he followed the man from the bakery out the back door that led to the alley. The next morning the bakery man was found dead in that alley.

Margo was involved in another little fracas one night. A photographer came to take pictures of the band to go along with a write-up in the paper. He was a shy young man about twenty-five. Some of the bosses decided to have some fun, so they called Margo in from the main room and made her sit at the bar with a few male customers. Then they collared the photographer.

They ordered Margo to turn around to face away from the bar, pull up her dress, and take her panties off. Then they forced the photographer down on his knees in front of her and tried to make him perform cunnilingus on her. The kid was scared, but he wouldn't do it. He fought and yelled, while Margo sat there, petrified. Seeing that their plan hadn't worked, the bosses took the kid's pants off, rushed him out the door, and shoved him down into a snowbank at the curb. They threw his pants after him and told him to stay out of the joint.

When these sorts of things happen, people get a little leery. Since we weren't getting paid, the boys in the band decided to get the hell out of there, but we were afraid to quit. We planned our escape, so that, one at a time, we would just fail to show up for work. Seely would be the next-to-last to leave because we couldn't go on without a piano.

As luck would have it, Smitty got a job with Louis Panico, a big-name leader in those parts. He was the first to go, leaving town with Panico to go on one-nighters. Tracy dropped out next; then Donovan. The last night that we worked, Seely and I played a duo. The bosses were fuming by that time, but I tried to explain that there was nothing I could do about it. I told them they might as well get a new band.

Then Seely stayed away, leaving me to go out and face the bosses alone. I had taken my sax home and left it, so I had only my clarinet to sneak out, but it was a problem. They expected me to stay on as leader and hire some other musicians. Frankly, I was very much afraid to let the bosses know that I had other plans.

I had become acquainted with the piano player who accompanied the singing waitresses. He had been there for several years and knew all the goings-on around the joint. In fact, he sometimes worked on the outside for the boys. When they had proposed that I peddle their beer for them, he had advised me to stay out of the operation. He had wanted to get away himself for a long time, but the bosses wouldn't let him out because he knew too much. Since he owned his own home, it would have been hard to just disappear. He advised me to get out while I still could, but without angering the bosses, and offered to help me.

I was to hide my clarinet under a loose floorboard on the bandstand. Later, he would sneak it out and bring it to me. I had no one to work with that night, so I went home. The next day I called Murray Humphreys to tell him I was quitting. He told me to get out of town. It sounded like a threat. I must say it made me feel a little uneasy to be ordered out of town by the Capone boys, especially since I couldn't leave. I didn't even have carfare to the bus station. I figured I'd just have to get over my fear. About a week later, the piano player called to tell me he had my clarinet and would bring it to me.

Dick Wirth, a local leader working out of an agent's office, had taken a job at the Brown Hotel in Louisville, Kentucky, for four weeks. He hired Seely, Tracy, and me for the five-piece band. Joe Kahn was the drummer, and Wirth played alto sax. We barely broke even at thirty-five dollars a week each. Since we were in debt to Wirth when we got the job, it took four weeks of working just to pay him back. I earned a few extra dollars, though, making some arrangements for the girl singer who was the floor show.

When we got back to Chicago, Wirth's agent had another job for him, in Nashville, Tennessee. On the way out of Chicago, though, Wirth informed us that actually there was no job for us in Nashville. The club owner there had canceled us but Wirth's agent, refusing to accept the cancellation, was sending us there just to show. He intended to hold the owner to the play-or-pay contract. I knew we would wind up with nothing, but Wirth said we had to go anyway so that the club owner couldn't say that we hadn't shown up. Since we were near-broke as usual, making a 450-mile trip down and back for nothing didn't make sense to me. If I'd had the money, Marge, Margie Drew, and I would have gotten out of the car and headed back to Chicago on a bus. Instead, having no choice, we went on to Nashville and made our show at the club. The only worthwhile part of that miserable trip was seeing Francis Craig and his band. They were playing at the Hermitage Hotel, and we could see them from the street, but of course, we had no money to get into the place to hear them.

Back in Chicago after the trip, Wirth got us two weeks in Ft. Wayne, Indiana. That wasn't quite long enough for us to become solvent again, but luckily, on Friday the thirteenth Seely won thirteen dollars in a floating crap game. We got back to Chicago in pretty good style.

It was a while before I got another job. Marge had to hock her wedding ring and go back to her mother in Dallas. Smitty's wife and son had moved to a two-dollar-a-week room downtown on Wells Street, while Smitty was on the road with Panico. He was sending her a few dollars now and then. After Marge left I stayed on at the Jackson Park Plaza for a few days, but I couldn't pay anything on the rent, and for three days I had nothing to eat but sweet potatoes. Finally, leaving everything behind but my instruments, I moved into a room next to Eula Mae. She did a little cooking on a hot plate for the three of us.

I got a good six-dollar-a-week job, as Eula Mae called it, in Berwyn—two bucks a night, three nights a week. As it turned out, although the boss furnished two glasses of beer a night, he didn't pay the band. Hiring us had been just a desperate attempt to enliven his business, but it hadn't worked. Borrowing streetcar fare from Eula Mae, I made several trips out there to collect my six dollars until, finally, the boss gave me the money just to get rid of me.

Musicians used to get together every Monday at Randolph and Dearborn in the loop. The commercial musicians met at the Capitol Building on the northeast corner, and the hot shots, our group, met at the Woods Building on the northwest. Our side reminded me of the Pittman Hotel in Dallas. You might say it was the seamy side of the street. Occasionally, someone on one side would venture to the other side, at risk of his prestige with his own group. Neutrals, looking for one kind of musician or the other, as their commitments demanded, would make both sides. I got a few jobbing dates, as one-nighters were called in Chicago. (They were known as club dates back east and casuals out west.)

Smitty returned to Chicago after his tour with Panico, and Marge came back from Dallas. Some of my friends and former bandmates from the Southwest began to drift into town too: Charles Lavere, who had dropped the Johnson from his name, up from Oklahoma City; Raby Cummings from Dallas, soon followed by Carl Shamburger; Fats Obenir from St. Louis; Mike Simpson, who came to town with Art Castle's band, quit the band, and stayed on his own; and Thurman Teague from Champaign.

Smitty got a job with Jimmy Green, a local leader who was getting some of the better work around town. Seely, Tracy, Teague, and I went to work with Joe Kahn, the drummer, at a place called the Wagon Wheel, playing for the Flo Whitman show. It was our break into the whirl of things.

Since Flo Whitman was delighted with the band, and her show was attracting good business, we had a good thing going for a while. The show consisted of a line of four girls and two nude dancers. The girls in the line wore only an eye patch over their shaved pubic areas and corn pads above, while the nudes had nothing but a couple of feather fans to wave. The club was so far out in the country that it was ignored by the law, so it became a hangout for the more libidinous people around town. It was also a favorite out-of-the-way place for extramarital affairs. Unfortunately, though, the Wagon Wheel became virtually inaccessible in the wintertime, so when summer was over, so was the job.

Toward the end of the season Kahn arranged an audition for us at another club. Usually, we left our instruments at the club to avoid the annoyance of lugging them back and forth, but the night before the audition, we had to take them home. I took my clarinet apart, wrapped the five sections in paper napkins, and packed them in my saxophone case, along with my sax-clarinet stand. I did the same thing after the audition the next day.

Teague had a sedan big enough to hold all the instruments, so we packed everything except Tracy's trumpet in the car and went our separate ways after the audition. Kahn drove home, in his own car, dropping Tracy and Seely on the way. Teague drove home alone. I took a streetcar. Teague was to take me to the job that night.

When Teague got there at the appointed time, he rushed up the stairs to get me, leaving his car lights on. Since I was ready and waiting, he wasn't away from the car for more than five minutes. When we got to the car, though, there was nothing left but Kahn's bass drum and Teague's bass fiddle. All the other instruments had been stolen. Luckily, Kahn had taken his "tops" in his own car, so the band was able to play that evening, but without me.

The fifty dollars I had saved to join the union had to be used, instead, as a down payment on new instruments. I had to alter my name for the new account because I still owed for the lost instruments.

The incident set me back six months getting into the local. I had served the three-month waiting period, so they allowed me to keep working a steady job. I had to redeposit my card, though, and wait another six months to become a full member.

Kahn didn't get the job we had auditioned for because it was to open before we finished at the Wagon Wheel. I was out of work again, but not for long this time because Flo Whitman booked the Gay 90's, a joint on Rush Street on the Near North Side.

During the interim I worked for a couple of weeks in a joint on Clark Street. One night as we were playing, my old Hi-Ho boss,

Murray Humphreys danced by. He recognized me. "I thought I told you to get out of town," he said, giving me a threatening look.

I was scared, but I didn't let him know it. I just grinned at him and shrugged. "Yeah," I said, "but I couldn't. You forgot to pay me."

Evidently, I had done the right thing. My apparent lack of fear amused him. He burst into a laugh and, raising his hand in a farewell gesture, said, "Carry on." He and his partner danced away, and I didn't see him again.

I had another visitor in that joint one night. Pee Wee Russell, who had heard of me from Raby Cummings, came up to make friends. Of course, I had been hearing about him for years and was pleased to meet him.

Pee Wee was out of it—broke, unemployed, and in need of a drink. I bought him a beer and lent him a quarter for another one later. I don't know what had brought him to Chicago that time. It was out of his territory. Pee Wee was an Oklahoman who had emigrated to New York. One thing the Depression taught us, though, is that being temporarily broke is no disgrace. Sooner or later we were all that way, but those of us who weren't used to lots of money didn't jump out of windows when we went broke—the way rich people were inclined to do in those days. We just struggled along waiting for better times. Pee Wee made out very well a little later, and so did I and the rest of my little clique.

Since Kahn could use only four men on the Gay 90's job, including himself, Teague left for Detroit. Seely and Tracy had taken jobs in other clubs when the Wagon Wheel job ended, so Kahn replaced them with Elmer Granger on trumpet and Lynn Hazzard on piano. Lynn had been the "floor" piano player there before we came in. He was an old-timer, who had been a theater conductor before sound movies came in and vaudeville went out. All we asked of him was to bump chords and stay out of our way since he wasn't a jazz player.

10

NONE OF THE JOINTS in Chicago where musicians were allowed to sit in was really set up as a showcase for talent—especially undiscovered talent. Smitty and I had sat in with Earl Hines's band at the Trianon, Jimmie Noone at the Apex, Boyce Brown at the Liberty Inn, and a few others, with no result except that we got better acquainted around town. The Three Deuces (222 North State Street) allowed celebrities to sit in, but we were not celebrities. The Gay 90's was ideally set up to fill the gap. It was located in a pretty good neighborhood that was convenient for traveling musicians playing the downtown hotels and clubs. So, partly because I thought Chicago needed such a place and partly for the fun of it, I began to turn the Gay 90's into a place where musicians could come to jam.

Shortly after we started the Gay 90's job, Ben Pollack's band came to Chicago, Ben's home town, for a lay off. At that time, Harry James, Dave Matthews, Stanley Wrightsman, and Sam Taylor, all of whom I knew from down home, were members of Pollack's band. Another band member I knew was Clarence "Shorty" Cherock, who later began spelling his last name "Sherock." I had been jamming around town with him before he joined Pollack. Beside these, there were Opie Cates, Bruce Squires, and others in the band.

When the boys from down home got in touch with me, I invited them to come up and sit in, and some of them did. For about six weeks we had a six- or seven-piece band every night that Pollack didn't book a one-nighter in the neighborhood. They would get there at starting time and stay all night. Harry and Bruce played all of the dance sets with us, and Harry also played Flo's show. Flo was delighted, even though our band drew about as much attention as her show. When the word got around, we had as many as ninety musicians at the bar, which was about its total capacity. Occasionally some of the more affluent ones would buy us drinks because we were all broke.

Flo Whitman had gotten Marge the job as hatcheck and cigarette girl because Marge had said she would rather work than stay home in a dreary apartment, and besides, we needed the money. I was trying to save fifty dollars again to join the local. "Aunt 'Raine" (Loraine Cummings) baby-sat for us.

Marge was very popular, and she made friends with some of the steady customers. One was a man who came in frequently just to sit at the bar and listen to the music. One night he asked Marge about me. "Who is the clarinet player? Do you know him?"

"Yes, that's my husband," Marge said, giving him my name.

"I'd like to meet him sometime," the man said.

Marge said she would tell me to come over and introduce myself. I wasn't particularly interested, though. The man always sat alone at the bar, and I figured he was just a square out rubbernecking. He didn't seem to know any of the musicians that came in. After a while, I got around to presenting myself, nevertheless.

"I'm Roy Shields," he said. "You're the best clarinet player I've heard."

I thanked him for the compliment, but it didn't mean much to me since I had never heard of this guy.

"How would you like to come to work at NBC?" he asked.

"You mean the radio station?"

"Yes," he said. "I'm the director up there."

"Well," I said, "I would like that but I can't work there. I'm not in the local yet."

He asked me when I would become a member and, when I told him June, said to come see him then. Later, I asked around about Roy Shields and found out that he was the head of the whole thing up there. (He later ran the whole NBC network.) No wonder he didn't make himself conspicuous at the Gay 90's, I thought, and no wonder that the musicians who hung out there didn't know him.

He was too far above us. A few nights later he quit visiting the Gay 90's, and I didn't see him again until October.

When Pollack went out on the road again he took Thurman Teague with him. Harry James had been authorized to find a replacement for Pollack's bass player, who had left the band, and had chosen Teague on my recommendation.

Our band was down to four again when they left, but others around town came up to sit in for kicks. One day, I met Jack Purvis at the Woods Building and invited him to come up. There's not a trumpet player in the world louder than Harry James. Purvis played pretty loud, too, but he made more noises with his feet than he did with his horn. Whereas Harry plays without even patting a foot, Purvis did so much stomping all over the stand that Billy Stern ordered me to get him off. He was too loud, the boss said.

Glen Burrs, the founder of *Downbeat* magazine, and Carl Cons, his chief writer and critic, had been coming to watch and listen to the goings-on. One night they brought Helen Oakley, an English-woman who served in the same capacity in England as Carl Cons did here. She had also been to see us several times while the Pollack gang was there. The write-up she gave us in *Downbeat* consisted simply of our names followed by, "They play pretty well for a bunch of kids." It was better than the silence Cons and Burrs had maintained, but I think it shows just how little music critics know about music. I had told Cons one night that I thought *Downbeat* was corny and had asked, "Why don't you guys learn to know what you are talking about?" Maybe that was one reason he never wrote us up. On the other hand, maybe it was sheer ignorance. What can a music critic say about something he or she knows nothing about? The critic has to be told by somebody who knows music before he can make a judgment. There was no establishment musician to tell Cons or Oakley that James, Squires, and others who played at the Gay 90's were good.

Lynn Hazzard quit, and at my suggestion, Kahn replaced him with Mel Henke. Henke had been working at the Gay 90's as the floor pianist and sitting in with us when we had guest players because Hazzard couldn't play jazz. The Pollack band was back after a few weeks for another lay off, and again our band was augmented. This time we usually had Teague on bass. In the meantime, Pollack had replaced Cates with Fazola (born Irving Prestopnik).

I'd heard various stories of how Fazola got his nickname. When he was coming to the Gay 90's, I asked him about it. "Well," he said, "you know how they teach you music in school. All that do-re-mi-fa-sol-la stuff. I remarked to some of the guys in the school band that I was tired of that fa-sol-la bullshit. I wanted to play jazz. They thought it was funny, and they began kidding me about being a fa-sol-la player. After a while I was being called Fazola."

About that time, Benny Goodman came to the Congress Hotel. Spud Murphy, who had become Goodman's arranger, came to see me, and soon, most of Goodman's men were coming around as well. Nate Kazebier, Pee Wee Irwin, Bill DePew, and Goodman himself, each sat in with us once.

When Spud told me one night that Goodman was looking for a trombone player, I told him Warren Smith was available. They were old friends, having worked together in Harrison's Texans, so Spud promised to arrange for Goodman to hear him. The trouble was that Smitty had given up on Chicago a few weeks before and gone back to Texas. It took me two or three days to locate him in Big Spring, Eula Mae's home town. He arrived in Chicago a few days later.

Spud arranged to have Goodman at the Gay 90's on a certain night, and I told Smitty to be there also. Goodman played a set with Smitty, Kahn, and Mel Henke, and afterwards he asked Smitty to come down to the Congress to see him the next night. Since it happened to be my night off, I tagged along. We had sat through a set when, suddenly, Smitty got up. "Let's get out of here," he said.

"Aren't you going to talk with Benny?" I asked.

"No," said Smitty. "I wouldn't want to play with the band if I got the job. Let's go."

When we got outside I asked him why he didn't want to wait and talk with Benny. "I'll tell you someday," was all he would say, but he never did explain. Smitty never said anything derogatory about anything or anybody, although he derogated himself often enough. Perhaps he thought that the band was too good for him.

Raby Cummings had gotten a job on Rush Street, too. Loraine would come to the Gay 90's once in a while to see Marge and wait for Raby. (There was another woman in our apartment building who kept Margie Drew sometimes.) One night Loraine was there when Spud, her former husband, came in. Even though neither of them knew that the other would be there, when Raby arrived, he imagined that Marge and I had arranged their meeting at Loraine's instigation. Raby proceeded to get drunk for the first time since he had sworn off booze back in Oklahoma before I knew him. He had told me that, at one time, he was drinking a half gallon a day but that he'd given it up because he had realized he couldn't handle it. He said he got mean when he drank.

Spud discreetly disappeared. When I got off work, Marge and I and Raby and Loraine took the el home together. Raby, refusing to sit with Loraine, sat in the back of the car mumbling to himself all the way to our stop at the end of the line. He wouldn't walk with her the few blocks home from there but, instead, followed along a little way behind us.

We all went to my apartment where the girls were going to cook breakfast for us. All of a sudden Raby stopped sulking and mumbling. Bursting into a rage, he came at me with an empty milk bottle. He was too drunk to hit me with it through the defense I put up, but he kept trying. I couldn't get him to stop his foolishness, so finally, I hit him—just once. I must have hit him pretty hard since I broke the outside knuckle of my hand. When his head hit the kitchen sink, it cut a gash in his forehead above one eye. I had hit him under the other eye, and it began to swell. Loraine screamed and went to call the police, but fortunately, she couldn't find a nickel for the pay phone in the hallway, so she came back. Raby had collapsed on the floor. He wasn't unconscious, though—just stunned and very drunk. Loraine and I got him up, took him to their apartment, and put him to bed.

Marge and I moved out the next day to an apartment on Ohio Street not far from my job. I didn't see Raby again for several months partly because, after his head and eye healed, he went on a job in Wisconsin for a while. When I did see him again, we shook hands and everything was forgiven and forgotten.

Once we'd moved near the job, one of Flo's dancers started dropping by almost every day since she lived somewhere in the neighborhood. Harry James and his wife, Louise (Tobin), were temporarily estranged, so Harry got a notion to date Jean, our dancer friend. We made up a foursome to go to the Three Deuces one night—really early morning—after I got off work. The Three Deuces being a late-hour joint, the action didn't really start until other musicians got off work around four o'clock in the morning. We got there early enough to get a table right in front of the band.

Zutty Singleton was on drums. I can't remember who was playing piano or bass, but Joe Masick was sitting in on tenor sax, and Shorty Sherock and Roy Eldridge were sitting in on trumpets. They had a pretty good session going, so we sat and listened for a half hour or so. Harry had a way of letting other trumpet players do their best stuff. Then he would take over and "cut" (meaning outplay) them. I had seen him do it several times, most recently at the Gay 90's with Malcolm Crain and Solly LaPertch. This time, though, when he took his trumpet out of its case and headed for the bandstand a waiter rushed up and took him by the arm. "Sorry, kid," the waiter said, "this is an invitation session." He ushered Harry back to the table.

We sat for a while longer, having a drink, until Jean got bored with the whole thing and decided to leave. Since she was only sixteen, Marge and I felt responsible for her, so we left with her. Harry wouldn't leave though.

Before long, the rush came and all the tables were taken. Customers were standing back by the entrance, but nothing would persuade Harry to give up his table for four. "It's my table," he said. "My friends will be back."

Downbeat later ran a photo—taken by one of their photographers that night—along with a little story about the kid who wouldn't give up his table. A few months after that, Harry would have been given the red-carpet treatment and a key to the joint.

Harry had a room in our apartment building across the hall from us and up a few doors toward the front of the building. Jean lived with an aunt who kept a pretty good watch on her. One night Harry had another date with her, not sponsored by Marge and me. Jean didn't come home from work that night, so her aunt came to see us the next day to ask if we knew where she was. She knew that Jean visited us nearly every day. Jean and Harry could hear her aunt talking with us, so they kept quiet, and Harry took the extra precaution of hiding in his closet, just in case we told her aunt where Jean was.

On Harry's twentieth birthday, he was sitting in with our band as usual, and as usual, Flo introduced him to the audience. Announcing that it was Harry's birthday, she said, "Let's get him out here to do a number for us," leading the come-on applause. Harry told me "Play 'Dinah' just as fast as you can," got up, laid his trumpet on his chair, and started out to the floor. We went into "Dinah" at a very fast tempo, having no idea what Harry was up to since he had left his trumpet on the stage. He ran out onto the floor and surprised everyone, including me, with a hilarious tap dance that broke up the house.

I talked with him later about it. "I didn't know you were a hoofer," I said. "You surprised us."

"Used to be," he said. "I was a tumbler and a drummer, too, back in my circus days."

"Oh?" I said. "Were you on a circus?"

"Practically raised on them," he said. "My father was a band leader."

Something clicked in my mind. "I'll be! Are you the little kid who used to come to our high school in Ada, Oklahoma, and play drum solos at the age of six or seven?"

As it turned out, Harry had been enrolled at Willard Elementary School in Ada when Honest Bill's circus wintered there for a few years. I always played the circus parade when the show opened in Ada in the spring. Honest Bill Newton's son, Clyde, who was president of my class, had been instrumental in getting Everett James to bring his son Harry to perform at our school.

One of the regulars at the Gay 90's was Joe Rushton, the great bass sax player who was with Benny Goodman later, and then with Red

Nichols. He sat in on clarinet, though, not bass sax. Guy Sanderson, the excellent clarinetist from Oklahoma City came in a few times. Then there were Murray McEachern and Buddy Rich.

Murray, who was then nineteen, had come down from Canada hoping to join Benny Goodman. A marvelous player even then, he sat in with us on trombone, trumpet, and saxophone. He made it with Goodman and the rest is a tale that's already been told.

"What's a guy like you doing in a joint like this?" I remember he asked me.

"Well," I said, "I need the money, and this is the best I can do, so far. Maybe I'll make it someday."

"Don't worry," he said. "You'll make it."

Two years later when I was with Harry James's band, I saw him in Oakland, California. "Hi," he said. "I see you made it."

Buddy Rich was also nineteen when he played with us. Since he told us at first that he was a tap dancer, we arranged for Flo Whitman to put him in as a guest in her show. Later he let us know that he was a drummer. One night when James, Squires, and Fazola were there, we asked him to sit in for a set. When it was over, Harry said to me, "That kid will be a good drummer someday." I agreed.

The Joe Sanders band had an engagement at the Blackhawk Restaurant down in the loop. Charles Lavere, who had joined Sanders—on trumpet instead of piano—brought some of the band to see us. Another of our regular guests was Edmond Benge, first trumpet with the Chicago symphony and maker of the Benge trumpet. He loved jazz and wanted to play it. He used to sit in occasionally, doing pretty well, too.

Another familiar face in the crowd, though not a musician, was a kid who peddled reeds at a discount, carrying his entire stock around in a briefcase. He would let us buy on the cuff if necessary. I had nicknamed him "the Spook" because everywhere I went I ran into him, even at the remotest joints in town. It was Willie Berg at the beginning of his business career. Later, he began manufacturing the famous Berg-Hume mutes, Berg music stands, and other band supplies. His factory and warehouses now cover five acres.

Since Spud Murphy was living in a hotel only a few blocks away, he came to our apartment almost every day for a while, always bringing a big bag of groceries. Sometimes he would go home with us after I got off work, and Marge would cook us breakfast. I went to his room one day. He was keeping some clothes and other things for Benny Goodman. Among the things, there was an original Goodman-designed clarinet mouthpiece, which Spud thought was a discard. He gave it to me, only to have to ask for it back a few days later when it turned out that Goodman wanted it.

I didn't get Goodman's mouthpiece, but I got enough of his discarded reeds to last me a couple of years. I had watched him change reeds on the stand the night that I went with Smitty to hear him. He would give them one toot and throw them on the floor until he found one that suited him. I mentioned it to Art Rollini one night.

"He always does that," Art said. "I pick them up later, but hell, I don't use them. Do you want them?"

I told him *sure* I did, so he brought me several boxes of them. (They come in boxes of two dozen with a spare on top.)

The last night that Spud was in town he walked out of the club with Marge and me. He offered to drop us off in his cab on the way to his hotel, but we declined, reminding him that it was only a couple of blocks to our place. Spud got into the cab, and as it took off, he looked back out of the window and thumbed his nose at us. It was the last time I saw Spud, although we've kept in touch.

Claude Maddox, another of my old Hi-Ho bosses, came to the Gay 90's one night. I was uneasy because, although Murray Humphreys had let me go, I wasn't sure about Maddox. It's true that he hadn't ordered me out of town, but I thought he might have had the same idea. It turned out that he had no hard feelings, though. He even had me join him at the bar for a drink. I suspect that the Capone boys had a little interest in the Near North Side because Humphreys and Maddox didn't seem to have anything to worry about in that territory.

Marge and I knew another businessman on the Near North Side, who came to the Gay 90's frequently. We called him "Red." He had given us a standing invitation to stop on our way home at the joint he owned a couple of blocks down Rush Street. We got into the habit of stopping there almost every night, and Red always bought the drinks.

One night a man sitting on the other side of Marge developed long arms. I told him to leave Marge alone, and he stopped for a while. When he started his pawing again, we started arguing. Marge went to the back of the bar where Red was lounging. "Red," she said, "there's going to be some trouble." She explained the situation.

"There ain't gonna be no trouble in *here*," Red said. He came over to the man at the bar, put one hand in the back of his collar and the other in the seat of his pants, pulled him off the stool, and headed him toward the doorway.

"I'm from the FBI," the man protested. "You can't."

"Bullshit, fella," Red said. "But that wouldn't make any difference. Get the hell out of here." He steered the man to the door and shoved him out onto the walk, face down.

We had nothing to worry about with boys like Red on our side. There were plenty like him around—men who were tough only with their antagonists. They wouldn't bother the "people."

The Three Deuces decided to experiment with using two shifts of bands. Since the second shift was to start at four o'clock in the morning, Joe Kahn booked our group there. The prospect of earning two salaries and being showcased at the same time made the future look a little brighter. Unfortunately, we played only one night before the union stepped in to stop us. It seems there was a local rule prohibiting musicians from playing two jobs. The one night we played was fun, though. Art Tatum was the main attraction, playing solo between sets by the band. He joined us on our last number, and we joined him on his last number to keep the music going without breaks.

The job at the Gay 90's lasted until May. We had been there about six months, and with Marge working, we had saved enough money for me to join the local union.

11

KAHN BOOKED a job in Benton Harbor for a big band under the ostensible leadership of Paul Ash, who actually had nothing to do with getting the band together or rehearsing it. He was just the front man on the job. We bought uniforms and rehearsed a few times. Then Ash walked out after the first night, and we were left to play out a two-week notice.

Jimmy Green, with whom I had played a few jobbing dates before going to the Gay 90's, hired me for a summer job he'd found at a ballroom on the South Side. I got Ray DeGeer, who had come to town from Oklahoma, on with the band, playing tenor. Kay Arman was our girl singer. It was mostly a commercial band, but Green paid a pretty good salary for those bad times—thirty-five dollars a week.

In the fall, I went back with Joe Kahn, who had booked the Silhouette Club on Marquette Road, also on Chicago's South Side. The emcee-comedian was Dick Buckley. At that time, he had begun calling himself "Lord," but it was some time later that he was billed as Dick Lord Buckley. Anita O'Day, his supporting act, sang with the band in the show but not on our dance sets. It was later, while she was with Gene Krupa's band, that she established herself as a band singer.

Mel Henke, who was with us on piano, had the yens for Anita, but since he was married, he didn't pursue her. There was a lesbian who had the yens for Anita, too, and she was usually at the joint when we got off work. To avoid her, Anita would ride home to the North Side with Mel and me. Mel and Anita would sit together, leaving the other girl, who rode the same el, and me on our own. She chose to sit alone.

One night we stopped off at Wilson Avenue for a jam session at a joint that was a few blocks out the street toward the lake. Mel and Anita walked together, I followed behind, and the other girl followed me. She wasn't invited, but she tagged along anyway, refusing, as usual, to walk with me.

That night I met Pete Daily, probably the most authentic Dixieland trumpet player of them all, with whom I was to be associated for many years, off and on. He was sitting in that night at the jam session with me on clarinet and Mel on piano. Pete was leaving soon for Hollywood with Mike Riley, and he wanted me to go with him. I was beginning to make a few contacts and getting known around town, though, so I preferred to sweat it out in Chicago.

It was against the local rules to sit in if your presence augmented the band, but we usually got by with it. (How we got by with it at the Gay 90's for six months is a mystery, considering all the publicity we had gotten.) The union raided that session, though. Pete went to an open window and tossed his trumpet down on an awning, I took my clarinet apart and stuck the parts in my pockets, and Mel left the piano. Nobody was caught in the act, but that broke up the session.

We left to continue our way home—Mel, Anita, and I, and the other girl, still walking behind. Angry and frustrated by then, she nasty-mouthed us all the way to the el. She was a beautiful girl, too. If I had been a woman . . .

Dick Buckley was the funniest comedian in the business. (So said *Esquire* magazine after his death some twenty years later.) He was the comedians' comedian—no zany antics, funny faces, or corny jokes that everybody has heard over and over again. Nor was he funny-ugly; he was a handsome distinguished-looking man, slightly bald. Buckley could assume an accent that made him sound more British than the British themselves. With that knack for sounding like an upper-class Englishman, he naturally dubbed himself Lord Buckley. Buckley liked musicians, so he used to make the Woods Building scene on Mondays once in a while. His stooge,

Junior, who had a Great Dane as big as a polo pony, would drive Buckley up to the building in an open-top car with that huge dog in the back seat. It broke up the musicians hanging around there.

One night Buckley invited Henke, Kahn, and me to his room a few blocks from the club to listen to records. He offered us booze and grass; we drank the booze, and he smoked the grass. (Buckley smoked grass even while doing his show.) After we'd listened to records till it got boring, Buckley invented a game. We musicians would select a record and play it, and if he didn't like the record, he would break it over the head of the one who had selected it and throw the pieces out the window. The further we went with the game, the more bad records we played, until, eventually, all the records went out the window.

One night Buckley brought his date to his room. Buckley got in bed first and, turning off the lights, he took off his toupee and popped out his set of false uppers. The girl stripped and got into bed with him, but for some reason, she had to turn the lights on again. When she did, she saw Buckley without his hairpiece and his teeth. It was too much for her. She screamed and ran out of the room; Buckley jumped up and ran after her—both of them still naked. He chased her down the hallway, down the stairs, and out into the street, where, as luck would have it, a cop happened to be standing. He took Buckley into custody but let the girl go. She was a minor, and her parents filed a complaint against Buckley. While awaiting trial, he was allowed to come to work nights in the custody of a guard, returning to jail after the job. Somehow the affair was finally smoothed over, and Buckley went free a little later.

Sometimes when Junior didn't show up, I had to act as Buckley's stooge in a couple of his bits. I was so bad that he thought it was funny and would break up at my attempts. When that job was over, he wanted me to go to Hollywood with him as his stooge—just for his own laughs, I suppose.

The last time I saw him before he left for Hollywood, he gave me a stick of grass. Since I had quit the stuff, I put it in my wallet and forgot about it till I saw Buckley in Hollywood four years later.

When the Silhouette job ended, Kahn got a job for a seven-piece band at a place on the South Side called the Beverly Gardens. Kahn, Henke, and I stayed on, and we added Stanley Story on tenor, Jack Herron on trumpet, Jimmy Hughes on trombone, and Johnny McFall on bass. Leaving his wife and kids back home in Dallas, McFall had come to Chicago to live with a woman. He'd learned to play bass fiddle because he wasn't good enough on piano to get the best work. In this case, I had gotten him the job for old time's sake.

I remember the audition for the job. The boss was standing in front of the bandstand, trying to be a know-it-all, and criticizing everything we did. None of us liked it.

"This guy is going to bug us," I said to Kahn. "Let's pack up and get out of here."

"That's a good idea," Kahn said, starting to disassemble his drums.

The boss put up his hands. "No, no, no," he said, "everything's all right. Do it your own way."

From then on, we did.

Harry James had joined Benny Goodman. We heard his first broadcast with the band one night on our break. It was a good moment for us—a friend making good. Apparently, a record Harry had made with Pollack's band some time earlier, combined with the urgings of his own brother, Irving Goodman, had persuaded Benny to hire him.

Things began to improve as I got better known around town. I went to Omaha for two weeks with Bill Hogan, a popular local leader, to play a theater. Al King was one of the trumpet players in Hogan's band. I had met him and his friend, Jack Fina, in a Chicago hotel room one night when they were with Clyde McCoy at the Morrison Hotel. Fina was just a kid. His parents had let him go out on the road at an early age under King's protection.

I worked for four weeks at the Sherman Hotel with Jimmy McPartland's seven-piece group. Joe Rushton was playing bass sax, and since Jules Stein (a nephew of MCA's Jules Stein) had the clarinet chair, I played tenor sax—as little as possible on the jazz numbers. It wouldn't have been polite to compete with Stein on clarinet unless I'd been invited to.

Although the Texas Centennial Fair ended in 1936, the show connected with it continued in Dallas in 1937 in conjunction with the annual Texas State Fair. One of my old friends, Jason Cox, who had the contract to furnish the band for the Road to Rio show, wired an offer. The job would last all summer and pay sixty dollars a week, so since I had no steady job at the time, I accepted.

My old boss, Jack Crawford, had been hired to conduct the band. He still had it in for me for having quit him, but when he started trying to make things rough for me, I went to Cox. He told Crawford to stick to conducting the band. Crawford and I didn't speak to each other for the rest of the engagement, but at least he left me alone. He had told us that there was to be no drinking on the job, so I went to Cox again. I told him that since we were paid only for the shows, we shouldn't be under Crawford's orders on our breaks. The job took about nine hours of our time, while our pay only covered the four hours of show time. Cox agreed. There weren't any boozers on the band, and besides, booze wasn't available by the drink in Texas, anyway. All we could buy was beer. Crawford was just being hard on the whole band because he didn't like me.

The show was a good one, emceed by Joaquin Garay. There were eight principals, sixteen chorus girls, and eight show girls. Margarita Cansino (who later changed her name to Rita Hayworth) was part of a family act, and Bill "Bojangles" Robinson was a guest dancer for a special occasion. The band was made up of thirteen of the best musicians in Dallas, most of whom were old friends of mine.

Our band, minus Crawford, was delegated to meet Benny Goodman's band at the railroad station when it came to town for a one-nighter. Harry James was the center of attention, of course, for all the Dallas musicians knew him. Harry never liked people to make a big to-do over him, and I think he was a little embarrassed over such an enthusiastic reception. He has never shown an inkling of conceit over his fame. On that occasion he just grinned, shook hands with his old friends, and mumbled he was glad to see them.

When I got back to Chicago in the fall, I worked the joints for a while, and Kahn, Henke, and I played a couple of jazz concerts. Al Golden needed some choruses on standard tunes written for three front-line instruments, without fill-ins, which would only become corny after a while, so I did them for him. I also did some full arrangements for Murph Podolsky. That was wasted work, though. Not only did he fail to pay me for them, he sold them to other leaders. I also rehearsed with a few bands. One of them was a band Red Nichols had put together in an effort to make a comeback. If he'd gone on the road we'd have been paid twenty-five dollars a week, but nothing happened. He wasn't able to get any bookings.

When the Bob Crosby band came to the Congress Hotel, I subbed for Gil Rodin for two weeks, thanks to recommendations from Warren Smith, who was playing with Crosby, and Hix Blewett, the band's copyist. Bob Zurke, whom I'd met in San Antonio when I subbed with Hank Biagini's Casa Loma Band, and Matty Matlock, whom I'd met once ten years before, were with Crosby, too. There was no reason for them to have remembered me, though.

I was a little excited about playing with the band, I guess—I forgot to take my clarinet to work. Luckily, though, I discovered my oversight in time to go back home and get it. The job didn't give me any chance to play jazz, but I must have demonstrated my ability on the written clarinet work because I subbed for Gil again a few months later when Crosby was booked at the Blackhawk Restaurant. I was working three nights a week with Jimmy Green at the ballroom on the South Side, and he wouldn't let me off. Luckily, the Crosby band's night off was one of the nights I was working with Green. They let me send a sub for the other two nights I had to play the ballroom, and I played with them the rest of the week.

Bob Zurke and I became reacquainted and developed a friendship mostly based on professional admiration since we had little in common. Zurke, who had become a hard drinker, was usually broke. I would lend him a little money now and then, even though some of the boys warned me that he'd probably forget to pay me back. To their amazement, he always repaid me when he had said he would. We remained friends until he died in Hollywood in 1944.

I played the rest of the winter and most of the summer with Green on various jobs. The Crosby band came into Chicago on the way to Minneapolis. Fazola had left the band, and Smitty and Zurke recommended me for his place. None of the others in the band had ever heard me play jazz clarinet, so we arranged for Eddie Miller and a couple of others to hear me. Joe Kahn and Mel Henke were to meet me at a joint about a block from my place, where a trio usually played. I had arranged with the leader of the trio to let us play a couple of numbers. Then I told Miller where the session would be.

Everybody showed up except Mel Henke, who also lived nearby. He told me later that his wife wouldn't let him out for the night. I thought everything would still be all right, though. The pianist in the trio was a good player, whom I had known for a long time, and he offered to sit in.

Miller asked me to play "just some blues." I liked to play the blues in the key of D-flat, but the piano player wasn't used to playing in that key, and he soon got out of hand. Before long I didn't know where the hell he was, so I stopped playing and went to Miller, who was standing at the bar. "I'm sorry," I said. "Something went wrong. My regular piano player didn't show up. Let's just forget it." It had been my chance to get into the big time, and I was pretty upset about it, but I didn't tell him that it was the piano player who had fouled up.

Later, the piano player apologized to me and explained that he had been playing "Smoke Rings," one of the few tunes of the time that was usually played in D-flat. Besides, he'd been nervous playing for the stars of the Crosby band. I didn't blame him much for his goof.

Green took us to Benton Harbor for two weeks, and then to a Chinese restaurant on Howard Street called the Limehouse. There was no sitting in since Green's was not a jazz band, but once in a while a few musicians would drop in to listen, and *Downbeat* knew we were there. We posed for a *Downbeat* photographer one night, and he got a picture that was pure corn. Green and the trumpet player sat in front on the edge of the bandstand, while I stood reared back with my clarinet pointed upward, the drummer had his sticks poised up around his ears, and Henke had his hands ready to pounce on the keyboard as soon as somebody goosed him.

Green's was primarily a commercial band, and I found the music I had to play pretty boring. One day Marge reminded me of the offer I'd had from Roy Shields at NBC. "If you have to play commercial," she said, "you might as well make more money out of it."

Since coming to Chicago, I had never been hired on the basis of an audition. The audition for Kay Kyser, for example, was a disaster. My old friend, Slim Brookins, from Dallas and Sully Mason, a friend of his who played saxophone in Kyser's band, had recommended me. Kyser asked me to come down at two o'clock and sit in at rehearsal, so I borrowed a dime for the el ride—a nickel each way. When I got to the Blackhawk, though, there was no rehearsal going on. I asked around and found that the rehearsal was to be at two o'clock in the morning after the band got off work. I stayed in town all day with no place to rest and nothing to eat and, then, didn't get the job. Kyser was paying $42.50 a week, which was below scale, and I heard that he was afraid to hire a local man. Besides that, he didn't want anyone with a moustache in the band.

The audition I had with Gus Arnheim was also at a rehearsal after work at two o'clock in the morning. Arnheim forgot I was there. The whole rehearsal went by, but he still hadn't called me to sit in. Finally, someone reminded him about my audition. Calling his rhythm section back, he let me play one number on the clarinet. Stan Kenton, the piano player, chose to play "Tiger Rag" in the key of C. Everybody, including me, was tired and uninterested. They played the number as fast as they could just to get it over with, and I didn't get that job either. Arnheim called in Joe Dixon from New York.

Other auditions had turned out just as badly. Finally, I resolved never to audition again, and except for auditions I had as part of a band or combo, I stuck with my resolution. I would tell anyone who wanted to audition me that, if my reputation wasn't enough, they could come out to hear me on my job. It worked out better that way.

When I called Roy Shields, he asked me to come down for an audition at the NBC studios. It was a tricky situation since I didn't want to seem conceited or uncooperative. "I can't play very well on auditions," I said. "You've heard me play. Couldn't we skip all that nonsense?"

"Oh, I know how you play," he said, "it's just a rule of policy here. Just come on down and we'll go through a mock audition."

That suited me because I knew he was going to hire me anyway. From the studios on the nineteenth floor of the Merchandise Mart Building, I could look down at the hotel where I had paid two dollars a week for rent a couple of years before. Shields had set up six music stands, all with sheets of music on them. There were all kinds of parts, from legitimate clarinet parts with cadenzas to saxophone parts on stocks and special arrangements. They were no problem, for I was still in pretty good practice. Then he asked me to play some jazz, with just him on piano.

"Aw, Roy," I said, "you've heard me play jazz before."

"Just a formality," he said, "we have to do it."

After a pretty bad chorus on a tune he chose, with him bumping chords, he asked me if I smoked marijuana. I told him no.

"Are you sure?"

"Scout's honor," I said. "I don't even drink much."

"There's no drinking on this job at all, and no smoking."

I told him that was fine with me, and he said he would call me later. By the time he did call several weeks later, Green had gone back to the ballroom on the South Side. Shields wanted me to start the following day, but Green wouldn't let me go without notice. I thought it was pretty selfish since there were plenty of saxophone players out of work that he could have hired. NBC was the best job in the country, and I might never get another crack at it.

Shields got around the problem by scheduling me so that I wouldn't have any night programs to play. None of the eighty-five staff musicians was allowed to work more than five hours a day, five days a week, because anything over that was overtime. Consequently, there were no set bands or orchestras, and nobody had fixed hours to work. I worked at NBC during the day and with Green at night for the two-week notice period.

Downbeat gave me a write-up that was even more fouled up than usual for them. Not only did they get my name wrong, calling me Drew Pierson throughout, but they didn't even spell Pearson's name correctly. I was fairly used to being introduced, sometimes by long-time friends, as Drew Pearson, but to spell the *wrong* name wrong was pretty dumb. A write-up like that wasn't what I wanted for my scrapbook. I've had derogatory things written about me that didn't bother me as much as that favorable mention, written in such a stupid way.

I was the only man on the staff who could play jazz. Some of the younger ones had been with dance bands as reading players, but most of the musicians were legitimate players. Some of them weren't very good at even that, but most of the work was simpler than that in a dance band. We were supposed to have the ability in reserve to play anything that came up, of course. Some did; some didn't. Unless a musician gets a chance to play different kinds of music, though, he forgets how. All I liked about the job was the money and the prestige. I would have preferred playing in one of the swing bands that were going strong in those days. A friend of mine, Don DeLillo, joined the staff the same day I did, and when I saw him in Las Vegas twenty-five years later, he had just left NBC. I don't think I could have stayed that long.

When Benny Goodman came to play the Chicago Theater, I went to see Harry James. He told me that he was thinking about putting out a sort of method book for trumpet and asked me if I would do the writing for him. We made a tentative agreement but never went through with it. Too many things were happening for both of us, and we were too far apart after he left town.

Harry, at twenty-two, had become recognized as the world's greatest trumpet player. Various trumpet makers were after his endorsement. My friend, Ralph Martiere, who was working at NBC with me, asked me to introduce him to Harry. After he and Harry got acquainted, Martiere asked us to dinner at his house. Harry and I took a cab over the next day between shows. When we got there, we were surprised to find Edmond Benge there.

The three great trumpet players and I relaxed in the living room.

Harry had heard of the Benge trumpet, of course, but he was sold on his Selmer at the time. Benge and Martiere were trying to persuade him to switch to a Benge, but Harry would listen politely, say "I like my Selmer," and change the subject, as if he didn't realize the pitch. That was all the response they could get, despite the fact that Benge was willing to *give* Harry the trumpet.

When my brother, Ben, died I went to Ada for the funeral. My old girl friend read about my arrival in the newspaper and looked me up. I had become a celebrity as far as she was concerned, and I played the part.

"I'm not very happy," she said when I asked her how she was doing. "I should have waited."

"You wouldn't have had to wait," I big-shotted, "but now you can wait forever. I'm not available anymore. Just listen to me on the radio." I hadn't been good enough for her back then, but now that my name had been in the paper, she wished she had waited. It was a lesson in understanding phoniness.

When the new contracts between musicians and NBC came up at the end of the year, some of the new men were laid off until the new contract was signed to include them. I was put on the standby list with some others. Although Shields offered to get me on the staff at another station or to put me on the National Barn Dance show and keep me on call at the studio, I preferred to try for something more to my fancy or not work at all.

I had no regrets. For about two weeks I subbed for Gil Rodin with the Bob Crosby band again. Charlie Spivak recommended me to Glenn Miller, who was planning to organize a band of his own in New York. Miller wasn't quite ready yet, though, so after I finished the sub stint with the Crosby band, I went into the Chicago Theater pit band.

The Chicago Theater was featuring the name big bands at that time. Jelly Caballero came there with Ted FioRito, and Thurman Teague with Vincent Lopez, but as things turned out, I didn't stay with the theater band long.

Dusty Neely (the drummer) got me a job with Lyle Griffin's little jazz band at the El Madena Club in Eagle Rock near Pasadena: Eddie Gilbert, Jerry Tubor, Griffin, Al Famularo, Neely, and me.

The Scat Davis Band playing the Roxy Theater in New York, 1942. The only clarinet work was in a number I had written, which we used as an opener on theater dates. Davis called it "Drew's Blues."   *Arsene Studio*

Marge and I get together with Eddie Pripps, who was working with me in Teddy Powell's band at the Paladium, 1943. Powell had a real swing band.

The best part of working in Phil Harris' band was playing second sax to the best lead alto player in the business, Les Robinson. We posed in front of his house in

At the Jade Club with Wingy Manone in 1944: Bill Campbell, piano; Roy Young, bass sax; Roy Hol, bass; Wingy, trumpet. Wingy and I got along fine as long as we didn't talk to each other.

Freddy Martin's band, 1945. Back row: Gene Conklin, Dale Stoddard, me, and Artie Brooks. Middle row: Jack Fina, Artie Wayne, Walter Kelsey, Irvin Weinper, unknown, True Boardman, and Jerry Jarnagan. Front row: Arnie Olson, Bob White, Dick Arant, Gotch Hughes, Harry McKeehan, Leroy Crouch, Stanley Wilson, and Freddy Martin.

I supplemented my pay at the radio station by working the clubs at night with various bands—the last of them was Joe Reichman's group. Here Earl Blue does some trumpet work. The Baker Hotel, Dallas, 1948.

Drew Page in 1956.

Dick Morris

A radio interview in Bakersfield to publicize the album, 1956.

Dick Morris

Charlie Ventura (standing at right) had been stuck for a sax player who could double on alto, tenor, and clarinet. I'm on the front line between two of Ventura's stars, Carl Fontana (standing at left) and Arno Marsh. My buddy Gene Barringer (wearing glasses) is directly behind me on the last row.

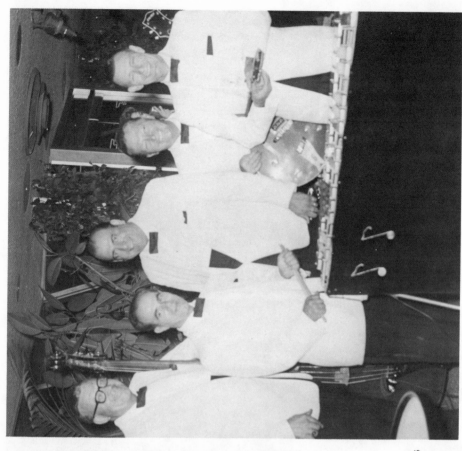

I filled in with Pete Daily's Dixieland band briefly. Front row: Pete, me, and Smitty.

Deacon Jones's band: Deacon, Johnny Cassella, Sandy Sandusky, Dale Osborne, and me. Phil Harris got us the job at the Desert Inn Lounge in 1960. It was before the days when musicians were expected to dance, sing, and hang by their tapeworms from the rafters.

The Freddie Masters Band: Masters, Bobby O'Connor (on drums), me, Russell Jones, and Meri Ellen—in Sondrestrom, Greenland, 1966.

The Russ Morgan Orchestra shortly before the accident: Russ Black, Ted Snyder, Eddie
Julian, Jack Morgan, Arno Marsh, Hal Hafner, Vince Shank, Gus Ehrmann, Brodie
Shroff, and me.

On the ferryboat that we missed.
The next crossing ended tragically.

Marge and Drew.

Good ol' boys reminisce: me, Charlie Teagarden, Henry Levine, and Bill Rand.

Drew Page.

Molly Parkes

12

When Harry James was at the Chicago Theater with Benny Goodman, he had told me that he was planning to start his own band, but it happened sooner than I had expected. I got his call from New York in January. He needed a trumpet player, a tenor sax player, and a bass player. I told him I could bring Mickey Tracy, Ray DeGeer, and Thurman Teague. He rejected Tracy, and I couldn't locate DeGeer soon enough, but Teague went to New York with me. I was to play second alto and baritone sax, as well as all of the clarinet, so I borrowed a baritone from Tommy Miller, a saxophone player at NBC, with a promise to buy it later.

In New York, we rehearsed for a few days in the building where the Roseland Ballroom was operating and then started on tour with a total of twenty-three arrangements in the book and a few "heads" (that is, arrangements constructed in our heads). Harry dictated the brass parts and Dave Matthews dictated the saxophone parts. Two of the heads became hits when they were recorded: "Two O'Clock Jump," which was Harry's version of Count Basie's "One O'Clock Jump," and "Lady Be Good," a series of riffs and solos not touching on the melody and retitled "Flash" on the record. Later, another head added to an arrangement of "Pagan Love Song" became a hit under the title "Back Beat Boogie." Harry began by dressing up the arrangement of "Pagan Love Song" with a tag. He developed the tag to such an extent that, finally, he threw the arrangement away, and we played the tag as a number.

When Harry first organized it, the band was composed of himself, Doc Toland (soon replaced by Tommy Gonsoulin), Claude Bowen, and Jack Palmer on trumpets; Truett Jones and Russ Brown on trombones; Dave Matthews, Claude Lakey, Bill Luther, and me on saxes (I doubled on clarinet); Jack Gardner on piano; Ralph Hawkins on drums; Red Kent on guitar; and Thurman Teague on bass. The girl singer was Bernice Byers, nee Beers. Harry didn't have a boy singer in the beginning, although Jack Palmer doubled on some novelty vocals. Jerry Barret was the manager; Andy Gibson was the arranger; and Al Monte, whose brother, Frank "Pee Wee" Monte, was managing Benny Goodman's band, was the band boy, sometimes called the "brack boy." Harold Blum drove the bus.

We toured for a few days in New England, but since Harry wasn't yet a well-known leader and the weather was cold, the attendance wasn't very good. When we began playing the Benjamin Franklin Hotel in Philadelphia, though, Harry began to draw attention and become publicized as a leader in the music magazines.

He had such a swinging band that we were anxious to go to work and reluctant to stop. There were no cliques or arguments or anything of that sort. It was a ball from the first note to the last every night—no matter how tired we sometimes were from long jumps on tours or lack of sleep.

It was to our advantage, I think, that eleven of the original band members were from the Southwest. Musicians from different parts of the country interpret the music—especially the rhythm and the back beats (syncopation)—differently. Some of them don't seem to *feel* the in-between beats; they simply play them mathematically. Harry couldn't have chosen a better area of the country from which to select a swing band because in those days the southwesterners were particularly unified in their interpretation of swing. Musicians there, although more scattered than elsewhere, got around quite a bit. They tended to know each other and to share the same ideas about music, whereas the musicians in the big northern cities tended to form schools or sects.

In those days, before World War II mixed people from every region of the country, it was possible to put together a homogeneous group with a unified interpretation. I'm not sure Harry planned it that way, but it's certain that he chose men with compatible ideas. Although his band grew after that, the original unit, according to

Harry himself, was the swingingest band he ever had. I think that, compared to the likes of Goodman, the Dorseys, Shaw, Miller, and others, Harry had the swingingest white band of the time. Miller's band didn't swing, nor did Shaw's and, in my opinion, Tommy's and Jimmy's were just so-so.

There have certainly been no swing bands to compare ourselves to since the early forties. As Phil Harris said on a television show, it would be hard now to find fifteen men in the whole country to make up even one swing band. The good teacher-whipped musicians of the early forties, who couldn't play it, invented ways of getting around it—bebop, progressive jazz, and other variants— until the public rebelled, turning to substitutes for music, like rock 'n' roll and country-western.

There was no room for a star clarinetist in Harry's band. (In fact, he didn't use the clarinet at all.) I couldn't blame him for that. To have featured a clarinetist would have matched me, as well as the band, against Goodman, Shaw, Herman, and Jimmy Dorsey. Besides, building a star demands that the band be centered around the star. Harry was more interested in building a band to be reckoned with than in singling out one or another of his musicians.

Having worked with Gonsoulin for quite a while on a couple of jobs back in Texas, I knew that he was a great player. As a matter of fact, he was a big name in the Southwest long before folks had heard of Harry James. Probably he, too, thought that he could become known by playing in Harry's band, but Harry couldn't afford to have another trumpet soloist either. Except for a few tenor solos by Lakey, Harry was the whole show—and quite a show, at that.

When we played the annual musicians' ball in Philadelphia later that year, we were received enthusiastically by all but one of the musicians, who must have been a trumpet player. Harry had played an exceptionally good solo, but the musician standing directly in front of Harry didn't applaud with the rest of the crowd. "Trick mouthpiece," he jeered.

Harry turned around to the band. "Just drums and me," he said. He and Hawkins started playing. The longer Harry played, the wilder he got. There's an old legitimate trumpet solo, called "Russian Fantasy," that has one very difficult variation, which Harry threw in just for laughs. He went up the chromatic scale, playing parts of it in all twelve keys. Then he went into swing rhythm, and topped the whole thing off with jazz, spending some time working up to a climaxing high note. During the whole performance, he didn't take the horn away from his lips. The applause grew and grew; the band was screaming. Finally, with a flourish, Harry threw his arm up and waved his trumpet. He looked directly at his heckler. "Trick mouthpiece, huh?" was all he said. It was the nearest Harry ever came to bragging, and he did it with his horn.

I was pretty disappointed that I had no chance to play clarinet since what good notices I'd had were as a clarinetist. Nevertheless, I saw to it that no one, except Teague, my roommate on the one-nighters, knew about my disappointment. It was enjoyable just blowing notes in a band like Harry's. I had a few offers—from Shep Fields, who was at the Waldorf Astoria with his all-clarinet band (I had subbed with the band on one of my nights off); from Bob Zurke, who was forming his first band in New York; from the Chicago Theater; and from Glenn Miller. I even had an offer of backing for my own band, although there was apparently a romantic catch involved in that proposition. I would have liked to play with Miller's band because of the clarinet lead, and I probably could have switched with one of the saxophone players since several of his men were eager to join Harry's band. Apart from the fact that I didn't think I could live on the $42.50 a week that Miller was offering since I was struggling to get by on the $75 a week I was making with Harry, I felt too much loyalty to leave.

With all the excitement and the hardships of one-nighters, some of us—Big Jack "Jumbo" Gardner, for one—were drinking a bit. One night in Philadelphia our bus conked out. We had to be in New York the following morning for a recording session, so there was nothing to do but wait around the garage, drinking. Since we hadn't slept during the last twenty-four hours or so, we were beat and irritated at the delay. The bus wasn't repaired soon enough, so we were forced to take the train to New York. We drank our way there, arriving in Pennsylvania Station around four in the morning.

By that time Big Jack was angry. He was also drunk, although he didn't look it since he never got unsteady on his feet when he drank. Ordinarily, he was the typical big man, gentle and well mannered, but that morning he was shouting. His voice echoed through the huge, nearly empty station. "A-a-ah! Fuck everything! Fuck everybody!" He even turned his belligerent eye on an inno-cent old lady we passed on the way. "Fuck you too, lady!" he roared. Some of the guys were trying to calm him down, but he wasn't in a conciliatory mood. None of us wanted to get into a disagreement with anyone as big as that, but something had to be done, or he'd wind up in the Tombs.

Big Jack and I had been good friends since my early days in Chi-cago. We looked out for each other in times of emergency. He knew that he could always get a drink from me if he ran out, and I could count on him for the same courtesy. I decided to try to pacify him with my Indian impersonation, which always amused him. Walking a few feet ahead of him, I turned to face him, put my hand up in the traditional Indian peace sign, and said, "Ugh, pale-face noisy. Paleface be quiet."

It worked. Big Jack grinned, put his arm across my shoulder, and walked out of the station with me. We took a cab together to the Forrest Hotel, where I got him registered and up to bed. Every time he started to sound off again, I just raised my hand and said, "Pale-face be quiet." By nine o'clock Jack was fine, and we made the re-cording session all right.

When the weather got warm, we began to play baseball. Harry James, in any kind of competition, was determined to have the best team. Luckily, all of us "ol' boys" from down in the country had had some practice at baseball: Red Kent had been a semipro sandlotter, while Harry, Lakey, Bowen, Brown, Teague, Hawkins, Palmer, and I had all played high school baseball.

At thirty-four, I was past my athletic prime, but I wasn't totally incapacitated. After all, I had had a fair chance of becoming a pro as a kid playing ball with guys like the Waners. I could still catch a ball, given a few chances, and I was able to hold down my position at third base, which seemed to require less moving around.

We made baseball fields out of cow pastures all over the eastern part of the country. We would practice all day, barely making it to that night's job. Since there were enough of us to make up two teams, we played regular nine-inning games. It isn't true that Harry wouldn't hire a musician unless he could play baseball, though. As much as he wanted a winning baseball team, his first consideration was always the band's music.

We beat every team we played, from musicians to bellhops, except the Steel Pier team in Atlantic City. It had been a close game, but Harry was humiliated as well as defiant when we lost. He was determined to win the rematch, so when Ralph Hawkins mentioned that he knew a pitcher back home who was one of the best in the country, Harry said, "Get him." He hired the boy for one day, putting him on the payroll as a member of the organization, not a ringer. The kid's first warm-up pitch went right through Jerry Barret's hands and we knew we had it made.

We beat the Steel Pier team that time, but I was a casualty in the game. One of the Steel Pier boys elbowed me as he came around third base. My eyes swelled, and I went to work with a purple face for a while. It was pretty embarrassing, especially when June, from Flo Whitman's show, came to see us a few nights later. She didn't even recognize me at first.

Connie Haines replaced Bernice Byers before Atlantic City, and after Atlantic City, when we played the Paramount Theater, Frank Sinatra joined the band. Harry put him in the show without a rehearsal. I knew that Frank was a good singer but I didn't know just how good until a few recordings later. It was difficult for me to judge a singer because I was preoccupied with doing my job, and besides, with all the horns between me and Frank, it was hard for me to even hear him. Frank's first recordings weren't very good. One of them, "All or Nothing at All," was shelved for quite a while. Once Frank became famous, though, it was released because, then, his name could carry it. I remember that Frank had some trouble recording it. The producer came out of the booth to coach him. "Don't say 'all or nothing a-*tall*.' It's 'all or nothing at *all*.'" Maybe that was the beginning of Frank's meticulous attention to lyrics. He certainly became the most articulate singer of them all.

Offstage, he was a very quiet kid, not at all a braggart. Contrary to some reports on the young Sinatra, I never noticed any cockiness in his attitude. Mostly a loner on the bus, he dozed, read magazines, and seldom said anything, but he readily responded to humor. He was easy to break up, especially onstage.

Soon after the Paramount job we played the Roseland Ballroom in New York. George Simon (author of *The Big Bands* and *Simon Says*), who was working for *Metronome* magazine, gave Harry some good write-ups that did a lot for his reputation as a leader.

Bands in those days wore uniforms, and Harry's band was no exception. We bought our uniforms at one time, at the same place, and, if my memory hasn't failed me, they consisted of a dark blue suit, a gray suit, and a reddish-colored herringbone suit with an extra pair of tan corduroy pants. We also had two pairs of shoes—brown and two-toned brown and white. We could combine the blue and gray suits in different ways to make four different outfits, and with the extra pair of pants, the red suit was two outfits. Altogether then, we had a total of six uniforms. The hardest part of working with the band was remembering what to wear, but nobody ever goofed.

For six weeks that summer of thirty-nine, we had a daytime job, playing in a band shell on the midway at the World's Fair. We had rain almost every day, but even when it wasn't raining, there wasn't much of an audience. Most of the people were just strolling rubberneckers. Near the band shell was a new curiosity—television. The picture was on a screen with the camera directly behind it. The transmission must have gone all of three feet. We didn't see much possibility of it coming into general use. Some engineers at the time said it would be impossible for television cameras to pick up more than three people at one time.

We played jobs around the East mostly until November, when we went to the Panther Room in the Sherman Hotel in Chicago for four weeks. It was there that I had the proposition to start my own band. There was a family that came to listen to the band several times a week—an older woman, about fifty-five; her daughter-in-law, about thirty-five; and her teenage grandson, who wanted to become a musician. The woman's husband was the head of a theater chain, and her son managed the theaters owned by the chain in the Chicago area.

They stopped me on my way out for a break one night and invited me to sit down. The younger woman asked me to get an autographed picture of Harry for her son. Later that night when I brought him the picture, I sat down at the table again for a bit. After that, I was the boy's special friend. He would stand at my side of the bandstand while we were playing to be close to the action, and at the breaks, he would lead me back to the table. I was becoming pretty chummy with the family, when, one night, the boy's mother began the pitch. "Drew, why don't you get your own band?"

I was surprised by the idea. "Who, me? I'm not a band leader."

"You could be," she said.

Her mother-in-law and the boy seconded the suggestion.

I told them that I had never thought about it much and that starting a band took more money than I had. They insisted that that was no problem because they were willing to back me. Evidently they had already discussed the matter between themselves. I thanked them for their interest and talked them out of the idea. I had no ambition whatsoever in that direction.

The next time they came in, I sat with them on the first break, but while we were playing the next set they acquired a new guest, Betty Grable. Harry, who had admired her for a long time, tried to get me to take him to the table to be introduced but I wouldn't do it. "I'm not going back," I said. "Not since *she* came in and joined them." I didn't want anyone to think I was trying to insinuate myself into the company of such a big star. I wished later that I had taken Harry over. I could have been the one to make their romance possible.

We had a show at the Sherman with the Boogie Woogie Trio—Meade Lux Lewis, Pete Johnson, and Albert Ammons, with Big Joe Turner on vocals—and a jitterbug team of eight kids. Jack Mathias, who had become Harry's arranger a while back, composed and arranged a real swinger for the show, called "Saturday Night Special," that drove the jitterbugs wild.

We were to go to Hollywood after the Sherman job. Harry was being considered to star in *Young Man with a Horn*, but as it turned out, he only did the trumpet playing in the picture. We were booked into the Palomar Ballroom in Hollywood, but the day before we were to leave for the job the joint burned down. MCA switched us to the Victor Hugo Restaurant in Beverly Hills.

It was a swank place, patronized by a lot of film stars, but it was as small as the parlor of a big house. Harry was not the kind of leader who opens with warm-up numbers to feel out the place. He came on with balls—to hell with sucking on the horns. We almost blew the place away on the first set. Afterward, when the manager protested the volume, Harry quit and got fired at the same time, but we had a contract to fulfill. Since we didn't really care what happened after that, we played so loud that the residents of Beverly Hills got an injunction to close Victor Hugo's. We ended up having to go to court to get paid.

In the meantime, though, most of the guys didn't have any money. I was one of the few who'd managed to save anything in Chicago, mostly because I'd known where to live. I doled out money to the boys who needed it, and Marge and I would have the guys come to dinner at our apartment. According to Harry, Frank and Nancy Sinatra were having spaghetti suppers for the band members, too. So we struggled along.

The day we got paid, we were waiting out on the courthouse steps, when Sinatra came up to me to show me a telegram that he had just received from Tommy Dorsey, who wanted Frank to join his band. "What do you think?" Frank asked. "Do you think I should accept it?"

At that time Harry was considering giving up the band reportedly because he was in debt. He had had an offer to stay in Hollywood and play at one of the movie studios. The band hadn't caught on yet, and it looked pretty shaky to me, so I told Frank that I thought he should accept Tommy's offer.

When we played the Paramount Theater in Los Angeles, I had my first and only chance to play clarinet in Harry's band. We had to accompany a dancer, whose music, a stock arrangement, had a semilegitimate clarinet part. It reminded me of NBC, where we did nothing much until the time came, but then we were expected to do the hard stuff. I enjoyed it.

We worked our way back to Chicago after the Paramount job, via Oakland (where I saw Murray McEachern), Colorado Springs (the Broadmoor), Denver (where I saw my old friend George Yadon), and St. Louis (Casa Loma Ballroom). Marge and Margie Drew stayed in California.

In Chicago we played the Chicago Theater with the Andrews Sisters. They liked the band so much that they proposed that Harry go with them on the rest of their tour.

When Sinatra had joined Harry's band, he had had to take some ready-made uniforms that didn't fit. After our first show at the Chicago Theater, the manager came back stage and told Harry to "take that little scarecrow out of the show."

"He's my singer," said Harry. "He stays in." About two years later the Chicago Theater was willing to pay $1200 a week for the "scarecrow" to sing.

We did a few one-nighters before playing the Chez Buffalo Theater in Buffalo with Red Skelton and Burt Lancaster. Burt was doing a trampoline act in those days. One night Frank was out front singing a song with no lighting except a pin spot. The audience couldn't see that Red was standing right behind him telling him jokes. Frank got so tickled that he had to give up on his song. Then Red stepped into the spotlight and finished the song while Frank stood by, laughing and punching at him.

In retrospect I suppose it was a notable gathering—Red Skelton, Harry James, Frank Sinatra, and Burt Lancaster together on stage. At the time, though, we were far more impressed by the people we played with who were stars already, like Connee Boswell, Anita Louise, the Andrews Sisters, Louis Armstrong, the Ink Spots, and Johnny Mercer.

I vividly remember playing for the Ink Spots at the Hippodrome Theater in Baltimore. It made not a bit of difference that they were famous—they were black. When Connie Haines's watch was stolen, the detectives just naturally had to hassle the only Negroes around. They gave the Ink Spots a pretty bad time before the watch was found stashed behind the plumbing in the ladies room.

We played with Anita Louise, the harpist, at a theater in Hartford, Connecticut. Her harp teacher, Catherine Jackson, who was traveling with her as coach and companion, asked me one night to escort them to an after-hours joint. For some reason, I was frequently chosen as an escort by women who were temporarily unattached. Usually all they needed was someone to walk across the street with them to a restaurant or some such place because it looked strange for a formally dressed woman to be walking around by herself. In this case I was needed because women didn't go to after-hours joints unescorted. Anita had evidently been invited to the place, for we had no trouble getting in, although her name would have been enough anyway.

In Boston I had another sort of experience with a girl. Every day a young and very pretty little girl would come to our show, arriving early enough to get a seat in the first row, right in front of the band. Using the railing around what used to be the orchestra pit for a footrest, she would spread her legs apart and pull her dress or skirt up above her knees. She didn't wear panties. I suppose the idea was to tantalize the guys in the band, but she was so young that we found it funny. Although fairly mature looking for her age, she was only thirteen. She found out where we were staying and showed up at the hotel one day. It seems she had chosen me as the object of her wiles, and when she cornered me in the lobby, I had a hard time getting away from her. I went up to my room, but a few minutes later she followed me. I had no intention of getting myself accused of child molesting. Although I managed to keep her out of the room and, later, to send her on her way, I was a little worried for the rest of the engagement that she'd make some sort of false accusation.

I was always bird-dogged by either very young girls or older women, I suppose because I looked ten years younger than I was. The young ones were looking for their father and the old ones wanted a son. Men usually considered me a kid until they had an emotional crisis, and then I became father superior.

We were playing Boston another time when Harry planned a weiner roast for after the job one night. There were lots of unattached women around the ballroom where we were playing, and every night when we got into the bus, we found it loaded with them. We didn't mind giving them a ride back to town with us, but the night of the weiner roast some of them wanted to go along. The idea didn't appeal to us, but there wasn't much we could do since they were determined to go. There was a woman on every double seat on the bus.

One woman, who had wrinkles that would hold a three-day rain, was walking up and down the aisle, saying, "Somebody take me. Why doesn't somebody take me? I'm the best fuck in town." Apparently, this wasn't an empty boast, for when we were in town for a subsequent engagement, one of the guys told me he'd seen her again. "Pooge," he said," You remember that old gal who said she was the best fuck in town? Well she was right. She is." (Close friends of that period usually called me Pooge because I'd once ordered peach pie. Somehow *peach* had come out *pooge*, and Smitty had picked it up, "Poogie P. Page and his pooch pie.")

We finally got underway, with some of the girls still on the bus. We had big boxes of weiners, buns, and other things to go with them. The roast was suppposed to be at the beach, but Harold Blum got lost on the way. He toured the whole city of Boston, its outskirts, and parts of the countryside. Finally we stopped at an eating joint, where Harry paid the cook to fix the hot dogs, and Blum got directions to the beach. By the time we got there it was almost daylight. We had eaten most of the hot dogs, and drunk enough beer and booze to make us feel pretty good, so we made a game of seeing who could throw a hot dog the farthest out into the ocean.

Back in town, it was almost time for the working girls to go to their jobs. Two of them said they lived too far out to make it home and back before work, so Teague and I said, "What the hell— come on up to our room and wait." He and I went to bed, and when we woke up, the girls were gone.

On the way to Boston that time we had played a one-nighter somewhere in Connecticut on a Sunday. We hadn't known that the sale of alcoholic beverages was prohibited in Connecticut after nine o'clock on Sundays, so everyone was out of everything. It was a true emergency, and I sprang into action. No one in the kitchen knew any bootleggers, but the cook came up with a beerlike drink called something like "grenay." It was my first and only encounter with it. I brought a supply of the stuff back to the band, and each of us who liked to drink had a couple of bottles of it.

It had an unusual effect, making us all giggly-silly. During the next set we were like kids on a pot jag. On the next break we had more of it. "Man, what is this stuff?" said Harry. "I'll never drink anything else!" The rest of us felt about the same way until the effects wore off later that night, and we were hung over and sick as never before.

I don't mean to imply that we were a bunch of drunks. We just nipped along normally. Actually, as a class, I think musicians drink less than most other people. Because we're in the public eye, though, everyone knows about the occasional drunk. It's true that some musicians have destroyed themselves with booze, but I haven't known many who were hooked on it. At least nine of Harry's band members either didn't drink at all or just had a social nip now and then.

Once, I decided to cool it for a while, so when we left New York for a short tour, I left my bottle at home. A couple of days out, we played a joint in Philadelphia where we had to do a half-hour broadcast. On a break just before the broadcast, I mentioned to Jerry Barret, who was standing at the steps to the bandstand, that I wouldn't mind having a drink, but that I hadn't brought anything. "Here," he said, pulling out a pint of Canadian Club, "I've got a bottle of Harry's. Take a sip." I accepted the offer at just the wrong time, for Harry saw me as he walked by on his way to the bandstand. He didn't say anything, but he looked displeased, not because he was stingy with his liquor, but because he had a position to maintain in the public eye.

It happened that toward the end of the broadcast Harry had to make a cut in the last number, leaving out some solos in one of the head arrangements, to fit it into the remaining time. Somehow the saxophone section didn't hear about the cut, so we kept playing background when the rest of the band went into the chorus. Harry was understandably peeved. It was the first and only time I ever saw him say anything to anybody in the band except "just play it right." I don't remember exactly what he said to us this time but it was something like "Well, you guys really loused up." The other guys just sat there looking humiliated, but I thought I knew Harry well enough to explain what had happened. "Harry, we didn't hear about the cut."

"If you'd lay off the booze you would have heard it," he said. "Pooge, I want to see you after the set."

"Fine," I said. I was waiting for him at the steps when he came off the bandstand, but he passed by without even looking at me.

I hailed him. "Harry, did you want to see me?"

He just shrugged and said, "Naw, Pooge. Forget it."

When the band played in New York, I usually stayed at the Plymouth Hotel. That was where I became friends with my boyhood idol, Rudy Wiedoeft. He was one, I think, who let the booze get him in later life. We had a few drinking visits in the Plymouth bar. Bob Zurke stayed there also, but since he was organizing his band and I was working, I didn't actually see him. He left Teague and me a message to call him. He wanted us to join his band, but we declined. The Plymouth was also where I met Wingy Manone, with whom I would later work.

Around the end of February, we went out on a six-day tour of the nearby eastern states. There were some bad jumps, so we didn't get much sleep. After a date in Pennsylvania, we drove for most of the night to get back to New York, where we were to open at the Apollo Theater in Harlem. We rehearsed in the cold, damp basement of the theater. When the first show ended, I couldn't get out of my chair because my legs were numb and my ankles were swollen.

Teague carried me up to the dressing room and called a doctor and a cab. Then he put me into the cab and took me first to the doctor and then to the Forrest Hotel. He took one of Artie Shaw's men back with him to take my place. Shaw's men were available because he had recently given up the band business.

Several days passed before I was able to get around. The band was getting ready to leave on another tour, but I knew I couldn't go along. The doctor had told me I had inflammatory rheumatism. Jerry Barret came to my room to tell me that Harry said I had better go home. I told Barret I was broke. All I had coming was

$42.50 for a recording session a couple of weeks back, but when Barret returned a little later, he handed me four hundred dollars. "What's this for?" I asked him.

Barret shrugged. "I don't know. Harry said give it to you."

I managed to hobble down to the front of the hotel as the bus was about to leave, and I tried to thank Harry for his generosity. He didn't want to hear it, though. "Forget it, Pooge," he said.

Musicians and show people don't waste time on fussy goodbyes. They know they are likely to run across one another again. Our partings are usually just "so long, I'll be seeing you." That's the way I left Harry and the boys in the band.

13

I WENT BACK to Chicago, not because I wanted to, but because I had a union card and a reputation there that I hoped would get me work. I had no desire to go back to Hollywood where I would have had to struggle along until I could get a union card, so I sent for the girls to join me in Chicago.

I got an apartment up on the North Side near a couple whose daughter had been Margie Drew's friend and playmate. The man, a physical culturist named Iver Iverson, who had formerly worked with the Chicago Blackhawks hockey team, had a studio downtown. I was still in pretty bad shape, so he and his wife took care of me, bringing me food and beer, which Iverson prescribed. After a few days, I was able to take the el to his studio for treatments, and pretty soon I was able to function again, but carefully.

My aversion to auditions kept me out of work for a while, but I think it was the right attitude to take. I got a call from the leader of the band at the 606 Club on Wabash in the loop. I didn't know the man, and he didn't know me, but he told me that somebody had recommended me. "Would you come down for an audition?" he asked.

"No thanks," I said, "I don't make auditions."

"You'd be taking Jimmy Morash's place," he said. "He's a pretty good clarinet player."

His tone of voice implied that Morash was so good that his replacement would only be tolerated. I had known Morash ever since I started getting around in Chicago in 1935. We had a good bit of respect for each other's work and were good friends besides. "Don't worry about it," I said. "I just left Harry James, and before that, I played first clarinet on the NBC staff." He wouldn't accept that, so I told him to ask Morash about me and hung up.

A half hour later he called back. "Would you come down and work for a week on trial?"

That irked me even more. "No," I said, "if my reputation isn't good enough, forget it." We let it go at that and hung up again.

An hour or so later, he called back again. I assumed that he had been calling other clarinet players without success. "All right," he said, "you can come down and go to work. Forget about the audition."

He sounded reluctant, though, as if hiring me were the best he could do, so I resented his tone. "No," I said, "I don't want your job."

The Great Depression was still with us, so Harry's four hundred dollars kept us going until I was able to get around and look for work. I went to the Sherman Hotel one night to see a friend who was there with Ben Pollack's band. Pollack, who had stayed in California when his band broke up in 1936, was trying to make a comeback with Los Angeles musicians. A Chicago buddy of mine, Hugh Hudgings, had gone to California, and he was with the band. Since Pollack had a good clarinet player, Bill Wood, I didn't get a job, but he turned out to be a valuable contact later on.

As fall approached I began dreading the Chicago winter. Finally, I got my chance to leave the town for good when, in October, I was offered two weeks of work at the State Fair in Dallas. This time it was with a local Chicago leader who was getting together a five-piece group for a sideshow of some kind. I took the job to get free transportation out of Chicago.

The only thing I missed when I left Chicago was the genuine friendliness of the musicians. There was no professional jealousy that I ever knew of. They were especially kind to out-of-towners who had drifted in and were down on their luck. I owe my survival to fellows like Sammy Saxe, who hired my whole little southwestern clique (Smitty, Tracy, Seely, Teague, and me) on the sly from his regular boys a few times. Kahn had hired four of us on the Wagon Wheel job. Green had hired Smitty first, then me on his recommendation, and later two additions to the clique, Ray De-

Geer and Mel Henke. Dick Wirth had hired three of us for the Louisville job. The sidemen were just as helpful. When a man got an offer he couldn't accept, he would recommend someone else, or even call someone himself. They did all they could to help a new man get started. I had become so used to the friendliness there that I never thought much about it until I went to crack Hollywood and Las Vegas. There, no one wants to jeopardize his own job by recommending someone else.

Marge and I took all our earthly trappings to Dallas because I was thinking of going from there to Ada to settle down and, maybe, teach school. I was disenchanted with the music business. Before I left Chicago I remarked to someone that I thought I would go back to Oklahoma and open a country grocery store. A couple of years later I ran into an old friend in Hollywood. "Well I'll be damned!" he said. "I thought you were running a grocery store in Oklahoma."

When the job ended, my half brother, Victor, drove down from Ada to pick us up. He made a pleasure trip of it, bringing Pop and Ava, my stepmother, with him. Ada hadn't been lively when I was a boy, and since the Depression, it was even worse. Rural communities had been hit hard. I applied for a new form of relief called unemployment compensation and began to draw sixteen dollars a week. We rented half of a furnished house for twenty-three dollars a month, including utilities. Victor thought the rent outrageous since he was renting a whole house for four dollars a month, although he had to furnish the house and pay about three dollars a month for utilities.

When I was a kid in Ada, Pop had been high-pressured, shirt-grabbed, and ball-fisted by a traveling salesman into buying a set of the *Harvard Classics* that hadn't been opened since. While I was in Chicago, Mel Henke had introduced me to literature, though, and now, I had the time to read. My favorites were Pliny the Elder, Pliny the Younger, and Cato, but Pop's *Harvard Classics* are full of underlined sentences.

I worked a little, too. Austin Kidwell, a music teacher in nearby Pauls Valley, had a jobbing band. My other half brother, Durward, who was playing lead sax in the band, managed to get me on with them. We played often but didn't make much money.

I was offered a teaching job that required traveling to a town thirty miles north and one fifteen miles south. I would have had to supply my own transportation, though, and I didn't have a car. Besides, the pay was only sixty dollars a month.

I decided to try private teaching, instead, but my fifty-cent fee, which was fifteen cents more than the other teachers charged, kept the kids away. I thought publicity might help, so I went to the local scoutmaster for help. He ran my picture with a write-up in the Ada *Evening News*, but the article was about my being an Eagle Scout. There was almost nothing about my musical career, and he didn't mention that I'd become a private teacher. He was just using me to make himself look like a great scoutmaster.

Eventually, I did give one lesson. The kid played tenor sax with a thin tone that sounded like eggs frying. "First," I said, "I'll show you how to blow that thing."

The kid was indignant. "I won the county contest," he huffed. "What can *you* show *me?*"

"If that's the way you feel about it," I said, "not a thing."

My reputation was better anywhere else in the country than it was in my hometown, but my ego wasn't too deflated. I knew that the folks in Ada hadn't even heard of the big-name leaders, much less the sidemen. Nevertheless, I could see that I didn't belong there anymore. I didn't look up any of my old friends in Ada because I was ashamed of getting paid for being unemployed. (There was still a good deal of stigma attached to any kind of relief, including unemployment compensation.)

By then the war was in full swing in Europe. There was every chance that we'd get involved, selling war matériel to both sides as a way of boosting our economy. I figured that my family would gain more benefit from an improved economy in a livelier place, so we went back to Dallas.

We had wanted to go back to Hollywood since playing there with Harry James. Soon after we got back to Dallas, Marge's brother-in-law, Russell Logsdon, persuaded us to go along with him to Los Angeles, where he had a job waiting for him. His coupe was too small for all of us, so he arranged for me to drive a used car out for a dealer, who paid for the gas and oil.

Although I had been working, I hadn't saved any money, and I had only a week's pay coming from the job I was on. I thought that I could get a good price for my spare instruments from a musician I knew, who owned a hock shop, but he only gave me twenty-five dollars for my flute and fifteen for my baritone, including the sixteen-dollar stand for it.

The money lasted just long enough to get us there with a dollar and change left over. The car I had driven coughed, sputtered, and fell apart just as I drove into the Los Angeles dealer's lot. We all moved into a rented house out near La Brea and Crenshaw in the south end of town. Russell paid the rent, bought the groceries, and lent me the money to transfer my card to the Los Angeles local.

Jacques Ordean recommended me to Stan Kenton, who was starting his own band. I was to join the band at a rehearsal, so I borrowed bus-streetcar fare from Russell. When I got there, the band was set up and running through a number. Ordean was playing lead sax, and there was another saxophonist sitting in the second alto chair, for which I thought I'd been hired. Ordean motioned me to come in, but I told him I hadn't come for an audition. "I'll see you later," I said. I left while he was trying to wave me back. Even in those dire circumstances, I wouldn't audition.

Irvin Verret was working with Phil Harris at the Wilshire Bowl, a swanky night club on Wilshire Boulevard that would later become Slapsie Maxie's. (At that time, Slapsie Maxie's was a small joint on Melrose.) Since I wouldn't borrow bus fare from Russell for a social visit, I decided to walk the four miles to the club. I intended to ask Verret for a five-dollar loan, but when I got there, my pride wouldn't let me. It was bad enough that he knew what I'd been doing since he last saw me. I couldn't admit to being so destitute. On the long walk home I was dreading having to tell Marge that I hadn't had the nerve to ask Verret for the loan.

A few days later, Ben Pollack called to ask me to go on tour with him. I reminded him that, because I was a transfer member, the union wouldn't allow me to take an out-of-town job until my probation period was completed. Pollack told me to meet him at the union. It seems that, as manager or, perhaps, part owner of a trailer park in Culver City, Pollack had provided a union official with shack-up facilities. The official who owed him a favor took care of the problem by slipping my card out of the files, where it would be replaced after the tour.

Originally, I was to play baritone sax, borrowing an instrument from Costello, the clarinetist in the band, but Pollack switched us. Costello took the alto-baritone chair, and I played clarinet. After a couple of rehearsals we went out on tour. There were a few one-nighters and a two-week stand in Albuquerque. Since Pollack paid pretty good money, I was able to save a few bucks, and when I got back, we found an apartment right in the middle of the Hollywood action. Actually a separate little house in a court, it was on La Mirada Street a half block off Vine Street between Santa Monica and Sunset Boulevards. Pete and Faye Daily lived across Vine Street at the St. George Hotel.

I had made two good friends working in Pollack's band: Johnny Fresco, the tenor man, and Dusty Neely, the drummer. Neely took me around town to jam sessions, which gave me the chance to sit in with good players, like Jimmie Rowles, Chico Alvarez, and Don Swander ("Deep in the Heart of Texas"). Fresco was eager to join Harry James's band, so, although Harry was still back in New York, I managed to get Fresco hired by mail, telephone, and a home recording.

Some weeks later, Neely got me a job with Lyle Griffin's six-piece band at the El Madena Club out in Eagle Rock near Pasadena. There was no floor show to hassle with. Griffin's good little band—composed of Griffin, who sang and played trombone; Jerry Tubor on piano; Eddie Gilbert on bass; Al Famularo on trumpet; Neely; and me—played mostly jazz.

I had seen Al Famularo playing in a theater in San Antonio, Texas, in 1926 but had never met him. He'd been in Hollywood for several years and was the best trumpet player in town. Unfortunately, he'd become too fond of booze, which, though it didn't affect his playing, made him lax about showing up for work at the right time. Famularo didn't play jazz, but he could swing the melody. I made some arrangements for the band that would show off his tremendous, infallible range and the most beautiful tone I'd ever heard.

The rest of the band members were part of a clique that got most of the sideline work at the studios. Because of that they could afford to play for almost nothing—our salary at the club was only twenty dollars. They were all well known around town. Other musicians began coming around to hear us, and before long El Madena became the hot spot in town. Harry Highsmith, who had formerly been a musician and music contractor at MGM, and his silent partner David Schnell, who scored and conducted pictures and was head of MGM's music department, owned the club. They welcomed the musicians who frequented the place, even though they didn't spend much money.

To my surprise and pleasure I became the soloist attraction because the fans were mostly clarinet players from the studios. Not jazz players, these guys were legitimate clarinetists, the elite of the town. The principal jazz player in town, also at a studio, never came because, I was told, he was afraid I would upstage him. Since I was being showcased, I practiced three hours a day at home, hoping to have surprises for my fans. My special number was a fast and technical bunch of nonsense, called "Clarinet Caprice Number One," which I had composed for drums and clarinet. The number usually ran on for about ten minutes, but once, when I'd been asked to play it on radio, I'd been allotted only three minutes. The announcer became so engrossed in the piece, though, that he forgot to call time, and I went on playing for over six minutes, wrecking the schedule for the rest of the show.)

Dave Schnell often came out to sit in with us on piano. Sometimes he brought some of his musicians from MGM. Lennie Hayton, his orchestrator and pianist, who later succeeded Schnell at MGM, sat in from time to time, as did my boyhood idols, Arthur Schutt (piano) and Manny Klein (trumpet).

I was offered sideline work at the studios, but I held out for recording. The music in movies was always separately recorded, and although the sideline musicians were the ones who appeared on the screen, they weren't the ones actually playing the music. Sideliners would listen to the playback of the studio recording and then mimic the playing. Even those artists who played their own music in a picture recorded the music in the studio first and then mimicked the recording when the scenes were filmed. A careful observer can notice that the musician's fingers are not always playing the same notes in the picture as are heard on the recording. Sometimes a wind player is taking a breath while the recorded sound goes on, or blowing through a rest in the recorded music. It's almost impossible to synchronize the music perfectly, particularly on an ad lib jazz solo. As a union transfer member, I couldn't accept the recording work I was offered until I'd been a member of the Los Angeles local for six months. I hadn't yet been in L.A. for even the six months it takes just to join the local.

Jelly Caballero had been in Los Angeles for some time and had his studio clearance, as they called it. So when, one night, Russ Cheever offered me some recording work that I had to turn down, I recommended Jelly. I assured Cheever that Jelly wouldn't disappoint him, and the next time I saw him, I asked him how Jelly had done.

Cheever chuckled. "I'll tell you," he said. "We ran through the stuff and Caballero played everything exactly right, note for note, the very first time. He laid his clarinet aside and waited politely for the rest of us to woodshed our parts."

Along about that time I got a call from Stan Kenton, who had booked a job and wanted me to join his band. Since I was happy at El Madena, I turned down that offer, as well as another from him shortly thereafter. Apparently, he had finally decided that I was good enough to play in his band without an audition.

Then Schnell got carried away one night after hearing me play "Clarinet Caprice" and offered me a job at MGM. "You're the best clarinet player I've ever heard," he said. "I've got an opening for you if you want it." I had to turn him down, of course, but he told me to let him know as soon as I got my clearance.

Besides practicing at home every day, I almost always walked up Vine Street to Howard Lockie's music store, a half block past Sunset Boulevard, where musicians hung out. I made some new acquaintances there and ran into a few old friends from other places—Matty Matlock, Clarence Hutchenrider, Hugh Hudgings,

Ernie Caceres, Dick Buckley, and others. Occasionally, I'd go down to Music City on the corner of Sunset and Vine, instead. The owner, Glenn Wallichs, who later founded Capitol Records, would let me sight read the melodies and chords on the new popular songs to arrange later. He had also recorded my guest appearance and performance on the radio.

I met Jackie Cooper at Lockie's one day. His mother wanted a record of him playing the drums, so he was looking for a clarinetist to play with him and Dick Winslow, the vibraphone player and movie actor. After we made the records at Wallichs', Jackie took Winslow and me to the club where Winslow was playing. He picked up a stack of about thirty stock arrangements to give me and then drove me home. Margie Drew, age ten, was outside when we drove up, and so she got Cooper's autograph to add to her collection.

One day I ran into Dick Buckley on Hollywood Boulevard. He walked home with me, raising his hand like a cop to stop traffic while we were crossing the busy streets. "I wish I knew where I could get some grass," he said, as we were parting at my house. "Do you happen to have any?"

"You know I don't smoke the stuff," I said. "But, hey! Do you remember giving me a stick the last time I was with you in Chicago? Come to think of it, I still have it."

I fished it out of my wallet. By that time it was flatter than a wet gunny sack, but Buckley was delighted. He rolled it back into shape, lit it, and took off, smoking the stick and waving good-bye.

There were some women who were habitués at the club, usually coming in on weekends, unescorted. Several romances developed into marriages, and a few triangles developed into divorces—two musicians even swapped wives.

One night two girls who hadn't been there before came in. They sat near the bandstand, applauding everything we did. When we met them, we discovered that they were married to musicians, who were out of town, and that they had come just to listen to the band.

Musicians tend to be skeptical of women who brag about the musicial ability of their husbands. Therefore, we took it with a grain of salt when Eleanor, one of the girls, told us that her husband, a trombone player named Burt Johnson, was good. I told her to bring him by when he got back to town, but since I'd never heard of the guy, I didn't expect much.

Johnson looked like a pro from the moment he took his horn out of its case and stepped up onto the bandstand. Eleanor, it turned out, hadn't been exaggerating. Without saying anything he took charge of the whole session. He had us yelling for more after his very first chorus. It was a kick to discover a real artist quite unexpectedly. Johnson was an excellent reader and a good composer, who eventually worked with most of the good bands around, especially the little jazz bands. I got him several good jobs with groups I was in.

Highsmith fired Griffin and promoted me to leader, giving me a five-dollar-a-week raise. I hired John Gruey, a tenor sax player, to replace Griffin, thereby changing the band's style from pseudo Dixieland to the Chicago sound. About that time Famularo got into some kind of mess and quit. He left his young daughter for Marge to take care of overnight and didn't come back to pick her up until a week later, I suspect because he had been hanging one on. I replaced him with Clyde Hurley, who didn't stay long because he played too loudly to suit Highsmith. Then Bert Moncrief replaced him.

The war was looking more and more likely. All of the guys seemed to be looking for other things—maybe for safer endeavors. Before long, I wound up with an entirely new band. Replacements were hard to get, especially on piano because the piano player had to play intermissions, too. Scott Seely, who had drifted out to Hollywood sometime before, worked with me for a while. With the threat of war hanging over us, I could see that the good start I had made in Hollywood would soon mean nothing. Then the bombs dropped on Pearl Harbor, and the bottom fell out of the music business—most of the joints folded immediately. I was pretty sure that El Madena would fold, too, so I gave Highsmith my notice, sent the girls back to Dallas, and appealed to friends in Chicago for help. I soon got a call to join Johnny "Scat" Davis.

14

DAVIS HAD JUST closed at the Blackhawk in Chicago and was going out on the road. Joining them in Aurora, Illinois, I spent about four months touring with the band. Mostly, we played one-nighters, although we also had two-week stints in Wichita, New York, and Baltimore. From Aurora we went west to Kansas, north to South Dakota, back through the Midwest, and as far east as Maine. We were in Old Orchard, Maine, on Easter Sunday, 1942, and although we were playing for the opening of an open-air pavilion, the weather was so cold that we had to play in our overcoats. We played the usual theater dates in Philadelphia, Boston, Hartford, and New York with acts like Jerry Lester, Jinx Falkenburg, and Connee Boswell.

While we were playing the Blue Moon ballroom in Wichita, which later became the Moose Club, Tommy Dorsey came to Wichita on a one-nighter, so our joint closed for the night, and all of us went downtown to hear Dorsey's band. Frank Sinatra was playing handball with a musician when I went backstage to see him at intermission. He was already pretty famous. We shook hands while the ball was on its way to his partner and back. "It's good to see you doing so well." I said.

"Yeah," Frank said, still playing, "I've come a long way since I saw you last, haven't I?"

I had resolved to myself never to approach anyone who had become famous—not even an old friend—because I didn't want to appear to be a toady. I had risked it in this case simply because I wasn't aware of how famous Frank had become. I was a little offended when he came out with that statement, but he didn't mean to brush me off. He was just going through a normal temporary reaction to instant fame. The next time I saw him, when he was a guest on a radio show I was playing a couple of years later, he came through the band at rehearsal to greet me. He did the same thing when I was at the Coconut Grove with Freddy Martin.

After the dance that night, some of the members of both bands went to a coffee shop in a hotel nearby. The place had two rows of booths with a traffic aisle between them. Mel Grant, our piano player, and I and a couple of others were sitting in a booth directly opposite Buddy Rich and his pals. Grant rarely got drunk, but when he did, he would sometimes become unruly. Grant didn't even know Buddy Rich, but he began telling me what an egotistical so-and-so he was, looking, all the while, directly at Rich, who was sitting four feet away. I tried to calm Grant down, without much success, while Rich just ignored the whole thing. When we had all finished eating, I risked approaching Rich. After I had introduced myself and reminded him of the Gay 90's, he recognized me, or, at least, he remembered the incidents I mentioned. I introduced him to Grant, and he invited us up to his room. We visited with him and his roommate for a few minutes. To my knowledge, neither Grant nor Rich mentioned what had gone on in the coffee shop. Rich had handled the situation so well that, from then on, Grant was convinced that he'd misjudged a good guy.

Things were jumping during the first few months we were in the war before rationing set in to hamper social and entertainment activities. There were good crowds at most places. We played a dance one night at the Astor in New York for the sailors of a ship that had just come in from an extended cruise. The boys hadn't seen hide nor hair of a woman for months, so the city had arranged the dance for them, enlisting the aid of several hundred unattached girls as dancing partners. The town had provided the booze as well, and everyone was lapping it up. Some of us in the band got shanghaied to the Copacabana Club after the dance.

That was the night a total stranger proposed to me. I was sitting with some sailors and the girls they'd paired off with when a girl came up to me. "Will you marry me?" she asked.

"I guess I might consider marrying you—or sumpin," I answered, trying to be cute.

"I mean it. No alternative." She was trying to look serious and sexy at the same time, but even though she was decked out in the latest fashion, augmented by quite a few fair-size diamonds, she wasn't very sexy.

"I'm already married," I said, hoping to get rid of her, or at least to change the subject.

"You could get a divorce."

"I couldn't support you on sixty dollars a week—sometimes anyway." I didn't mention that sixty dollars was top pay—my usual salary was closer to twenty.

"I don't need support," she said. "I have the money." She went on to tell me about the family home on Long Island and a winter home in Florida and how wealthy she was.

"No cash dowry?" I asked, still trying.

"You wouldn't have to work. I wouldn't let you."

"Anyway, that's better than making me quit the music business and go to work," I said. "No thanks." I know everybody has his price but I wasn't for sale at that moment. I found out later that her girl friend had made the same proposition to one of my bandmates. He had seen them drive away from the club in a big limousine, so maybe they weren't kidding about their money.

The tour was rough on us. The jumps were long between one-nighters, and since the bus wasn't comfortable, we did most of our sleeping on the job. Besides, the only clarinet work in the band was in one number I had written, which we used as an opener on theater dates. It was just a combination of brass and saxophone riffs in twelve-bar blues chord structure—up-tempo—that Davis titled "Drew's Blues." The thing was such a simple little piece; I had written it standing up at a dresser in my room one night, without even scoring it. Since I wasn't too happy just playing written notes most of the time, I had tried to quit the band several times out in the middle of nowhere but was persuaded to stay on because there were no replacements available. When we played New York, though, Davis found a replacement, so I played out a two-week notice with the band in Baltimore.

On the last night there Davis announced that I was leaving and asked me to play a farewell solo. I had to try to live up to the flattering things he'd said about me. Besides, my replacement, a kid of seventeen whom I'd never heard of, named Buddy DeFranco, was waiting in the wings. I was thinking, as I had with Jelly Caballero years before, that I would give him a lesson. Some of the dancers had stopped to watch when Davis made the announcement. I began to play "I Surrender, Dear" and, as usual, to improvise with my eyes closed. As I played, more and more dancers gathered at the bandstand. I played choruses for about ten minutes, and when I stopped, I was suprised to hear applause. Looking out, I saw I had stopped the dance. The whole crowd of about six hundred people had gathered around the bandstand to listen. Davis was leading the applause for an encore, so I played "Drew's Blues" until I was exhausted.

When it was over, Davis came over and put his arm around me. "Man, I didn't know that you could play like that."

"You never asked me," I said.

He called a break, and we headed for the bar to take on a little altitude.

The playing was nothing to brag about, but the incident demonstrated to me again that people can't tell whether something is good or not until someone tells them. I was to become more and more aware of the phenomenon when I played on radio shows and saw the hosts telling the audience when to applaud, using hand motions, holding up APPLAUSE signs, or encouraging laughter by laughing themselves. The applause Davis milked out of that crowd didn't do much for me because I knew how phoney it was. The only kick I got out of it came years later when I was reminiscing with Buddy DeFranco and he told me he'd been "scared to death" to follow me. That was the best compliment I've ever had because De Franco is the best jazz clarinetist ever.

I had written to Roy Shields from Baltimore, and he told me I could come back to NBC in Chicago. In the meantime, I was offered a job with Goodman that I didn't even consider. I arrived in Chicago at night and checked in at the Chicagoan Hotel. The next morning was dreary, sunless, and foggy, just as it usually was in Chicago. When I looked out the window, I remembered why I'd so wanted to leave the place. I packed my bag and took the next train to Dallas.

The war had created a shortage of musicians, many of whom either enlisted or were drafted, while others took defense jobs to avoid the draft. Because I was over the draft age, I was never classified, and when I tried to enlist, I was turned down. There were more jobs in Dallas than I could handle, although I tried pretty hard. I worked a ballroom job seven nights a week. During the day, six days a week, I played at two radio stations. Then on my day off, I worked a special Sunday program for yet another radio station, rehearsing at nine in the morning and doing the show at three in the afternoon. Since two of the stations were downtown and the other was at the fair grounds, much of my off time was spent riding street cars. Otherwise, I slept three hours at night and two in the afternoon. Marge had to tell me when I woke up whether it was morning or afternoon so that I would know which job to go to.

Old friends—Glenn Hughes, Chuck Franzen from Wisconsin, and some old boyhood buddies—came through, but I didn't have time to see them. Louise Tobin, whom I'd known before she met Harry, called me at work as she was passing through on her way to Juarez to divorce him. My father came through Dallas on his way to Oakland to work in the shipyards, and many old friends had to leave without a "so long."

The war panic subsided somewhat, and things began to get organized. I wanted to go back to Hollywood where the pay was better, since, for all the work I was doing in Dallas, I was making less than eighty dollars a week. The Southwest has always been in the starvation wage bracket. Whereas Hollywood had three scales—A, B, and C—Dallas had only one—C-minus, compared to anything in Hollywood.

When the ballroom job folded after a few months, I was down to radio work and jobbing dates. A man came to the union hall one day to organize a band for the army. Some of the boys joined right away with the assurance that they would be stationed in Waco, but I was undecided because I was over the draft age. Although the man, a warrant officer, offered me the rank of staff sergeant, I didn't think I was enough of a bully. Still, he finally talked me into considering it. I got a physical from a private physician, who told me that my double hernia would make it impossible even if I wanted to join. The warrant officer had told me they'd do a repair job as soon as I joined, but I figured, since I didn't have to go, I could put it off. Then the warrant officer died, and the boys were up for grabs. Most of them, including Truett Jones and Curtis Hurt, wound up in the infantry. They started out in the same outfit, but later, Hurt was sent to Iceland. The story is that his hair turned white overnight when he was injured and had to lie in the snow all night before help came. Some of the others saw action in the Pacific, but luckily, none of them were killed. Garner Clark, the great Dixieland trumpet player, enlisted as a band director and took Ray Leatherwood, his bass player with him to Long Beach, California. I was with them the night before they left.

I worked in Dallas for more than a year because I didn't have the money to move to Hollywood. Finally I got a fill-in job with a traveling band at the Baker Hotel. The Dallas hotels didn't use local bands; they wanted "names", no matter how lousy the bands might be. It's the name that counts since no one knows the difference. Some traveling bands were all right, but some weren't. Booking agents, acting on the principle that anything from out of town was better, would exchange bands. Since the band never stayed in any one place for long, by the time anyone discovered how awful a band was, it was on its way somewhere else.

I worked for Freddy Nagel, who had one of the good bands. He wasn't a big enough name to get by with a lousy one. Since I was playing a noon session with him as well as night, and I was still doing radio work, too, I was pretty busy. I worked night and day again, but the job paid pretty well, so by the time it was over— about six weeks—I had saved enough money to buy a second-hand car and make the trip to Hollywood.

We took Marge's mother with us. Between the wartime speed limit of thirty-five miles an hour and the gas rationing, it took several days to get there. I shut off the motor and coasted on all downgrades. Motels were beginning to appear everywhere, although the ones in the sticks were still pretty primitive. We stayed in some that had chickens roosting on the roof.

15

MARGE WENT TO work at the Ranch Market on Vine and La Mirada, and I got a job with the "Take It or Leave It" radio show. Phil Baker, the host, had brought the show from New York to Hollywood for a thirteen-week run. For a while Johnny Richards led the band, but he was too good for the show. He was making special arrangements for the tunes contestants had to guess in the music category, but all Baker wanted was somebody to fake a few bars. So he imported his New York leader, Jacques Renaud, who knew the routine.

A block down from my house there was a joint on Santa Monica where Benny Carter and his band were playing. One night I ran into Garner Clark there. He needed a trombone player for his army band. I knew that the trombonist on the radio show was being drafted, so I offered to bring him to Long Beach the next morning to meet Clark. Since I had been putting Clark back on the bar stool all night, I wasn't surprised that he was still asleep when we got to the base. While we were waiting for him, I had a little reunion in the band room with Russ Cheever, who was practicing his clarinet, and several other musicians that I had known in Hollywood. Garner showed up after a while and arranged to get my friend in his band.

Hollywood began to be dominated by old friends from Chicago and the Southwest—Pete Daily, Hugh Hudgings, Jules Stein, Al Golden, Julius Kinsler, Carrol Fuller, Dick Buckley, Earl and Bud Hatch, Roy Young, Warren Smith, Spud Murphy, Gus and Jerry Jarnagan, Lloyd Snyder, Glynn Harris, Glenn Hughes, Red Cooper, Matt Blair, Harold Barnett, Bob Ernst, Grady King, Ace

Estes, Sam and Larry Taylor, Wingy Manone, Matty Matlock, Eddie Miller, Ray Baduc, Bill DePew and Bob Zurke. The town was swinging. Between the scarcity of musicians caused by the war and leads from friends, I had no trouble getting started in Hollywood the second time.

I played some casuals with Muzzy Marcellino and with Freddy Nagel (using the same uniform jacket that I had worn with him in Dallas) and subbed a couple of weeks with Emil Baffa at the Florentine Gardens, backing Sophie Tucker and the Mills Brothers.

Hugh Hudgings, who was Horace Heidt's personnel contractor, hired me for Heidt's band. We played at Heidt's own joint, the Trianon, six nights a week and on his weekly radio show. Heidt was one of a kind. Not a musician, at all, he began his career working with a trained dog. In his early days as a band leader, he had had an amateur-contest show similar to the popular Major Bowes show and discovered Art Carney, Dick Contino, Fred Lowery, and others. His chief talent, though, was making money. The doorman at his joint frisked the musicians he suspected of drinking on the job. Heidt didn't care whether we drank, as long as we bought our drinks at the bar.

I was supposed to be just filling in with the band until Fazola could join, although I don't know why Heidt wanted Fazola. There was no clarinet playing to be done in the band, but I suppose Heidt intended to create some work for Fazola. I wasn't happy about filling in because the man Heidt wanted wasn't yet available, and the booze rule didn't sit too well with me either. I made my feelings known on the way home one night. A day or two later, when we were rehearsing for the radio show, Heidt said he had decided to "try a new boy."

"Would right now be too soon?" I asked, putting the reed caps on my mouthpieces, ready to take off immediately. He wanted me to stay for the broadcast, but we agreed that I wouldn't come back after the show. That was the end of my first time with the band.

At Lockie's music store one day I lucked into two other jobs, and since they didn't conflict, I accepted both of them. One of them was a job two afternoons a week at KHJ radio, and the other was with a five-piece group at Slapsie Maxie's, mostly playing shows.

Ben Blue and the team of Patty Moore and Benny Lessey were the regulars, while the other acts came and went. Sometimes Maxie himself took part in the show. The show featured blackouts. A performer would deliver a one- or two-line gag from a little theater above the bandstand, and then the joint would be blacked out. It was my job to stand in front of the band so that I could see the performer and cue the band after each gag. The joint was a hangout for movie stars and other celebrities and occasionally they'd do the blackouts.

In one of the gags a girl in a Salvation Army hat carrying a bass drum would say, "I used to smoke, but I don't do that any more. I used to drink, but I don't do that any more. I used to go out with boys, but I don't do that any more. All I do now is (bang, bang) beat on this *ga-awddamn drum.*" I looked up one night to see Martha Raye doing this bit with nothing on up top but a brassiere.

Marion "Pee Wee" Adams, the drummer, was the leader, Baird Jones was on piano, and Harry Harrison was on trumpet. I got Burt Johnson a job with the band, and we had a ball with the little dance music we got to play.

I also got Johnson on at the radio station. We played in a legitimate orchestra that had a woodwind section of two clarinets, flute, oboe, and bassoon; a trumpet and a trombone; a piano; drums; and a string section—about fifteen men in all. The conductor was Leo Arnaud, from the Paris Conservatory. The orchestra was used mostly to back singers, but we played one or two instrumentals in between. I found the work interesting since most of the parts were for A clarinet and had to be transposed a halftone down.

Both of my jobs lasted for several months, and in the meantime, I started working a third job—the Jack Benny show with Phil Harris' band. On my night off from Slapsie Maxie's I also played the Hollywood Canteen with Gil Bowers for free. All the performers there had donated their services, including the act that performed with Bowers' band, Betty Grable.

Harry James, who was in Hollywood playing his radio show, would come to the canteen to see Betty Grable, whom he'd met by that time. He was as big a celebrity as Grable, so he took pains to avoid being spotted by his all too eager fans. He would come to the stage door and open it just wide enough to peek inside. A time or two he saw me first. "Psst! Hey, Pooge," he would stage-whisper, "is Betty there?"

Along about that time Slapsie Maxie's closed for a while to move to the Wilshire Bowl, which was a bigger place. Hudgings called me to fill in with Heidt again, so I spent a few weeks with him until Irvin Verret called me to join Phil Harris' band. When I called Hudgings to quit I told him, "Tell Heidt I've decided to try a new band."

Harris' band had been holding forth at the Wilshire Bowl when it became Slapsie Maxie's and had been kept on as the house band. Most musicians loved working for Harris, so almost no one ever quit him. He was losing musicians to the draft at that time, but that wasn't why I was hired. One of his saxophone players, who had replaced a draftee, got an overload of beer one night. Apparently he couldn't wait until intermission and was too drunk to care, so he took a piss in a false palm pot on the edge of the bandstand in front of everybody in the house. Phil was ordered to let him go.

The best part of working in the band was playing second saxophone to the best lead alto player in the business, Les Robinson. I had heard him on records he'd made with Artie Shaw, had met him a few years before, and now was sitting beside him listening to every marvelous sound he made. The fact is, most players made the alto sound like flies buzzing. I had never liked the sound of an alto sax until I heard Les Robinson, who made an instrument of it. He credited Artie Shaw with teaching him how to play the sax. "I was playing with a cornball band, trying to sound like Wayne King," he said, "when Shaw happened to hear me. He told me I sounded so bad he just wanted to see if he could teach me to play right. He had to hire me to do that."

There were three other saxes in the band—Julius "Julie" Kinsler, my old friend from Chicago, on tenor; Hollis Bridwell also on tenor; and Jack Mitchell who played baritone. All of them were good players, but since their experience had been more commercial than swing, they played the notes exactly as written. Les Robinson knew ways to make written notes sound as fresh as if they had been improvised, though, and I think I did too. Leaders like Benny

Goodman and Harry James wouldn't even allow pencils on a rehearsal because they expected their musicians to know how to play the notes and because sometimes marking parts can result in utter confusion. The arrangers would mark the music; then the swingers or the Mickey Mouses would put down contradictory markings; and the leader would top it off with markings of his own.

At first I thought Les was quiet because he was stuck-up, but after we became good friends, it turned out he had thought the same about me. Neither of us was a talker, and perhaps that's why we got along so well. Les and his wife, Evelyn, and Marge and I became a social foursome for a while. Each of us got along with all three of the others. We alternated spending our days or nights off in each other's homes. We played miniature golf, went to baseball games, and did a little social drinking later in the day. Then the visiting couple would stay overnight. Most band couples talk nothing but shop when they get together, but we seldom mentioned music or musicians, and we never went to bars or shows.

Since Les was new to Hollywood, he didn't have his studio clearance, and therefore, had to turn down an offer from MGM. As soon as he got clearance, though, he went to Warner Brothers and stayed there for many years until the studios discontinued contracting musicians.

One of Harris' arrangers, when he was available, was Joe Haymes, a fine creative musician who had built several good bands only to lose them to more prestigious and solidly established leaders. Tommy Dorsey took twelve of his men when he split with brother Jimmy to organize his own band. Joe had given up the idea of his own band and had taken up drinking instead. Sometimes he had to be wrung out for a couple of days to get back in shape to work, but he was one of the most likable persons I had known. He and I became good friends later on.

Sammy Lewis, Patty Moore's husband and former vaudeville partner, was still the manager at Slapsie Maxie's, and Patty, Benny Lessey, and Ben Blue were still the house entertainers. There were bigger stars with them than there had been at the old place, though—Joe E. Lewis, Danny Kaye, and Phil Harris himself.

I remember that Phil didn't like his bit in the show, something about a hosanna-howling country preacher, coming on with arms raised and hands waving, shouting "Hallelujah!" One night he was irked to the point of expressing his displeasure. "Hallelujah!" he announced. "Halle-goddamn-lujah!"

Phil Harris created an image for himself as a boozer, but that was just a gimmick. In all the time I was with him, I only saw him with a drink once, and that was in the band room. At least fourteen men in his fifteen-piece band were bigger drinkers than he was.

During the war, Jack Benny did some of his shows at nearby military bases. Benny and Don Wilson traveled to the bases by car, but everyone else rode in the bus. Bonita Granville was one of the guests the day we were doing the show in Fresno. She sat near the front of the bus. There was also a stranger riding with us, sitting in the back. "Who's the cornball in the lumberjack outfit?" Les asked me.

"I don't know," I said. "Probably a stage hand or the bus mechanic, just in case."

The man was still hanging around that afternoon, doing nothing. As the rehearsal progressed, though, we found out that the "lumberjack" in jeans and a checkered shirt was John Charles Thomas.

The Jack Benny Show was on prime-time radio, seven-thirty to eight, if I remember correctly. We broadcast it live at four-thirty for the listeners back east. The program would be recorded at the same time in other time zones via closed-circuit radio (on discs since tape hadn't yet been invented) for later rebroadcast. The musicians' union required that we be paid extra for the recording. However, they thought it perfectly all right for us to play a show twice in one day, live, without additional pay.

The servicemen usually supplied drinks for the cast and musicians. The day we did the show in Fresno, we took the leftovers along to help shorten the trip back to Slapsie Maxie's. Eddie "Rochester" Anderson was my drinking partner for the two-hundred-mile, four-hour journey. The only casualty of the trip was Frank Remley, who, because he rarely drank, overestimated his capacity. He recovered quickly, but at first all he could do was sit there, holding his guitar like he didn't know what it was used for. Luckily, Harris wasn't the sort of leader who reprimanded his men for every minor infraction. Tyrannical leaders never seem to understand that, while they can get precision, they can't get warmth or loyalty and dedication from musicians who despise them. Tyranny seems, instead, to breed negligence. There's no reason to make a scene just because a musician is incapacitated for once in his life. I've worked with more drunk leaders than drunk sidemen, for a boozed leader can still wave a stick, but a boozed player can't play well, and he knows it.

Phil Harris had begun his career as a drummer. His father, Harry, who had played E-flat clarinet in a circus, was the steward on the Benny show (and later on Phil's own show). He told me that Phil had been in his family band as a kid but didn't particularly care about playing music. At fourteen he had run away to Hawaii. I suppose that Phil just drifted back into doing the thing he knew best, but he didn't try to pretend that he was a show band leader. He would say to Chet Ricord, his drummer, "Chet, I'll give the downbeat, and from then on it's all yours." Then he would follow Chet, and things would go smoothly. I know leaders who should take a lesson from him.

I was pretty disappointed when Phil Harris decided to give up the band business except for the radio show. The job had been too good to last. Although there was some talk of keeping us as the house band at Slapsie Maxie's under another leader, the idea didn't catch on with the bosses. Instead, they brought in Leighton Noble, a handsome man, whom, it was reported, a movie studio had signed to a contract for no other purpose than to keep the competition from getting him.

Except for the Benny show, which didn't pay enough to support me, I was out of work again. I had time to run around with Joe Haymes, who still wasn't doing well. I would lay a couple of bucks on him once in a while, and I tried to keep him supplied with cigarettes. We would talk about the band we intended to start someday.

I saw him late one day at Lockie's music store. "How would you like to go with Teddy Powell's band?" he asked me.

"Who's that?" I had never heard of Teddy Powell.

"A band leader. He's at the Palladium."

The Palladium was only a block away on Sunset Boulevard, but I hadn't noticed who was playing there. It seemed to me that if any band of note was there I would have heard about it. "I guess I wouldn't be interested," I told Joe. "Something will turn up."

"But you've got to hear this band. You'll like it, and he needs a clarinet player."

"I wouldn't spend the money to get in the joint," I said. I knew that the Palladium was virtually crash-proof, and although it's a piddling consideration, musicians are averse to paying admission to a joint that doesn't recognize the profession.

"Don't worry," Joe said. "I know how to get us in."

Reluctantly, I agreed to go with him. We passed the time at a cheap eatery nearby until the Palladium opened at eight o'clock. Joe was able to get us in at the stage door since he knew the door-keeper. We stood in front of the bandstand to listen. I was duly impressed by the band, and was delighted when Powell hired me that same night on Joe's recommendation alone.

Powell had a real swing band—five brasses, five reeds, and a rhythm section. Some of the band members were Charlie Ventura; Mario Saratella, with whom I had worked in Scat Davis' band; Ralph "Bubbles" Copsey of Ben Pollack renown; Dick Mains; and my old friend from Chicago, Eddie Pripps. The vocalists were Peggy Mann, my favorite girl singer, and Gene Barry, who later became an actor. Because Fazola was my predecessor, there was a clarinet solo in almost every number, and I had a ball.

Ventura was one of the most conscientious musicians I have known and a perfectionist on his horn. At intermission he spent most of his time trying new reeds, looking for one that was just right. We became good friends, and since he wouldn't take time out to go to the bar himself, I would bring him his drinks. I usually gave him and Peggy Mann a ride to their respective hotels after work. He had appointed himself Peggy's chaperone.

There were all kinds of entertainment specials for the GIs at that time. The Palladium got together a band leaders' band for a little show one night. Bing Crosby sang, while Harry James, Phil Harris,

Teddy Powell, and Sammy Kaye played in the band, with some others whom I've mercifully forgotten. Harry was probably the only one who had touched an instrument during the previous twenty years, so the music was pretty bad. They mostly laughed and clowned around, enjoying it as much as the kids did—it was a huge success.

Ben Pollack, who was still around, making stabs at getting back into the whirl of things, brought a group of singers backstage one night to audition for Powell. It was Mel Torme's group. Powell couldn't use them, but they got started soon after that, nevertheless. Another night Buddy Rich sat in on drums for part of a set.

The Palladium was a public ballroom where anybody could come to dance, pairs or singles. There were lots of unescorted girls there, probably because of the war. Many of them were wives and girl friends, left behind by their men in the service and looking for a little romance on the side. There were a lot of WAVEs around, too, some of them brazenly on the make. A WAVE propositioned one of our trombone players one night. "I'm horny as hell," she said. "Would you take me out tonight and fuck me?" I never heard the outcome of the invitation, but the trombonist was unmarried and away from home, and she promised to furnish the issued condom.

The band was to go on tour after the Palladium engagement. We had uniforms made at Sy Devore's little tailor shop on Vine Street, a couple of doors down from Lockie's music store. I paid for mine in advance, even though, at seventy-five dollars, it was pretty expensive, but the others made only small deposits on theirs. In the meantime the tour was canceled, except for one date in El Paso, after which the band was to break up. The boys didn't see any sense in paying for a uniform suit for only one night, but Sy didn't think I should have mine either until theirs were also paid for. I didn't blame Sy for trying to avoid getting stuck, but I wanted what I had paid for. Finally, my rights prevailed, and I became the owner of a fancy suit that I had no earthly use for, although, if I had dropped dead, I'd have had just the thing to wear in the coffin.

I hadn't used public transportation since the war started, so I had no idea what was in store for me. I wasn't even obliged to make the trip to El Paso, but I went because it was free transportation halfway to Dallas. I wanted to show the hometown boys that they had been wrong to ridicule me for wanting to go back to Hollywood. We had to travel by troop train. (The GIs always seemed to be on their way to somewhere else.) The train was so packed that I had to stand in the vestibule of my car or sit on my saxophone case all the way to El Paso. A convict just out of solitary would have developed claustrophobia on that train. I don't recall having anything to eat, either.

After the one-nighter in El Paso, I was on my own, so the next day I crossed the border to Juarez and bought a quart of booze to shorten the trip to Dallas. Again I was on a troop train, although this one wasn't as crowded, and I was able to find a seat. The only other civilian in the car, a young woman, cottoned up to me as a sort of defense against all of the attention the GIs were giving her. I even acted as a screen for her once, so she could change clothes in her seat.

Since many of the GIs were drinking from their own bottles, I assumed it would be all right to bring mine out. Evidently, though, civilians weren't allowed the same privilege, for when the conductor passed by, he confiscated mine. I could live without the stuff, but the trip seemed much longer without it. I'm sure that the conductor hoped to keep it for himself, but I saw to it that he returned it after the trip, as promised.

In Hollywood again after that little joyride, I worked for Wingy Manone a while at the Jade, a joint on Hollywood Boulevard near Vine Street. He had a good little band that included Bill Campbell on piano, Roy Hol on bass, and Jake Flores on trombone (later replaced by Roy Young on bass saxophone). Since Wingy didn't like anybody's playing unless they were from Louisiana, I wasn't offended that he didn't like mine. We got along fine as long as we didn't talk to each other.

Red Nichols dropped in at the Jade one night. He was trying to get a little band together for a job downtown in the Alexandria Hotel, but since he wasn't yet eligible to contract a band in Los Angeles, he wanted me to act as contractor, for contractor's pay. Unfortunately, Wingy wouldn't let me go without a two-week notice, so I had to tell Red I couldn't make it. It was a disappointment because I thought Red's job would be far more interesting than playing choruses on corny old Dixieland tunes. His band would play arranged music with no faking except on solos.

A few nights later Johnny Schmidt, a clarinet player, dropped by the joint, looking for work. Wingy told me I could go work with Red if I wanted because he could replace me with Johnny. That was fine with me. I told him to go ahead and hire Johnny, but when I called Red the next day it was too late. He had already hired somebody else.

I worked a little while with a six-piece band led by Dale "Deacon" Jones at the Palladium. Stew Pletcher was the trumpet player in the group. Deac and I got along well, and when Red Nichols called me a few weeks later, he let me send a sub so I could accept Red's offer. I didn't care that it was too late to be Red's contractor. I just wanted to play in his band.

It didn't turn out to be the paradise I'd expected, though. Red was drinking quite a bit, and he was cranky. A perfectionist, he insisted that we play only the plain sheet-music church chords and nothing else. Once, the piano player altered some chords in "Body and Soul" because he didn't know the simple original chords. The next night Red brought in the sheet music and slammed it on the piano. "Here it is," he said, "and, by God, I want it played exactly as is."

Another time, he made a recording date without telling me about it. Instead, he used another clarinet player. It irked me that he'd done it secretly, but I didn't complain about it. I just let Red know I wasn't that stupid.

Glenn Hughes, who was with Freddy Martin at the Coconut Grove, told me that Freddy needed a replacement for a draftee and asked me if I would be interested in the job. "Sure," I said, "if you can get me on." I told him I didn't audition, so he offered to bring Freddy down to hear me on their night off.

When I told Red about it, he thought I was making it up as an excuse to leave him. He was pretty drunk and got so nasty about it that we almost came to blows. The next night I got to the joint early, as usual, and there was Red, sitting at a table all by himself.

He came to me and apologized—something I admire greatly, for most people would rather be despised than admit they are wrong about something. After that there were no hard feelings between us. He was surprised, though, when Freddy Martin came in to hear me play. I started with Freddy two weeks later.

16

I HAD TO QUIT the Jack Benny radio show because Martin was playing the Jack Carson show, and union rules wouldn't allow me to play two radio shows and a steady job as well. Had I been working casuals I could have worked seven nights a week and still done all the shows I wanted. The Jack Carson show was one that was broadcast live twice—once for the east coast and again for the west—rather than being recorded for rebroadcast. Because of the union rules about live and recorded performances, we worked all day getting the Carson show done and made about twenty dollars less than we had doing Benny's recorded show.

During the two years I spent with Freddy Martin I never heard him criticize anybody's playing, nor did he ever give a music lesson. Freddy always assumed that he'd chosen good musicians from the start. He and leaders like Phil Harris and Harry James knew that anyone good enough to play in their bands didn't need music lessons. Freddy was also glad to see anyone make good, even if it meant losing his stars. He would release a man to go on to bigger things and give him his blessing. Russ Morgan, Murray Arnold, Jack Fina, and Merv Griffin passed through his band at one time or another, but no one ever quit Freddy out of dislike.

During the war years, Hollywood musicians played for celebrities, civilian and military. Besides the numerous benefits and rallies of those years, we played for celebrities on the radio show and at the clubs. I got a little blasé about such people, losing my country-boy awe of them as I began to realize that famous people are just human beings. Even so, I always showed the proper respect. At the Grove we played for Generals Vandenberg, Doolittle, Patton, and

Eisenhower; Admirals Halsey and Nimitz; Majors Boyington and Bong; Jack Dempsey, Arthur Treacher, and Jimmy Durante. Gary Cooper sat next to me on the bandstand when he and his mother, a colonel in the WACs, spoke at a war bond rally.

I met Irving Berlin under rather embarrassing circumstances. Since the band room had no toilet and the nearest rest room was out around the dining room and dance floor and across the huge lobby of the hotel, we used the little lavatory on the wall of the band room in emergencies. Freddy never came to the band room, so he didn't know about the little convenience, which I happened to be using when he brought Berlin to meet us. He began introducing him around before he realized what I was doing. I think Freddy was more embarrassed than I was.

The Grove was a pretty informal place that, like the Palladium, the Jade, and the Alexandria Hotel, did not exclude singles. Some schoolteachers, most of them women, who had come to town for a convention, spent a few evenings at the Grove once. Although not as rowdy as some conventioneers I've seen, they were pretty uninhibited. One of the women cornered me at the back of the bandstand in a long hallway. The lady wanted to get together with me then and there behind the drapes that covered the rear of the bandstand. People who are away at conventions will do things they'd never dream of at home. The trouble was that I wasn't away from home, so I declined the invitation.

Two weeks after I joined Freddy Martin's band, our second daughter, Netta, was born. That night Les Robinson, whom I hadn't seen for quite a while, came to see me. Even though nonessentials like liquor and cigarettes had become scarce, I managed to keep a supply of both items because I had a priority rating at the Grove drug store. So Les and I started in on the fifth of bourbon I had stashed away.

"There's an opening on saxophone at Warner's," he said, "and I'm delegated to bring on whoever I want. You can have the job if you want it."

I was working in an established band, which I'd wanted to join for a long time, and making good money. Besides, I was really enjoying working for a good-guy leader. I told Les that I was satisfied where I was. I didn't want to leave, even for more money, especially since he was offering a saxophone job, while I wanted to stay with jazz clarinet. Les did his best to change my mind, but booze always made me stubborn. The more we drank, the stubborner I got until, about eight hours later, we ran out of bourbon. We left the argument hanging: I told Les I might take the job if the clarinetist ever quit.

About two years later when Les tried again, I was still sitting pretty good. The Grove job, the Jack Carson show, and lots of recording work kept little checks for one thing or another coming in almost every day. For the second time I turned the job at Warner's down. Then the war ended, and my job was reclaimed by a draftee under the law that guaranteed the soldiers their old jobs back. Martin had no choice, but at least he warned me a couple of months in advance that he would have to give the man his job back when he got out of the service.

About that time Jack Fina notified Martin that he was going to leave to form his own band. In the meantime Mel Henke had come to town with Horace Heidt's band. One day he went with me to our rehearsal for the Carson show. During the break, Henke fooled around at the piano for a while. He was such an artist, though, and had developed such technique from years of practicing ten hours a day, that, even fooling around, he was fantastic. His improvisation was like a new piano concerto. Martin, who happened to be within hearing distance, asked me to introduce him. He and Henke talked a while—Mel told me later that Martin had offered him Fina's job. But even though Mel was unhappy in Heidt's band, he turned down Martin's offer. Soon after that he quit Heidt and went back to Chicago.

Jack Fina, who left Martin's band the same day I did, offered me a job with his band, but I preferred to stay in Hollywood, where I thought I had it made. But things had changed in the years I had been coasting with Martin. Suddenly, there weren't many jobs not only because the war was over, but also because people virtually stopped dancing, and the big bands died out.

There were a lot of causes contributing to this decline. The war had really hurt the big bands. Transporting them became impossible because of gas rationing and troop movements that tied up the trains. The draft made it extremely difficult to keep a band together at all. Music itself had also changed. Bebop, with its strange undanceable rhythms, became popular for awhile. Then the musically uneducated kids developed rhythm and blues and rock 'n roll. Country-western became popular because, aside from the big band dance music, it was all that the older dancers could understand. Of course, all music doesn't have to be dance music, but ballroom dancing had made my living for a lot of years. I couldn't play bebop, rock, or country-western, and I wasn't about to learn how.

There were no big bands in Los Angeles and only two or three little jazz bands, so I subbed for an old Dallas friend, Bob Ernst, for a while at a burlesque joint called the Burbank Theater. Lili St. Cyr and Betty Rowland were a couple of the stars, and later June Knight, my old friend from Flo Whitman's show in Chicago came to work there and was arrested for indecent exposure. These days she would probably be considered fully dressed. During lulls in the show we would pass the time counting the men in masturbation row in the balcony.

Later I got a job in a joint called the Silhouette. Larry Taylor, Sam's brother, was the drummer; Don Morris was the tenor sax player; Skip Anderson was the piano player; and Bill Jones was the bass player. Ack Kavish, whom I hadn't seen since 1926 in Laredo, sat in with us a few times on clarinet, and Louise Tobin, Harry James's first wife, sang with us on occasion.

When the joint changed bands, bringing in Barney Bigard to replace us, I contacted Jack Fina, who was at the Claremont Hotel in Berkeley, and he hired me. I sat in with the band for the first time at a recording session in Hollywood the day Fina made his recording of "Flight of the Bumblebee" with just the rhythm section. (He had recorded it earlier with Freddy Martin's band.) I saw Anita O'Day, who was there recording with another group, but all we could do was wave and pantomime to each other through the glass wall of the studio.

I was uncertain about whether I'd stay with Fina. We had a house, a big yard, and a dog, and although Margie Drew had gotten married, Netta was still at home. So for a few weeks, I commuted from Berkeley to spend my day off at home. The trip took up most of my free time. I would take a bus from Oakland after work and arrive in Hollywood at noon, then stay up the rest of the day and sleep a few hours that night. Early the following morning I'd leave by bus for Bakersfield where I'd change to a train, which would arrive in Berkeley just in time for me to go to work.

One day when part of the train was derailed past Fresno, about a hundred miles north of Bakersfield, we got a ride back to Fresno and caught a plane. As we were flying over the wrecked train the man sitting next to me said, "Look! A train wreck!"

"Yeah, I know," I said. "I was on it."

It was obvious from the look he gave me that he didn't believe me, but I didn't bother to elaborate. There's not much point in trying to prove a thing like that.

Because of the housing shortage in Berkeley the only place I could find to live in was a dump of a hotel downtown. My half brother, Victor, who had come to Richmond, a few miles from Berkeley, at the beginning of the war to work in the shipyard there, had stayed on after the shipyard closed. Although the housing for shipyard workers had been condemned, some of the apartments that hadn't been destroyed yet were still being rented out. Vic and his family were living in one of them. He was able to get apart- ments for all of the married men in the band. Marge and Netta and I spent about four months there.

When the band closed at the Claremont, I sent the girls back to Hollywood and went with the band to the Chase Hotel in St. Louis. The first night I was there I heard a marvelous piano player named Ralph Sutton who was playing solo in the lounge. He played his own jazz versions of most things but was also doing Fina's arrangement of "Flight of the Bumblebee" as a throwaway. He asked me whether he should go to Hollywood or New York to try to break into the big time. I recommended Hollywood, but as it turned out, he wound up in New York.

After the Chase job, which lasted four weeks, we did a recording session in Hollywood backing the King Sisters. (The famous tenor player, Babe Russin made that session with us.) Then, on our way to Chicago to open at the Palmer House, we played some one-nighters, the last one in Hamilton, Ohio.

We had played a private party in Chicago the night before, so we had to travel overnight after the job to make a matinée at the theater in Hamilton. We arrived just in time to set up and play the first show in our travel clothes and without shaving. After the show I was just getting settled in my hotel room when a newspaper reporter showed up asking to interview me. I suppose that I was the only one of the band members he could find. I enjoyed myself, making up the answers as I went along, but never saw the write-up, for we had to leave for Chicago after the last show that night. The reporter was so young that he may have been doing an assignment for his journalism class in high school.

At the Palmer House we played for the floor show—the Muriel Abbott dancers and Herb Shriner, who were still unknown at that time. We had to pass through the girls' dressing room—a long narrow hallway—to get to the little stage that was set up for us at one side of the dance floor. The girls would enter from one side of the bandstand and use the dance floor for a stage, while Shriner would make his entrance from wherever he happened to be waiting—he had no dressing room. Muriel Abbott was so pleased with the band that she gave each musician a money clip adorned with a silver dollar.

Fina had a good hotel band—three fiddles, two trumpets, five saxophones, and a four-piece rhythm section. The guitarist was the featured vocalist. If the big-band style had lasted, he would probably have made it big. But even though Fina was a great guy to work for, I was getting restless. Playing with a commercial band—even a good one like Fina's—was about as exciting as working in an office. So I gave my notice after four weeks at the Palmer House and took the train back to Los Angeles, seated facing a pair of school-teachers from L.A. who tried to convert me to communism.

Things weren't any better in Hollywood. Although I had been in the cliques that got all the good work, I had lost my place at the hog trough by abandoning it for a while. Starting over is harder than breaking in the first time because people figure you lost out through incompetence and because those who take your place guard their jobs with their lives and try to keep you out. I had been in the joint clique, too, but there still wasn't much work for joint bands.

Marge's sister and brother-in-law, the Logsdons, were pestering us to come back to Dallas, so we decided to try it again. I knew I could work there. After selling the house, on which we made a sizable profit, and the furniture, we were solvent again. My kid brother, Durward, sold me back my 1936 Buick for six hundred dollars. (It was the car I had bought in Dallas five years before for two hundred dollars and sold to Durward for three hundred.) We loaded it up with our little personal things and took off "never to return."

17

AS USUAL WHEN I went back to Dallas, I immediately began working day and night. Arriving just before the State Fair opened, I got the job as first clarinetist with the official concert band. I also began working nights with Jimmy Thornhill's band at Abe's, a night club in downtown Dallas on Commerce Street by the Baker Hotel. After the fair was over I worked with Thornhill on the radio staff at WRR.

We stuck it out in Dallas for eighteen months despite the drawbacks. The radio station job brought in a steady eighteen dollars a week, which I supplemented by working the clubs at night with various bands. (The last of those jobs was with Joe Reichman at the Baker Hotel.) But even though I had the best jobs Dallas had to offer, I wasn't making much money. Marge and I weren't used to Dallas weather any more, either. Besides, although Dallas was filling up with refugees from the North and the East, I was still scorned as a damyankee convert. Northerners were still the enemy.

Eddie Pripps, my friend from Chicago and, more recently, Hollywood, was the arranger and conductor for the Spike Jones show, which was on tour with Doodles Weaver. When he came to town, I invited him out to the house, and to make a little party, I invited a couple of my local friends. We ran out of booze after a while, and when I returned with a new supply, I found out that Pripps had gone to bed. "What's the matter?" I asked him. "Are you sick?"

"No," he said, "your friends insulted me. Fuck 'em."

"Tell me about it."

"Nothing important. They just don't like people from the

North. To them, I'm a yankee son of a bitch. I didn't argue the point because they are your guests."

"Don't mind these Texans. Most of them think they are better than anyone else from anywhere."

"You don't."

"No," I said, "I got over the idea when I was twelve. I stayed over it, too."

"Your friends will never get over it."

"As of now, they're not my friends any more."

Dallas has become much more cosmopolitan since I left it. Its population has doubled, largely because of an influx of outsiders. In 1950, though, it was still a city inhabited mostly by natives, where outsiders were unwelcome except as cheap labor. I didn't want to stay in a place where my friends were despised simply because they were from the North and where I myself was treated with suspicion just because I'd gone elsewhere to better myself. So back to Hollywood we went—broke again.

The clique had what little work there was left in Hollywood all sewed up. The movie studios began using free-lancers entirely instead of keeping musicians on contract. This state of affairs deprived a lot of good players of a steady income. There were a couple of hundred excellent musicians out of work and scrambling for every job that came up. Many of them lost the fancy homes they could no longer meet the payments on. Those of them who had gotten their studio contracts by agreeing to kickbacks found out that ordinary jobs couldn't be bought. In Hollywood, almost everybody was scrounging.

Marge went to work, and after a couple of weeks, I got a job, too. Will Osborne was going on tour with a pick-up group that was just so-so. He was just the sort of leader I enjoyed working for—no disdainful words or looks and no music lessons. The band had a bebop rhythm section that made my job tough, though. Actually, I think by that time the rebels were calling their thing "progressive." The bass player was straight, but the piano player and the drummer—a couple of bombed out kids who were just experimenting—played mysteriously. The drummer played quarter-note triplets (six beats in a four-beat measure) on the bass drum and accented up beats on the tops against the piano player, who was doing just the opposite but worse. It was no way to hold a band together. One night on the road I stopped playing in the middle of a solo. I looked at Osborne apologetically and said, "I just can't play with this erratic rhythm."

Osborne shrugged and, shaking his head sympathetically, "I don't blame you," he said. "I couldn't either."

I was making ten dollars for every day I actually played on tour—a maximum of seventy dollars a week—but there were quite a few days off, as well as some long jumps. Once we went from Denver to Fayetteville, Arkansas, and back to Denver without sleeping, besides having to work the night before we left Denver and again the night we got back. A day off figured in there somewhere, but Osborne paid us for that one.

Shortly after that, we got a real day off. My old friend, George Yadon, invited me to a jam session in Colorado Springs, about ninety miles south of Denver, at Merle and Ruth Alderman's house. Ruth is better known by her maiden name, Ruth Etting. Her husband Merle, an excellent piano player, was well known for his movie scores—he won an Oscar for one of them—and his conducting. The fun started about four o'clock that afternoon and lasted till four in the morning with frequent breaks for goodies and drinks. All but Ruth, who doesn't drink, wound up half smashed.

Ted Rodgers, a good ol' boy from Ada whom I'd known since he was a little kid, had become a band leader. He came to the session with his trombone player, Howard Cooper, who turned out to be a marvelous player. I later got him a tryout with Osborne, which unfortunately was unsuccessful. The book was pretty limited, and he had no chance to solo. After that, I made up my mind never again to recommend a player for an audition. I always advise a leader to skip the audition and just hire the man. I feel that it's a reflection on me if a player doesn't make it on an audition. I heard from Rodgers some time later that Cooper had drowned himself soon after the session in Colorado. If he had gone on, I am sure he would have made it before long.

Our tenor man left his horns in the lobby of the joint we played in Durango, Colorado—the second job of the tour. When he missed them he called and gave instructions how to send them to him, but they never arrived. After that the guy had to borrow a tenor in every town we played for the rest of the six-week tour. Every day he had the hassle of finding someone who was willing to lend him a horn, which he would then practically overhaul before he could play it. He sanded quite a few mouthpieces open, which probably didn't suit the owners when they got their horns back. After he was finished with it, he also had the chore of returning it. This procedure took up all of the guy's spare time every day. I would have given up the first day and told Osborne to hire someone else.

The second of the tours I made with Osborne was worse than the first. After six weeks of hard travel, the fellow who drove the car I was riding in, wanted to make a side trip to see the Grand Canyon on the way home. We couldn't talk him out of it, so our lead trumpet player, Clyde Reisinger, and I got out of the car. I took my horns and travel bag and told the driver to go ahead. He couldn't very well leave us stranded out on the highway, so he gave in.

I was out of work again and thinking more and more about getting out of the music business. There wasn't much music business left anyway. Marge—unlike most musicians' wives—didn't want me to quit unless that was what I wanted. I decided to get away from the whole scene and try something completely different. So I wrote to a friend in Albuquerque who built houses. Having helped to build a few houses in Ada when I was a kid, I was a fair hand with carpenter tools. The man was willing to hire me, but I didn't have the money to go there and survive for a week. About that time, Victor, who had moved to Fontana, about fifty miles from Hollywood, came up for a visit. When I told him I wanted to quit the music business and mentioned the proposition I had from Albuquerque, he offered to get me on, instead, at a big construction job he was working in San Bernardino.

I liked construction work—no travel, no worries, no hassles—but at the same time, I kept my options open. I transferred into the

San Bernardino musicians local and began working at a joint in Fontana with my own trio three nights a week. Weekend work was no problem because I had all day on Saturday and Sunday to sleep. The trio was composed of clarinet, piano, and guitar. The guitar was still primarily a rhythm instrument in those days, and I felt that this guitar player could provide a much better beat than any of the drummers were putting out.

The joint became a hangout for the more elite of the local riffraff. A free-lance writer gave me a few plugs, and I became a local celebrity. Among the musicians who came around to check out the newcomer was a drummer named Billy Roe. He asked me if I would be interested in rehearsing with him and a piano player. I explained that I was quitting the business but agreed to keep it in mind for later, just in case. He didn't have a job for his trio anyway.

Some weeks later, he came by to see me on the construction job, by coincidence just before the job was finished. Walking alongside the ditch I was digging, he asked me again if I would rehearse with him. Since I had quit my playing job in the meantime and had no work of any kind coming up, I agreed to rehearse with him. I was disgusted with music mostly because of the new conception of rhythm that the drummers were experimenting with, but I was pleased to find that Billy Roe was not an experimenter. Nothing could budge him from the beat. He kept time as well as any drummer I had ever worked with probably because, like Buddy Rich, he had been a tap dancer. He never tried to play drum solos behind me or the piano player Tim Talbot either.

Roe and Talbot were both excellent musicians who had lately played with Bobby Sherwood's band in Hollywood. I had such a fine time rehearsing that, when Roe got a job in Riverside a little later, I went with him even though it meant playing music six nights a week while working construction five days a week. I also started doing a television show on Saturdays mostly for the prestige it gave. Television was certainly no money-maker then. I drove a hundred miles at my own expense and spent the whole day doing the show for thirteen dollars. But I was busy in music again, and I liked that.

When the job in Riverside ended, Roe booked a job in Bakersfield, about 150 miles from the San Bernardino-Riverside area. For the first few weeks, I drove home on my day off, but when it looked like the job would be steady, I moved the family there, furniture and all.

18

MAISON JAUSSAUD, a beautiful place built of rough stone and located on the prairie about a mile from downtown Bakersfield, looked more like a country club than a French restaurant. The Jaussaud brothers, Martin and Babe, had decided to add floor shows to their big club section, which consisted of a long bar, quite a bit of table space, and a twelve-by-eighteen-foot dance floor. We were provided with an inverted tabletop raised about eight inches from the floor to use for a bandstand. Likewise, the floor show performers had their tabletop, which we musicians carried out and placed in front of the bandstand before each show. Like most places at that time, Jaussaud's had no dressing rooms. The performers who had costumes got into them in the office at the front of the house. They had to come through the audience to get to the stage.

The star of that first show was comedian-singer Joaquin Garay, with whom I had worked in 1937 when he'd been emcee and star of the Road to Rio show in Dallas. He went over big, and so did the Billy Roe Trio. I had never seen such a reception for a small group. The joint was packed every night. The acts liked us, too, because we were all experienced at playing shows, so we never loused up an act. Many of the performers said we played their acts better than even the Las Vegas bands had ever done.

Business was so good that the Jaussauds expanded the club into a real show room with a stage big enough for dancing between shows, two dressing rooms, and a professional light man. Of course, as usual, the architect didn't include a band room, so we still had to pack our instruments and take them home every night.

At first, we had one night a week off, but because the joint was open seven nights, they had to use a sub band once a week. This setup created problems for the sub band and especially for the acts because they were forced to do a long afternoon rehearsal with the sub band every week. I remembered that the musicians at the Chicago Theater used to work seven days a week for six weeks and then take a week off, so I suggested that arrangement to the Jaussauds, and it became the policy. Playing every night gets to be a drag, but after all, at one time I had worked seven nights a week year round. Six weeks brought us just to the verge of collapse, whereupon we had the week off to get ourselves back in shape to do the same thing again.

Although the Jaussauds paid well enough to attract decent acts, they could never have afforded to bring in big stars. The club's location, though, made it an ideal spot for performers to stop on their way to Hollywood. The pay was good enough to interest a star who needed a jump breaker, while those who were breaking in a new act needed a place like Jaussaud's that was close to Hollywood. Carol Channing did a week there without pay, according to Martin Jaussaud, simply to try out some new material. Rudy Vallee broke in an act there, as did Gabe Dell, Mickey Shaughnessey, George DeWitt, Irene Ryan, Lillian Roth, and Gary Crosby. Many of the acts filled in for a week or two before or after playing Las Vegas, Los Angeles, or San Francisco. Up-and-coming stars like Marty Allen, Dick Contino, Paul Gilbert, and Pepper Davis used the place to fill gaps between their more important engagements.

Walter Gross was one of those who came to Jaussaud's to break in an act—he was accompanying a girl singer. Gross liked to drink, but he had been on the wagon for quite a while before coming to Jaussaud's. I had just gotten over an attack of bursitis that had put me on the wagon, too, so I bought a fifth of vodka to celebrate my recovery. After work one night when Gross and I were talking out in the parking lot, I asked him to have a drink with me. That drink primed him, and after we parted he got started on a binge. The next night, during an argument with his girl singer, he roughed her up, and she had to cancel out. Gross filled in her spot in the show, playing the piano, mostly his own composition, "Tenderly," and trying to sing. The Jaussauds canceled him, and he went to Las Vegas to pursue the idea of doing a single.

There was a lot of new money in Bakersfield, generated by the discovery of oil in what had been a purely agricultural area. These country boys had gotten rich but their manners were still pretty raw. At first, while the acts and the band were still on the table tops, we were practically in the ringsiders' laps. There were those who got ringside tables just so they could participate in the acts. They'd heckle the stand-up comics or join them on the floor with a cigarette in one hand and a drink in the other. These guys would sing with the soloists and the quartets, pretend to trip the dancers, and pat or pinch the butt of any girl performer they could reach. I've had such people try to snatch my clarinet or saxophone while I was playing, and that sort also liked to pound on the drums or whack the cymbals. The new stage prevented a lot of this non-sense, but the bolder ones still came up on the stage to join the acts. Imagine a man in a T-shirt, Levis, and cowboy boots with barnyard crud all over them coming up to put an arm around Carol Channing and pat and tweak her behind while she is performing.

Of course, the audience wasn't entirely composed of clods. Most folks were pleasant and enthusiastic. We also had some pretty distinguished guests from time to time. I remember Dan Dailey, Ernie Ford, John Ireland, Gil Bowers, Harpo Marx, Molly Jordan (of "Fibber McGee and Molly"), Freddy Martin, Jimmy Durante, Jimmy Rodgers, and Buddy Hackett. Hackett and Rodgers would play once in a while at a joint down the street called the Saddle and Sirloin. My old friend Jack Ordean had a trio there.

The Jaussauds had told us that we could stay on the job as long as we wanted to, so I settled down in Bakersfield. I had a steady job and was teaching at a music store six days a week besides—just coasting along—until, in 1955, I was in a car that was hit broad-side by a freight train. I was able to walk away from it before passing out, but my injuries incapacitated me for three months. A trade magazine hinted that I was all washed up, but I still had some Texas stubbornness that I hadn't used yet. I went through a couple of months of physical therapy for a broken hand, but what really helped was the encouragement I got from the almost daily letters that Peggy Mann wrote me.

When Scott Seely wrote asking me to make an album for him, I agreed mainly to prove I wasn't washed up. Seely had started his own recording company, Accent Records, in Hollywood. He had put out a few singles, but albums were a new gimmick in 1956. Mine was the first album issued on the Accent label. It wasn't very good partly because I wasn't as ready as I had thought. Nevertheless, the album got some good reviews, and I was on every disc jockey's show in Los Angeles and Bakersfield. Unfortunately, we never sold many copies, but the effort did me a little good anyway. Because I'd recorded some of my own compositions, I became eligible to join ASCAP some years later.

The radio interviews went fine in Los Angeles because I was alone, but in Bakersfield, Ralph Yaw and Georgie Starbuck Galbraith kept me company. Yaw, who had been the arranger for the Roxy Theater in New York and later for Stan Kenton and others, was one of my best friends at the time. He had composed two of the numbers I had recorded, and Mrs. Galbraith had written the lyrics. Because Yaw knew all the radio and television people in town and Galbraith knew the newspapermen, they arranged the interviews. I met Galbraith when I went to her house with Yaw for a newspaper interview she had arranged. (The *Saturday Evening Post* had already run their photo with a write-up.) Despite the fact that her lyrics hadn't even been sung on my record, the story that subsequently appeared was mostly about Gailbraith, with secondary emphasis on Yaw and a bare mention of me. The paper also mixed up the caption information that accompanied the photo so that I was identified as Yaw, and he was called Drew Page, a "trumpeter." It seemed to me that the fanfare was misdirected. After all, I had written three of the numbers and had played all of the music on the album.

The first television interview turned into a battle between Yaw and Galbraith for the spotlight. Again, my only significance was that I'd recorded their songs. I just sat on the sidelines listening to their squabbles. The rest of the interviews—another newspaper article, a few radio shows, and another television appearance—all turned out the same. It seemed to me that we should be plugging the album, not the composers.

Finally I went to see Galbraith about it. After I had explained how I felt, she immediately called the newspaper to set up another interview. More pictures were taken, but this time Galbraith wrote the interview herself, concentrating entirely on me. It made me feel a little better.

I had gotten used to running into old friends in strange places, so I wasn't surprised when Johnny McFall showed up in Bakersfield. He didn't stay long, but his visit woke up my restlessness again, and I began to think about moving on. I had become bored with the job since shows had become so important that we didn't play much dance music any more. I was tired of being a mechanic instead of a musician, and I knew that there was no hope for advancement. I was at the top of the Bakersfield heap. McFall became the manager of a big apartment house in Hollywood and offered us a free apartment until I could get started again. So in November, 1957, I moved back to Hollywood.

19

JUST AFTER I got back to Hollywood, I lost the ball of a finger in a mechanical door that malfunctioned. The lawyer I hired got me five hundred dollars compensation, which came in handy while the finger was healing. Shortly thereafter, I was hit on the head with a beer bottle while walking along the street one night. My skull was fractured, and I cut my hands on the broken glass when, unconscious, I fell to the sidewalk. There was no one to sue, though, since I didn't know who hit me. After my finger healed I had the tone-hole ring for that finger on my clarinet made into a pad that covered the hole, so I was able to play again.

My first job was with Mike Riley, who was booked into the Brass Rail in Chicago for four weeks. Riley had a good little band, composed of himself on trombone, Gerry Burns on trumpet, me on clarinet, Will Bradley, Jr., on drums, and a piano player whose name escapes me. We also had a comedian who pretended to double bass.

The joint featured music, and we were one of three groups playing there at that time. Jimmy Ille's four-piecer was there with a girl singer, a real belter, who was the boss's girl. The other was a rock group led by a singer, Steve Bledsoe. Rock was just getting started, so that was the first rock group I had ever heard in person.

Since we were sharing the time with the two other groups, the job was pretty easy. In fact, we didn't get to play enough to suit me. There were good audiences that usually included a few "important" figures. We were invited to parties, which we couldn't attend, were given tickets to baseball games, which we couldn't attend either, and some of us were offered other jobs. I was offered three jobs while I was there—one to put my own group in a joint. An agent, who came in every night for a while, wanted to make a "star" of me and offered to get me straight with the union. I hadn't kept up with the dues since leaving Chicago, so it would have cost a hundred dollars to rejoin the local. I didn't want to live in Chicago again, though, and besides, I never dwelt on praise. I've seen it ruin too many good guys, turning them into strutting egomaniacs, making them so undesirable that they wind up out of work. Then too, I was wary that this guy's backing would turn into an obligation that I didn't need or want—I didn't want to risk it.

One day I ran into Marvin Hamby, who was attending a convention of musicians' officials with Jack Foy, president of the Las Vegas local. I had known Hamby since 1935 when he was with Louis Panico, and we were living in the same apartment building. A few years back, he had migrated to Las Vegas and had become vice-president of the musicians local there. I had written to him recently about the prospects of working in Vegas. The conditions he and Jack Foy described seemed favorable except for the scarcity of casual work. Somehow, I would have to survive until the three-month prohibition against steady work expired. Nevertheless, I began to think about making the move.

I had planned to go back to Los Angeles by train, but I was talked into a deal by three boys in the band, who were going to drive a car back for a used car company. Since Riley had given us our transportation allowance in cash, the boys thought it would be cheaper to drive the car, and even cheaper than that if I joined them. As it turned out, they had actually invited me along because they were broke. One of them had spent his money on a ring, bought from a street hustler, that had already turned green and begun to slough off its plating. It was worth about fifty cents in a dime store. I don't know how the others came to be broke, but there wasn't enough money between them to run that car to Los Angeles, or even to St. Louis. We made the whole trip without stopping to sleep—all at my expense. Of course, they were going to pay me back later, but I'm still waiting for that.

Back in Hollywood, I had a couple of propositions from men who had heard my album. One was from Professor Wolfe at the Los

Angeles Conservatory, who wanted me to teach clarinet. The other was from Herman Lansinger, head of Golden West Publishing Company. Having heard the record on a jockey's show, he had traced it back to Scott Seely, who called to tell me about it.

Lansinger told me that he wanted to publish my record solos in a folio if he could get the copyright from Seely. He also wanted to produce another album of my own compositions, publish my solos in a folio, and sell album and folio as a package. Finally, he wanted me to write a book of exercises and paraphrases and then a full method book for the clarinet. Since Seely wouldn't give him the copyright, Lansinger couldn't put out the folio. That part of his offer would have been the easiest for me because I would only have had to write down what I had played. The other parts of his proposal would have entailed a lot of time and work for years to come. Still, I began to put together the little inventions I had been jotting down for a long time. I am still working on it. (I had the first batch of stuff almost ready for Lansinger's fall printing in 1960, but I lost it and was too discouraged to start over.)

In September, 1958, I came to Las Vegas, applied for unemployment benefits, and settled down to "sweat out my time," as musicians put it. At that time musicians transferring into a different local still had to get transfer slips from their home locals. When I went to put my card in, I told the secretary, Orion Sims, that I didn't want to play shows, that I wanted to play nothing but clarinet—no saxophone, flute, or any of the other doubles. I was tired of playing a bunch of nothing behind acts, most of whom it fit perfectly. But there wasn't much work for a clarinet player. I played a few casuals with small groups in the first three months, and I was rehearsing with a group: Darryl "Snooper" Rogers, Gene "Sandy" Sandusky, myself, and a girl singer, Betty Artese. Nothing came of it, but I got acquainted around the union.

Among the casuals was the opening of the Convention Center, which I played with Ted Vesley's concert marching band. Eddie Fisher was one of the stars of the show. As I came to the entrance of the hall that night to go to work, I was caught up in a flurry of commotion. Just then a cab pulled up and Elizabeth Taylor got out. Later, she sat on the makeshift stage with Fisher, who introduced her when he went on to perform. She was the star of the whole show without doing anything.

The part of the show that I enjoyed most was Charlie Teagarden and his little jazz band. Sitting in the balcony, we in Vesley's band faked riffs behind one of his numbers. It was the loudest background I ever heard behind a soloist, but of course, Charlie had the mikes, while we were playing dead. We didn't drown him out, but even though the Convention Center is a big place, we must have filled it, with enough noise left over to fill another one. Charlie got a big ovation, especially from all of the musicians there.

One night Snooper Rogers and I went to a rehearsal of Charlie Ventura's band. I told Rogers that Ventura had been a friend of mine years before. He had since become famous mostly because of his recording of "Yesterdays." There was a vacant saxophone chair that night.

"Why don't you go up and talk to Charlie?" Rogers said. "He might need another sax player."

I was still ineligible for steady work, though, and was reluctant to talk to him anyway because of the tendency of the famous to forget their former friends. Besides that, under union rules musicians aren't allowed to solicit steady jobs while on transfer. (Until recently we weren't allowed to solicit anybody's job at anytime.) So even though Rogers tried to talk me into it, I wouldn't do it.

A few days later, just as my time was up, I got a call from the union. Ventura had heard that I was in Las Vegas and had left word with the union that he wanted me to see him. I found him to be the same down-to-earth person I had known before. He had been stuck for a man to fill that vacant chair, which entailed doubling alto, tenor, and clarinet. Since I didn't have an alto at the time, Ventura borrowed one for me.

Ventura's was a thirteen-piece swing band, composed of a brass section, three saxes (besides himself), and a four-piece rhythm section. We played at the Thunderbird Lounge after the last show was over, usually around midnight. By that time, the Las Vegas opportunities and high salaries had begun to attract good players from all over the country. Ventura, who knew them all, also knew which ones would suit him best. His outstanding stars were Gus Mancuso on baritone horn, who was later replaced by Carl Fontana, and Arno Marsh on tenor sax. I became well acquainted with our second trumpet player, Gene Barringer, who was just filling in a lull in his regular job as arranger, lead trumpet player, and right-hand man for Milton Berle.

When we heard that Carl Fontana was joining the band, Barringer told me about him. I had been out of circulation so long that I hadn't heard of him. "This guy," said Barringer, "plays so good he makes you mad. You wait for him to make a mistake and he never does." Arno Marsh is a tenor player of that order too, and of course, there was Ventura. Musicians from other jobs began dropping in, and Ventura would put on impromptu jam sessions, featuring Fontana, Marsh, and himself, that got pretty wild. Everybody else, except the rhythm section, rested their fingers and went to school. Ventura kept after me to join in, but I declined because, frankly, I didn't know what the hell they were doing—only that it was good. The only time I played a solo with the band was the time Ventura got a request for "Jazz Me Blues," and I was the only one who knew it, verse, interlude, chorus, and all. Even then, I played only the straight melody. To request a Dixie tune from a band like that was ridiculous anyway.

Vido Musso, who had moved to Las Vegas, came in a couple of times, greeting me the first time he saw me with a bear hug and a kiss on the ear. Willie Smith, who was with Harry James, dropped in regularly. He was in hot pursuit of Margie Drew, who had moved to Las Vegas, too.

"I used to listen to you on the old Jimmy Lunceford records," I said one night. "It's good to know you after all these years."

"Oh, that wasn't me," he said. "That was my uncle. Where's Margie?"

"I don't know. I guess she's home," I said. "Don't give me that 'uncle' bull. You're the oldest man in the business." He looked about forty.

He laughed. "That *was* a long time ago, wasn't it?"

Willie was an unusual looking fellow—a black man who looked more like an Oriental. He told me a guy had once asked him, "You're Chinese, aren't you?"

"Naw," Willie answered, "I'm a nigger." That became his stock answer to the inquisitive.

That job lasted for thirteen weeks, the usual quarter-year in the cycle of music and show business for steady jobs. On broadcast shows the layoff is thirteen weeks, with thirty-nine weeks of work.

As in Hollywood, I found quite a few old friends in Las Vegas. From back home in the Southwest were Roy Young, Larry Sockwell, George Hill, Dale Osborne, and Guy Sanderson. Some of the guys I had known in Chicago were Don Owens, Doc Rando (Grillot), Jack Cathcart, Harry Jaeger, and Phil Dooley. From Hollywood were Bill Jones, Garwood Van, Wingy Manone, and Dale "Deacon" Jones. Merle and Ruth Etting Alderman were there, as was Max Day from Bakersfield.

The famed trumpet player, Wild Bill Davison, who had come to town to organize a band, had Merle Alderman recruiting for him. Remembering me from the jam session at his house in Colorado Springs, Merle chose me to play clarinet—I didn't have to double. The group was a sort of Dixie combo, with Tommy Turk on trombone, Gene Sandusky on guitar, and Johnny Cassella on drums. Alderman did the arrangements. We made some demo records and rehearsed several times. It was all fun, especially the rehearsals, because we took breaks now and then to taste the beer and booze that Alderman always had on hand. Nothing ever happened, though, so Davison gave up and went back east.

Ruth was usually around at rehearsal, but even though we kept after her, she only sang for us once. One day after a rehearsal, she gave in and sang one song with no accompaniment other than Merle on piano. That was soon after her life story had been filmed in Hollywood, and knowing about her fabulous career, we thought it a real treat. She was in her early sixties at that time and had been retired for several years before the picture was made.

My next job was with Wingy Manone at the New Frontier. Wingy's son, Jimmy, had grown up and was playing drums, and Tommy Turk was on trombone. Wingy is one of the most colorful personalities in the music business. He can be grumpy at times, but most of the targets of his temper don't take offense. I knew him well, having worked for him three times. Of course Jimmy knew him well, too, but nevertheless, he said the old man bugged him so much that he was looking for another job. Turk and I shrugged off Wingy's remarks about me to Turk and about Turk to me. Turk couldn't limit himself to playing merely the Dixie tailgate style that Wingy wanted, and I'm not a Dixie player either, although I have been accused of it at times. Naturally, according to Wingy, we didn't fit in with his style. When I left the band, before the engagement ended, I no longer seemed to be in Wingy's good graces—if I ever had been.

While I was in Bakersfield for a job, I contracted valley fever, an infection similar to rabbit fever that nearly everybody in the San Joaquin Valley gets sooner or later. In the meantime Gene Barringer had gotten me a job with him on an upcoming tour with Milton Berle. The salary was to be three hundred dollars a week with twenty-five dollars per diem whenever we were away from home, so I wanted to make it. Consequently, I got out of bed to come back to Las Vegas, the fever lingered for several weeks, and I couldn't make the tour.

About that time Johnny McFall, who had quit playing by then, came to town. He went to work managing an apartment house only a couple of blocks from us. Roger Boyd and John Haynie Gilliland also came to town with Smoky Stover for a few weeks. Boyd told me how Louis Armstrong had once tried to hire him.

"We were in Reno," he said, "and Louis was there. He came in one night to hear the band. I found out later that he wanted to hire me, but he didn't tell me about it. He talked to Smoky and asked him if he would let me go. Smoky said no, that he needed me."

"Why didn't you go and see Louis about it?" I asked.

"Hell, Page, I didn't know about it. I didn't find it out till just the other day."

Boyd wrote me a letter a few weeks later, asking how things were in Las Vegas. I told him to come out, that I would try to help him find a job, but he didn't come. He shot himself soon after that. I heard that the had been having trouble with one of his legs and was afraid he would have to quit playing, but I think the real reason was that he was despondent over missing his chance of a lifetime to make it big.

Pete Daily was in town for a while, but there were no jobs for Dixieland trumpet players in Las Vegas. The last time I saw him was the night we went bar hopping together. He got loaded and wanted to fight me all the way home. I managed to get him into the house, and the woman he was living with called AA for a drunk sitter. I had enough experience with drinkers to realize that Pete's belligerence wasn't directed at me, his old friend. He would have tried to pick a fight with anyone.

I rehearsed for several days with the five-piecer that Deacon Jones was organizing, but although we auditioned a few times, nothing happened. When Phil Harris came to town to do some shows at the Desert Inn, Jones and I went to see him one afternoon. We had a friendly get-together, and Harris got us the job in the Desert Inn Lounge.

The band consisted of Jones on bass and valve trombone, Dale Osborne on vibes, Johnny Cassella on drums, Gene Sandusky on guitar, and me on clarinet, flute, and bass clarinet. We played five days a week in the lounge and one night for dancing in the Sky Room. It was before the days when musicians began to be expected to do acrobatic choreography—dance, sing, and hang by their tapeworms from the rafters. We just played music. In the lounge we weren't supposed to attract anybody's attention except those who were taking breaks at the bar. Because we were supposed to simply provide background for the gambling, we didn't play much jazz. We found that continuous medleys were the most appropriate thing for the situation. Sometimes we would play a medley for the whole thirty-minute set. Our alternate background-music maker, Milt Herth, did the same thing on the organ. The money Jones got for the group was the only consolation, for he split it five ways. In those early days of lounge, or stage-bar groups, it was customary to split the money evenly. The groups were mostly temporary get-togethers of the local men, the leader being the one who got the job. The next time, one of the others might be leader. If a guy took the leader fee he'd have a hard time getting the right men to work with him. Later the lounges began using name groups.

Since I didn't want to play shows any more, I had to depend on lounge work. There were no dance bands—dancing was taboo because it could lure gamblers away from the tables. The Sky Room was the only place in town where dancing was featured, and it was a small room consisting mostly of a bar and tables. The dance band was Sam Melchione's trio of himself on accordion, a clarinet player (first Bob Riedel and later Arno Marsh), and a bass player.

Lounge work was pretty uncertain. Operators didn't like to see the same musicians coming back in a new group even though the loose structure of the groups coupled with the sporadic work meant that musicians were constantly moving from group to group and joint to joint. Since almost all of the customers were transient, it didn't make sense for the operators to demand new faces. Nevertheless, some musicians couldn't be hired because they had been in the same place before with other groups. Age also made a difference to some bosses. A friend of mine, who was prematurely gray, was fired on the spot one night when the boss, noticing the gray hair, told the leader to "get that gray headed old son of a bitch off that stage." Besides that, musicians who could play jazz were assumed to be unable to play shows. It has always been that way. Most jazz players have been asked time and again whether they could read. The reverse is also true—show musicians are asked if they can play jazz.

While I was with Jones, the musicians' officials had their national convention in Las Vegas. Attending some meetings with one of our delegates, I saw the three Dallas delegates, all of whom I knew very well—Bill Harris, Jack "Boxie" Russell, and Les Lester. They all urged me to come home. Russell told me that Dallas had become one of the biggest producers of jingles and that some of the musicians were making five hundred dollars a week. He would see that I got in on it. "Go home and pack a bag," he said. "I'll pick you up and take you back." I was tempted, but I couldn't forget why I had left Dallas for good. Even that kind of proposition couldn't lure me back, and besides, since Netta was in high school, I didn't want to move away.

After the stint with Jones I played various lounges with other groups. I worked for four weeks with Henry "Hot Lips" Levine's Dixie-type band at the Flamingo, playing three sets a night in six hours, not enough to keep warmed up. Della Resse, backed by a big band, was one of two alternates playing there. I spent most of my time off in the coffee shop reading books. The coffee shop night manager tried to persuade me to take a job as host there, but even though I was pretty desperate for a steady job, I declined. I would have been seating mostly the bosses and the performers, which would have included Harry James and his boys, and I wasn't eager to be considered a has-been. I did feel that the offer was a compliment because such a job demands a personable man.

When I played the Ringling Brothers Circus for two weeks, it was like going home after thirty-five years. I had always wanted to play the Greatest Show on Earth, but the pay wasn't good, and the job was tough to get. By that time, the circus had stopped carrying a band. Instead, they kept a leader and a drummer, hiring local musicians in each town to make up bands of different sizes depending on the town. In Las Vegas the quota was twelve. We had two clarinets, and I took first chair, which was all right with Joe Cervelloni, the other clarinet player. We both played the first clarinet parts, sometimes alternating when our lips got tired on some of the long background numbers for the acts.

Merle Evans had been the leader for forty years, except for a five-year leave from 1956 to 1961. He was an old friend of Harry James's father, Everett, and of Harry himself. He told me that Harry usually came to see him when they played day-and-date jobs and would sit in as conductor. He asked me to locate Harry, who was in town at the time, and bring him by. Unfortunately, it was Harry's night off at the Flamingo, so I couldn't find him, and the circus closed the next day. It would have been fun sitting in a circus band with Harry as the guest leader.

Bob Crosby spent a year at the New Frontier. I went by occasionally to see Matty Matlock, Eddie Miller, and Hilton "Nappy" Lamare. At one time when I wasn't working, I had stood by for Matty for a few days while he was having some dental work done. When I mentioned to Matty that I was playing the Ringling show, he said, "Man, those notes go by one beat to the page." Which was about right. When marches are played in one beat to the measure at a fast tempo, the clarinet players are pretty busy with all those notes.

My father thought that playing the Ringling Circus was my greatest musical accomplishment, especially under his idol Merle Evans. It was something for him to brag about. From my point of view, it helped to put down the myth that jazz players couldn't read. The entire band was composed of jazz players, including Carl Fontana, who got such a kick out of playing the show that he asked for a picture of Merle Evans. A couple of weeks later he received a package from Evans, containing an autographed picture for every member of the band.

At that time Evans was trying to restore the old policy of carrying a band, and he promised me a job if he succeeded. I got a letter from him some time later, saying that he had failed but that I could play his show anytime we were in the same town. It was one of my most fondly remembered compliments.

Soon after the circus job, I decided that I would probably be better off playing in a show band. It was too late to expect to get anywhere as a clarinet player since the rock bands were taking over, and traditional music was just about out. I was also getting older by the day. The only hope left, it seemed to me, was to make a little money and forget about enjoying playing.

It happened that Garwood Van needed an extra saxophone player, so I called him and went to work in the house show band on baritone, tenor, and clarinet. It started as only a temporary augmentation, but Garwood kept hiring me back week after week, and I was there for several weeks. Then the hotel changed to a policy of bringing in Broadway shows with their own conductors. The first show conductor brought his key men, fired everybody in the house band, replaced some with musicians who had come out and put their cards in for that purpose, and hired back a few local men who had been in the band. Most of us were out, but I found being a musical mercenary to be not quite as humiliating as it had been when I was playing shows with dance bands.

The old policy of the Thunderbird had been to bring in acts of high professional stature. The show would open with a line of dancing girls doing a routine to the band's overture. There was some fast-moving clarinet work for all the clarinet players in unison. It was only simple scale and arpeggio stuff that I went through as a matter of course. But I found myself alone—the other reed men weren't playing it, so I asked about it later.

"What about the clarinet work in the opener? Am I supposed to play it?"

"Sure," said the man next to me. "Hey, that was good work."

"I just wondered," I said. "It's unison, isn't it?"

"Yeah, we can't play it."

It is true, despite this incident, that some good players who have not had any show experience get lost after the downbeat and stay lost, whereas experienced show players, even those who are not expert musicians, know where they are and can fake through a show. When I was playing the Chicago Theater, we sometimes had subs from the Chicago Symphony who couldn't keep up with what was going on—one of them knew nothing but the third trombone parts in the symphony numbers. The other reed players in the Thunderbird band were also excellent flute players. There was one that I wanted to take flute lessons from, and one who wanted to take clarinet lessons from me. The arranger for the NBC staff in Chicago had once wanted to trade me lessons in legitimate writing for lessons in jazz writing. Nobody knows everything.

At the Thunderbird I played with the Andrews Sisters, Edie Adams, and Gogi Grant. Twenty-three years had passed since I first played for the Andrews Sisters in Chicago, so I felt a touch of nostalgia about that. Edie Adams and Gogi Grant were impressive performers and persons, and I enjoyed playing their acts, too. It's the big-heads that turn musicians off.

I began to get the message that Las Vegas was not the place for me to be. There was no clarinet work, and out-of-town musicians, mostly from back east, were taking over the show work. Many of them had their jobs before they came to town, despite union rules to the contrary. Leaders would get permission from the union to import a trumpet player, say, because he doubled mandolin, not-withstanding that there is never any call for mandolin. A googol of tricks was used to get by with importations. Whole sections of some bands were made up of men from the same town.

Since Netta was only a few months from high school graduation, I didn't want to leave right away. Besides I was broke again. I'd had my horns in hock so many times that I got to know my "Uncle Ben" personally. I told him once that he could probably play them better than I could by now. I put them in again and applied for a job at the Nevada Test Site. The government security guys took six weeks to check out my background before I got my clearance and went to work. I goldbricked there for two months before pressure to hire minority groups put me out of a job.

By that time Netta had finished high school. She worked through the summer and saved a thousand dollars for college. We moved back to California. Marge, who had been working at a chain drug store in Las Vegas, was able to transfer to a store in Studio City. When Netta left for Colorado State College in Greely, Marge and I had to get used to being alone with each other again for the first time in thirty-two years. We moved back to Hollywood soon after.

20

MARGE'S JOB WAS much better because the salary in California, a union state, was twice what she was paid in Nevada. She got all the fringe benefits, as well, of which there were none in Nevada at that time. I filled in with Pete Daily's band, which included Warren Smith, and then took a job at Big Bear Lake, high up in the San Bernardino mountains about a hundred miles south of Los Angeles—not as the crow flies, but as the mountain road corkscrews out of the city of San Bernardino. It wasn't a music job, though. My half brother, Vic, who was building a big recreation center up there for a church organization, gave me a job as general factotum, including duties as labor foreman over the only laborer—me. I stayed there for nine months, driving home for weekends, until Vic got a job as inspector of construction for the state at UCLA (a fifty-year construction project), and there was nobody to hold my job for me. The church job was almost finished anyway. It was too cold up there in the wintertime to work much, and my job lately had been mostly to watch the place to prevent the kids from stealing the buildings. After Vic left, I worked for a while as a plumber's helper, before I decided I'd had it with physical work. I hadn't touched a horn for over a year, and I was itching to play again.

While I was in Las Vegas, I had been recommended to Freddie Masters, a jazz band leader from New York who had moved his base to Rockford, Illinois. Masters played clubs and military bases around the eastern states and overseas. I had written him a letter at the time, but because I had asked for too much money, he hadn't

hired me. This time when I wrote to him, I told him I would accept whatever salary he could pay, so he hired me, by mail and
telephone. I met him in Rockford, and we drove to Chicago to
pick up Art Santley, his guitar player. From there we went on to
New York to gather the rest of the band—Bobby O'Connor, the
drummer; Bob Dorough, the piano player; and Melodie Lowell, the
singer. Our ultimate destination was Thule, Greenland.

We had one rehearsal, mostly for the singer, before going down
to McGuire Air Force Base in New Jersey for shots and to board the
plane. Everything going in or out of Greenland goes by plane, except that, during the summer (between June and August), the ice-
breakers make it in to deliver the heavy supplies. A few fishing ves-
sels also visit the southern part during summer.

Five hours after taking off, we were in another world. None of
my experiences had prepared me for Greenland. Thule is the name
the Greeks and Romans gave to the northernmost human habita-
tion they had discovered. Greenland's Thule is an Eskimo village
of about a hundred people where the United States maintains an
air base and a Distant Early Warning station. In 1965 there were
about 2,700 air force men there, with two women who were
nurses.

We checked in at the Visitors' Officers Quarters, and the next
day, we were briefed on how to behave while we were in Thule.
(Actually, it was difficult to tell one day from the next because the
sun didn't set.) The briefing officer spent some time explaining the
weather. The wind can change and the temperature can drop to
zero or below, as he put it, "quicker than a cat can lick his ass."
Wind speed might climb to fifty knots per hour. These blizzards,
the officer told us, are graded according to their severity. In a Phase
1 storm it's unsafe to leave the area; Phase 2 means a man doesn't
go outside alone; during a Phase 3 blizzard all outdoor activity
ceases—no one goes outside. An ear or a nose can freeze while a
man is crossing a twenty-foot street, and if touched, will fall off. In
extreme cold, a man can die within fifteen seconds. We were told
to breathe as shallowly as possible to prevent frostbite of our lungs
and never to hurry. The air force issued us parkas and offered us
"iron pants," which are cumbersome insulated chaps to be worn

over regular pants, and mukluks, which are heavy insulated boots. (We were expected to furnish our own gloves.) Masters, who had been there before, told us we wouldn't need the pants and mukluks because we wouldn't be outside any longer than it takes to get from the door to a taxi and back to the door at our terminus.

Besides the weather warnings, the briefing officer gave us some rules to follow. We were told to avoid the women's quarters, for there was an armed guard posted at an observation window twenty-four hours a day who had orders to shoot any intruder. In fact, we never saw either of the women while we were there. We were also warned about smoking grass. "Anyone caught with it up here has had it," the officer said. Finally, we were told to stay at least twenty feet away from the Eskimos to protect them from any virus we might be carrying that they would have no resistance to.

We played three hours a night, including breaks, alternating with two other bands among the three clubs—the officers', the noncoms', and the airmen's. The other bands were a rock-and-roll group and a country-western group.

During my year and a half with Freddie Masters I made five trips to Greenland, all of them much the same, except that three of the trips were to Sondrestrom in the south. We were not USO units, but professionals earning a buck or two, and so some of the groups engaged in a little under-the-table mischief. Their girl singers would turn tricks on the side. Some "groups" were just a few hookers and a pimp. Men who hadn't seen a woman for months were glad to pay a franklin for a lay. At ten tricks a night for four weeks a girl could go home and retire for a while. Two of the girl singers in one of our alternate groups were hookers.

The men were so accustomed to this state of affairs that one of the airmen approached our singer quite openly one night. Melodie slapped him, and that brought Masters over in a hurry. "Stupid," he grated, "there are other ways of turning a man off." The kid was just inexperienced—that was her very first job. Some time later, she came to see me for advice.

"I guess I shouldn't have slapped that kid," she said, "but what's a body gonna do in a case like that?"

"I don't know," I said, "but when a woman waves a hundred dollar bill at me and says 'how about it,' I tell her okay if it's all right with her husband. That usually stops them."

"You're being funny," Melodie said. "What if she says she isn't married?"

"Oh, I have an answer for that, too," I said. "I tell them I've got the clap."

The bizarre conditions there are tough on the men. One day at the base exchange, I overheard a conversation between two airmen. "I've been real jittery lately," one said, "so I went to see the doc about it."

"Yeah? What did he say?" The other one asked.

"He said it was tension."

"And what did he say to do about it?"

"He said to masturbate."

"Hell," his buddy said, "he wouldn't have to tell me that."

Some of the cases aren't so simple, though. There are men who go beserk and others who just sit, staring at the walls. Those who become really disturbed have to be sent home. Something like that happened to Santley. After a week or so in Thule, he stopped speaking to us. He wouldn't even show any signs of recognition except to turn away whenever he met us, and he ignored us on the job. He never said a word to anybody, not even on the way home or when we parted.

I didn't hear any possible causes for the mental problems mentioned, but surely isolation from the world was one of them. There was no television, and local radio was broadcast infrequently. Occasionally, they were able to get long-distance radio by satellite. Mail was delivered by supply planes that came in only about three or four times a month.

We all had strange feelings at times. I attributed mine to the static in the air, which is as good a reason as any for feeling goofy. It's quite a chore to take off or put on a nylon shirt that's sticking to you like a leech because the climate is so dry. The dark winters have an even worse effect, as I discovered later when I spent four weeks in darkness up there. It's a weird feeling to see the full moon circle the earth in full view and to look straight up to find the

North Star, which we think of as a direction finder. Every direction there is south.

We musicians had it a little better than the noncoms and the airmen since we were given the hypothetical rank of a commissioned officer. We ate at the officers' mess and were invited to some of their little parties. The parties were nothing more than bull sessions with tape-recorded music and plenty of booze. There was such a spirit of comradery that the drinkers could always borrow from another quarter's supply, leaving an IOU to replace the stuff later.

A place even more desolate than Thule was the outpost on P mountain, where we were invited to play a concert on one of our nights off. There were only about twenty men, most of them commissioned officers, up there. The trip up was a two-hour drive at fifteen miles per hour. We followed a snow blower on our way out. Off to the sides of the road at intervals were survival huts to be used in case a party got in trouble. They were stocked with food, heaters, and first aid supplies.

About halfway up, we passed an Eskimo whose sled had broken down. The bus driver explained that the man was waiting for help from his own people. He had tried to hitch a ride with our driver on a previous trip that day. "He was waiting here by the road with his dogs," the driver said. "I could have taken him, but man, I wasn't about to take those dogs. They would have torn this bus apart, and me with it."

A blizzard was beginning to blow in just as we reached the outpost. If it had started an hour earlier, we would have been in trouble. As it was, we were phased in while we were there, but there was nowhere to go anyway. The phase lasted for three hours after we played the concert, so we passed the time kidding around with the officers and having breakfast. The officers had their own makeshift amusements. The ice for drinks was in a bed pan; the mixed drinks were served from bed urinals. They put on a parade and concert for us using such instruments as a string on a mop stick, toilet paper tubes, and a few broken instruments. The music was mostly verbal, with some noises on the horns. One officer, who had passed out, lay on the floor, ignored by the others. A good time was had by all. When the phase was over we took off down the mountain, passing the Eskimo on the way back. He was still waiting with his dogs by his broken-down sled.

We went one afternoon to the crowning of the Eskimo queen, the grand event that took place in one of the aircraft hangars. Everybody who wasn't on duty—including the base commander—came to see it. Our ambassador to Denmark was there, along with a few American and Danish dignitaries, and most of the Danish civilians employed on the base also attended. The little girl, dressed in a formal gown, sat there smiling. She didn't seem to know what it was all about.

We had taken taxis to the coronation, but with everybody trying to leave at the same time when it was over, there weren't enough taxis. Since it was a bright, calm day, we decided to walk back rather than wait for the taxi. Although we had less than a mile to walk, the going got tough about halfway there. We made it back to our quarters, but we were exhausted and pretty near freezing when we got there. My windpipe was frostbitten, so I had to go to the base doctor the next day. For a few days afterward, I was a little apprehensive because of the rule that those under a doctor's care don't get to go home. The injury wasn't serious, though, and I managed to fake a cure before it was time to leave.

In the wintertime Thule, in constant darkness, gets much colder. We were once phased in for thirty hours. Each building in the living quarters had its own store of emergency food supplies—perfectly good bread and other stuff left over from World War II. I heard one of the officers estimate the temperature combined with the wind chill factor at more than 120 degrees below zero. No matter how the thermometer registers, it's just as cold as the *wind* says it is.

The rules are a little different in Sondrestrom. Eskimos are allowed in the Danish places, so we saw quite a few of them around, dressed as outsiders. The climate in Sondrestrom is also quite different—not as dry. I once saw it snow there, an unusual occurrence in Greenland. Most storms just blow the snow that's already there.

My southwestern accent came in handy when we got back from Greenland one time. We didn't need passports, but this time we were questioned about our nationalities. Everyone but me had identification that suited the customs inspector, but I didn't even have a driver's license because I didn't own a car at the time.

"Where were you born?" the man asked.

"Mineral Wells, Texas," I said.

"I have a Texan working here," he said. "Wait, I'll get him over here."

When he came back with his Texan he said to me, "Now talk to the man."

I did, running the whole gamut of Texanese.

The Texan laughed. "He's from Texas, all right," he said. "No doubt about *that*. If he wuz any more Texan, even *I* couldn't unnerstan 'im." I was allowed to pass.

The country had become involved in Vietnam, so most of the jets were being used to transport our troops. After our first flight to Thule, we took the four-prop C-118s or chartered civilian planes. These planes had to be refueled at Goose Bay, Labrador, before going on to Thule or Sondrestrom.

Once, while we were waiting to take off back home, I was sitting with a man in civilian clothes who was obviously loaded. He would get up once in a while and stagger around the room, out the doorway, and back. I figured he was going for another nip and wondered who the hell he was. He was in the same condition on the plane for the first hour or two. He kept walking up and down the aisle, and after a while, he sat down by me.

"Well, I finally got this old crate on course," he said.

"What do you mean?" I asked. "What do you have to do with it?"

"Oh, I'm the navigator," he said. "I didn't know where the hell we were for a while."

Another time, when we were heading out of Goose Bay after refueling, one of the four engines failed. To reduce the risk of explosion or fire and to lighten the load, the pilot circled over Baffin

Bay for an hour dumping the fuel. When we landed back at Goose
Bay, the fire fighters and ambulances were waiting, and a helicop-
ter, equipped with foam hoses, hovered above us. We had to spend
two days at Goose, ostensibly for engine repairs, but more likely for
the fishing, for we had heard the crew planning the trip.

We stayed at the Polaris Hotel. I passed some time in the lobby
watching Eskimos lose their money to the slot machines there.
One of them, dressed in the traditional costume of sealskin boots,
fur parka, and fur pants ran out of money. Seeing me standing
there, she came up to me.

"Loan me five dollar?" she asked in pretty good English. "I pay
you back."

I couldn't really afford to throw away five dollars, but this was my
first and only opportunity to meet an Eskimo. I thought I might
learn something about their way of life, so I lent her the five dollars. She lost it and came to me for more, but I refused to invest
any more in her enterprise. Instead, I got her into a conversation
about Eskimo life.

The woman was quite willing to talk to me. She even gave me a
picture of herself, on which she wrote her name, Rachel Henry.
She had been married to an American airman, and had spent two
years with him in Louisiana. After he had deserted her, she had
returned home to Happy Valley, a settlement of a few hundred
souls about seven miles away from the International Base at Goose
Bay. She was working as a maid in a private home.

In turn, I told her who I was and why I happened to be there.
She was sympathetic. "I do anything you want me to do," she said.
I had no interest in getting to know her intimately, though. Eskimo
women are not terribly appealing to a refined sense of smell. As the
old boys used to say back home, she would have stunk a dog off a
gut wagon.

Some time later, on another trip when we played the clubs at
the Goose Bay air base I received a message upon deplaning at the
airport that Rachel Henry was waiting for me in the lobby. It took
some skillful maneuvering on my part to avoid another encounter
with her. Needless to say, I had to take some ribbing from the boys.

Our status at Goose was the same as it had been in Greenland. We were invited to parties and taken on a tour of the Hudson's Bay Company trading post in Happy Valley. One night we went to a Christmas party at Major Short's house. (Some of the officers with families had civilian houses there.) His young and beautiful wife was a clarinet-saxophone player and leader of the base dance band. Their hobby was snowmobiling. After booze had livened things up a bit, the Major took us all, one at a time, on a snowmobile tour of the part of Labrador he claimed as his back yard.

There was a good-looking Canadian woman working in the souvenir concession at the air terminal. We had been there so many times en route to Greenland and back that she had become an old friend. She longed to come to the U.S., and while we were waiting to board the plane home on that trip, she asked me, "Why don't you marry me and take me out of here? You could divorce me after I got set there."

"It's too late for that," I said, "but if this was thirty years ago I'd take you up on the offer." I wonder if she ever made it to the States.

21

BETWEEN VENTURES to the polar region, we made trips to Cuba and Puerto Rico, and we played some clubs and military bases in the eastern states. All of the jobs were for a week or two—Masters didn't play one-nighters. He didn't work all of the time, either. For Masters, the tours were breaks from running a couple of businesses in Rockford. While he was home, tending to business, I would go back to Hollywood to job around until the next tour. Masters paid my fare to and from Rockford for the tours.

I think we might have set a distance record for jumps between engagements once when we went from Thule, near the North Pole, to Jamaica, down near the Equator, and from there to Guantanamo Bay Naval Base in Cuba. We had to approach from Jamaica because Castro only allowed a fifty-mile-wide approach channel. Planes that goofed and flew over Cuban territory were subject to being shot down. After a twenty-four-hour layover, we boarded a small navy transport plane with the other band, the Roy Scott–Meri Ellen group. We were welcomed with a show of brass and a formal to-do. A group of officers, accompanied by the base newsman and a photographer, greeted us. There was a twenty-foot banner on the side of the bus that read: "HELLO STATESIDE REVIEW. WELCOME TO GUANTANAMO BAY, CUBA. WE HOPE YOU ENJOY YOUR VISIT."

The accommodations were grand—a huge house for the men and another for the two girls. Both houses had so many rooms that I never bothered to count them. There were also two refrigerators in each house, stocked with beer and soft drinks. We were given a schedule for each day that showed where and when we were to eat, work, and play. Golfing, swimming, horseback riding, and other activities were compulsory. They were out to show us a good time whether we liked it or not, and of course, we had a ball. The bus and a driver, a Cuban named Pecko Robinson, were on full-time duty to take us around.

The work was a breeze. We alternated forty-five-minute sets with the other group on the jobs and played one television show and a concert on the aircraft carrier *Enterprise*. We also played at an officer's private party after work one night. The invitation was like most of the ones that musicians get: "Y'all come—and don't forget to bring your instruments." The party was a ball. After a few pick-me-ups, we played a few of our special numbers and wound up in a jam session with the other band. There was a woman there who decided I was just what she wanted. Fleeing her was worse than staying with the crowd, because she kept in hot pursuit. The house was encircled by the typical screened veranda, which made a fair track for a foot race, although it wasn't long enough. After a few tags I hid in the crowd.

The flight back from Cuba to Norfolk, Virginia, wasn't nearly as much fun. We went on a troop transport plane that was equipped with one long bench seat along each side of the plane. It was noisy and the cabin wasn't pressurized. Even though we flew low, the altitude, combined with the noise, was hazardous to the ear drums. They issued us wax to put in our ears.

That engagement brought Freddie Masters and Meri Ellen together in a temporary partnership. Freddie also hired Meri's singer–bass player, Russell Jones, and her drummer, Al Page. They were with us for our next tour, which took us to Puerto Rico, where we played the Sheraton Puerto Rico in San Juan. We got our rooms free at the hotel as part of the deal. The job was a nightclub on the ground floor, alternating on the bandstand with another group.

Just before leaving Greenland for San Juan, I had blown another hernia, so most of the time, a local clarinet player filled in for me. Since the patrons expected rock music, we went over on that job like a skunk at a lawn party. I sat at the bar one night, listening to the bartender who was making some derogatory remarks in Spanish about our band. He didn't realize that I was getting the gist of it, so he wasn't very careful about what he said. After a while, I decided to shut him up. "Dame un' otra botella de cerveza, por favor," I said in my best beer-ordering Mexican.

I got the beer—not very graciously—and silence ensued. But I knew what the help thought of us.

Shortly after I got back to Hollywood in January, I tried to make arrangements for another hernia operation, but they couldn't schedule me right away. I called the hospital a few times and got the usual runaround. Finally, about the middle of April, I said to the receptionist, "Look, I'm a musician and I *blow* my instruments. I can't work till I get fixed."

"A musician?" she said. "So is my husband. What do you play?" I told her.

"That's a coincidence," she said. "So does he, and he had to have a hernia fix. Wait just a minute."

I waited, and when she came back, she said, "All right, you are scheduled for the day after tomorrow."

After the operation and some recuperation time, I went to Las Vegas to see what was going on. I went to see Freddy Martin, who was playing at the Top o' the Strip at the Dunes Hotel. He had tried to hire me back when he played Bakersfield, and I hoped he might still want me. He did, but since he would need a pretext for firing the clarinet player he already had, Martin wanted me to learn enough oboe to be able to say I could double on it.

I went home and rented an oboe from Claude Lakey, my old buddy from Harry James's band who now had a big music store in Sepulveda. I had spent a few days mastering the oboe, when I got a call from Thurman Teague. He said Gil Bowers was looking for a saxophone-clarinet player for the touring production of *Hello Dolly*. When I expressed interest, he told me to contact Abe Siegel, the bass player, who was Bowers' close friend. As a result, Bowers called me from somewhere near San Francisco and hired me to join the band a few days later in San Bernardino.

The Broadway shows on tour are governed by the rules of the

American Guild of Variety Artists (AGVA). These rules, which are enforced as strictly as those of a prison, make life on the road so much easier for performers that we wouldn't get rid of one of them.

Time of departure from a town was 9:00 A.M. The bus pulled away from the hotel or motel at exactly that time. Anyone a minute late had to get to the next town on his or her own.

After three hours of travel there was a one-hour stop for lunch—no more, no less. If the destination happened to be only a few minutes away, there had to be a vote on whether to stop for lunch or not. We would only continue on without lunch if the vote were unanimous on both buses. One bus couldn't stop while the other went on.

After lunch we were allowed to travel only four hours more. If the trip took longer because of some mishap or misjudgment, we were paid five dollars an hour overtime for riding.

After the final curtain, we had to be given time to get at least eight hours of sleep, so the ten hours after the final curtain were free time.

We got one day a week off. The rules allowed us to travel on days off as long as we stayed where we were on every fourth day off. If there were a long jump on the travel days off, we went halfway each day for two days. On trips like that we usually stopped out in the middle of nowhere for the night. I suspect the schedules were arranged to make the union's rules backfire on the performers—employers' revenge. The places we had to spend the night were surely the only conspicuous drawback to traveling under AGVA rules.

Once, on a two-day jump fromn Albuquerque to Sacramento, we stopped at a motel out in the desert near Seligman, Arizona, only 180 miles from Las Vegas. We had had to spend the previous day in Albuquerque because it was our no-travel day off. Most of the show's people, having never been to Las Vegas, would have preferred to travel on the day off or to go the extra miles on their own time. We had to go to Las Vegas the next morning anyway to catch a plane from there to Sacramento. Some of the more eager kids chartered a small plane in Seligman and flew in for the night, but the rest of us spent a dreary night in the hinterlands.

Another time, on the way from Portland, Oregon, we took the tortuous route down the Pacific coast as far as Santa Cruz, California, on our way to Fresno. We spent our night off that time in Crescent City, California, with about the same accommodations as Seligman had offered. I asked our bus driver why we didn't go down the Highway 5 expressway. "The office routes us," he said. "We can't change anything. I think they're afraid somebody might go out and get drunk and have a hangover on the show." I figured that was more likely to happen in a little rolled-up town like that as a sort of revenge.

On another two-day jump we spent a lonely night off in a motel in Minnesota across the Red River from Fargo, South Dakota. I don't know why we couldn't have stayed in Fargo.

All hotel or motel rooms were reserved a week in advance. We were given a choice of two hotels. Their names and rates were posted backstage and each member of the cast, crew, and orchestra signed under the name of the one he or she preferred. Usually, we all signed for the same place. On arrival our keys would be waiting for us, each in a separate envelope with the person's name on it. We didn't even have to register because the manager would take care of that chore.

The bus drivers loaded and unloaded our baggage for us. Since the tours were long (about nine months), it was practical to have two bags—one containing things for immediate use and one with others for future use. The drivers learned which ones to take off and which to leave on the bus. If we were playing as long as a week, they knew to take them both off. The buses would also take us to work if the theater were more than a couple of blocks away.

Everything possible was done for the convenience of the cast and musicians. It's a complete contrast to the ordeal that dance bands are put through when they travel. After getting used to touring with a road show, it can be quite a shock going back to dance-band tours. Most of the musicians were New Yorkers who hadn't done much traveling with dance bands and, therefore, didn't realize the difference in conditions. They would complain about things that seemed like luxury to me.

One other consideration that made traveling more bearable was the unwritten code that made peace and quiet the rule on the bus. There was no piped-in music, no radios or tape players, no loud talking, and no horseplay. Actually, almost everybody on the show was a loner, especially on the buses.

There were thirteen musicians on our bus. The other passengers were the ladies' hairdresser, the "book" man who passed out programs in the theater lobbies, a few of the dancers and bit players, and a few dogs and cats. The principals were in the other bus, and the star, Dorothy Lamour, traveled in her own Cadillac with her husband, Bill Howard.

The sets and props were transported in two trucks, and the stage crew and the wardrobe man rode in another bus. These units left after packing up at night to get there ahead of time so they could set everything up in the next theater. Their bus was equipped with bunk beds for the night travel.

I didn't know any of the boys in the band before I joined it, except former Chicagoan Frank Pichl, the bass player. Most of them were show musicians—good ones—rather than jazz players. They were accustomed to playing the shows as a sit-down job back home, and so they considered touring to be emergency work. The hiring forms ran from the beginning of the tour in September till mid-tour, which meant that a performer couldn't quit or be terminated before the form expired around the end of January. At that time anyone who was staying on signed another form for the rest of the tour.

We played the last six weeks of the tour with *Dolly* at the original Theater in the Round in Lambertville, New Jersey. At first all of us stayed in a motel across the Delaware River in Hope, Pennsylvania, but eventually everyone but the guitar player, who had his own car, and me moved to Lambertville to be near the theater. I preferred to stay in Hope to develop my friendship with Dr. H. W. Gabriel, author, ghostwriter, editor, and literary consultant. He was a fund of information on all sorts of subjects, and he introduced me to some of the interesting residents of Bucks County, Pennsylvania.

After a hiatus of a year and two months, which I spent with Freddie Masters, playing overseas and in clubs around the East again, I toured with another road show—*Cabaret*.

One of the few big bands still struggling along was the Glenn Miller band, which was then under the direction of Buddy DeFranco. We ran across the Miller band in Akron, Ohio, while I was with *Dolly* when their bus pulled in at the hotel right behind ours. They were playing a one-nighter at that hotel. I got back from work that night in time to catch the band's last set, after which I spent a few minutes with DeFranco in his room. He wasn't exactly ecstatic about doing one-nighters, he said, but he didn't mind the thousand dollars a week. He told me their next stop was Lexington, Kentucky. Two years later, our *Cabaret* buses had just pulled up in front of a hotel in Lexington, Kentucky, when the Miller bus again pulled in behind us, and again I saw DeFranco. "Well," I said, "it sure took you a long time to get here."

Gil Bowers was satisfied with my work and my behavior. He told me once that I could have a job with him any time he had one for himself as conductor. Since the favorable work and travel conditions made road show tours seem like paid vacations to someone like me who had traveled with dance bands, I began to think about finishing my career playing the bus-and-truck shows. I wasn't a kid anymore at sixty-five, but I still found the work easy. There was a problem to consider, however. The New York shows usually don't hire people outside of New York because the union requires them to pay the musician's transportation to and from New York. I would have had to either move to New York or impose on Bowers to "talk me on." Although he had succeeded in getting me hired for *Cabaret*, I was afraid the string pulling would get to be too much of a hassle if it went on.

22

I WENT BACK to Hollywood after *Cabaret* closed in Montreal. Since Gil Bowers didn't go out as conductor that year, I had to find other work, and decided to try Las Vegas again. When I ran into Charlie Teagarden at the union club, I asked him if he knew of any job openings. It happened that Jack Morgan, who had become the leader of the Russ Morgan band after his father's death, needed a lead saxophone player. Teagarden called him and recommended me for the job, and Morgan agreed to see me. I was a little uneasy about playing lead sax because, since I'd specialized in jazz clarinet, I'd always taken the third saxophone chair—the clarinet chair. I just wasn't as good on sax as on clarinet. When I told Teagarden about this, he arranged for me to begin on second alto, instead.

I was still worried because I had heard that Morgan was tough on his men. Nevertheless, I went to his house for an interview. Morgan had apparently accepted Teagarden's recommendation of my musical ability, for he didn't ask about my experience. He simply wanted to know if I could put up with the hardships of touring and if I was sober on the job. My answers must have satisfied him because he hired me. It was the beginning of six years with Morgan's band.

We started a tour of one-nighters in Albuquerque, New Mexico. The tour covered forty towns and fifteen states, mostly in the Midwest and Southwest in twelve weeks. We covered most states more than once, going, for example, from New Mexico to South Dakota, down to Texas, east to Illinois, west to Colorado, and back to Iowa; then from there to Kansas, and from Kansas to Arkansas, to

Nebraska, to Oklahoma, to Wisconsin. Not every jump was direct, but there weren't many stops along the way either. The last jump we made was from San Antonio, Texas, to Las Vegas.

This wasn't the luxury travel I did with the shows, but it wasn't too bad after we got started on a jump—getting started was the problem. The departure time that was always set only meant that we wouldn't leave any *sooner*. Actually, we invariably left thirty minutes to two hours later. We usually arrived at our destination just in time to set up and start playing, no matter how long or how short the jump was, and sometimes we were late. Frequently, running late robbed us of our lunch and dinner stops. We played some jobs without having eaten since breakfast. Sometimes, because we didn't have time to check in for the night, we had to change into our uniforms in the ballroom's toilet.

This slapdash way of traveling is typical for dance bands. Although the musicians' union has rules similar to those of the AGVA, the bookers and leaders don't pay much attention to them, and the union doesn't try to enforce them. To complain about rule infractions is to rebel against the leader himself. Such things are taken personally, unlike rebellions against a faceless businessman in a New York or Hollywood office somewhere. So to stay in the good graces of a leader, the sidemen don't make waves. They just gripe among themselves about annoyances. Occasionally, I've seen a group of sidemen get together and elect spokesmen to present their gripes to their leaders, but inevitably, when the time came, everybody backed out, leaving the spokesmen holding the bag.

After that twelve-week tour, we had a few days off for Christmas. I thought of quitting the band but decided against it. I'd gotten used to the traveling again and had made friends with Morgan, so I thought I might as well finish my career with the band. There was a possibility that the band would go back to the Dunes Hotel in Las Vegas, where it had been for several years before Jack took over. The band had been playing one-nighters for five months before I joined it. While we were laying off, Jack succeeded in booking us back into the Dunes to open in late February.

In the interim we toured for nine weeks—five of them at the Willowbrook Ballroom in Willow Springs, Illinois, near Chicago.

Because the Chicago local limited musicians to a five-day work week, we booked out two days a week at jobs that had to be at least seventy miles away from Chicago. Once we played Green Bay, Wisconsin, one day and Austin, Texas, the next. Of course, we had to fly to Austin and actually spent less time than usual in transit. We even got some sleep in Austin, which was a welcome break, for we hadn't slept the night before in Green Bay. Since the job, playing Governor Dolph Briscoe's inaugural ball, was important to Morgan, he payed our motel bills as a bonus.

What solo work there was in the band was for trumpet and tenor sax, but there were no jazz solos except in some of the old stock arrangements and two of the flashy show numbers. The flash numbers were used to close the sets before intermissions. Their length could be modified according to how much time we had to fill. There was a spot for me in each number, but it was used only when the time allowed. Usually, because Morgan didn't like clarinet, my solos were omitted. We also had a Woody Herman arrangement, which had a clarinet solo, but we seldom played it because it was not in the Morgan style. Since my clarinet work amounted to about one solo a month—not enough to keep up a lip—I asked Morgan to eliminate my solos altogether.

When the band opened at the Dunes in February, 1971, I decided to move back to Las Vegas and began looking for a house to buy. For the remaining five and a half years that I spent with Morgan, we played two four-month shifts a year at the Dunes and made two tours a year.

Our drummer was Ray Cooper, a Britisher just over from London, where he had worked in all types of bands for a long time. While I was sharing an apartment with him and our piano player, Ray Andrews, during the five weeks in Willow Springs, Cooper had learned that I knew Harry James. He had long been a James fan and had even written Harry for a photograph. Harry was playing at the Desert Inn Lounge in Las Vegas, and Cooper wanted to meet him. I arranged to meet Cooper at the Desert Inn on our night off to try to introduce him, although I wasn't sure that I would have the chance.

On the appointed night I took Margie Drew along. Cooper brought his wife and another couple and we got tables in front of the band. Knowing that Harry wouldn't be able to see us in the audience because of the spotlights in his eyes, I told Margie to write him a note, "Margie Drew and Pooge are here." When the waitress handed Harry the note, she indicated where we were sitting.

We went on with our conversation, and pretty soon Harry began talking on the mike. I wasn't paying attention to what he was saying, until Margie nudged me. "Daddy, he's talking about you!"

"Ladies and gentlemen," he was saying, "I'm going to do something tonight that I have never done before—introduce a guest in the house." He went on to say a few things about our association in the old days and asked me to stand up and take a bow. I was flattered to be the only one Harry had ever thus distinguished. No doubt, during his long career, he had had quite a few real celebrities in his audiences.

I went to the bar by the stage door to wait for his break. There, I ran into Murray Arnold, whose group was alternating with Harry and his band. Twenty-four years before when Murray had replaced Jack Fina in Freddy Martin's band, I had met him while he was sitting in with the band for a few days to break in before Jack and I left. Even though that was the extent of our acquaintance, he remembered me. We visited at the bar till Harry took his break.

He and I had a drink together, after which Harry was delighted to go to the table with me to meet my friends and see Margie Drew. While he was with us at the table, Murray Arnold took his turn at talking to the audience about me, exaggerating a bit about our long friendship, but making it seem to the audience that I was of some importance in the music business. I was more surprised at his attention to me than I had been at Harry's, but Las Vegas is the place for such doings because visitors like to feel that they're on the inside.

I made many new friends in our semiannual tours, and since we covered about the same territory each time, every town began to seem like home. The tours were rough, but so was playing at the Dunes, where we did six hours a night, as opposed to four hours a night on tour. To my way of thinking, it was a toss up whether the hotel or the tours were more tolerable to a musically jaded rounder like me. Both were boring after a month or so, but the one-nighters were more adventurous. On a one-nighter anything might happen—nothing ever happened at the hotel. Even though I was weary of playing the same music, the same way, in the same order every night, I was just as alert as always to what was going on in the world—to people's changing manners, morals, and inhibitions. The best way to keep up with such changes is to travel and observe. For that reason I almost always preferred traveling to staying in one place.

One of the annoyances that sidemen must endure when traveling is compulsory visiting with fans. Those who invited us went to a lot of trouble and expense, but nobody really enjoyed it. Since Morgan was a socializer by nature, our visits were too numerous to list. Some of them were for dinner or lunch, and some just for a couple of hours of howdying and knee-slapping, but inevitably, there was a tour of the house. Every visit cut into our sleep time, for we would have to get up and on our way earlier in order to make them.

For about four years, or eight tours, we traveled in vans—seven of the men and their personal luggage in one van and Morgan, Ray Andrews, and I with the big instruments, the books, and the stands in the other. Those in the first van didn't have to make all of the drop-in visits. They only attended the command dinners, lunches, and after-work parties and breakfasts, but Ray and I had to make them all.

I remember on one occasion the jump was from Des Moines to Springfield, Missouri, about 350 miles by the map. We were late getting started because of a flat tire so that it was already ten o'clock by the time we left. Such a distance was a good ten-hour trip in a heavily loaded van over secondary highways. Nevertheless, Morgan had met a couple at the ballroom the night before, who lived about eighty miles south of Des Moines, and we decided to drop by and visit them. The woman cooked a meal, and we ate, and still we sat around gabbing. I reminded Morgan that time was running short, but he paid no heed. Finally, I got desperate. "Jack," I said, "we've got only five hours to make over 250 miles, we'd better get going."

As it turned out, because Ray neglected to open a fold in the map when he was figuring the mileage, Morgan thought we had only 150 miles to go. What followed was one of the wildest of all the wild rides I made with that band. We ran a gauntlet of cars and trucks for five hours, stopping only for gas. To make things worse, we had a heavy rain most of the way. At a quarter to nine we pulled up in front of the Grove Supper Club in Springfield. The other men were waiting for us, and they unloaded our van and set up the band while we changed clothes in the men's room. Morgan even managed a quick shave, and we made the downbeat at exactly nine o'clock.

There are a couple of good things about arriving late, though. The waiting crowds make heroes out of us, as if we have made a superhuman effort for them. Then, too, the people feel like insiders, seeing something of us offstage. Most people are like the little kids who love to watch the circus unload and set up. The musicians take a little pride in their efficiency, too. In Morgan's band we did our own setting up. The huskier guys unloaded, while the less brawny guys set up the stands. One man would pass out the stand lights; another would hook them up. One set the books by the stands and, in emergencies, opened the case and put the music on the stands. Doing it all in fifteen minutes was a pretty good display of teamwork.

Aside from the loss of time, there were other things that made those visits unpleasant. Some hosts bored us playing old Russ Morgan records the whole time we were there, as if we didn't hear enough of the music out of our own horns four hours a night. Some of them spent the time showing us evidence that other bands had been there—autographed photos, the bed where so-and-so slept, and the bottle he drank from. Once, I got so shaky after enduring a combination of inflictions for three hours, that I couldn't stand it any longer. I went out and sat in the van.

"What's the matter?" said Morgan when he came out, "You sick or something?"

"Yeah," I said, "sick of those phonies. That's one time I could have used a drink."

"Why didn't you say so? Hell, the old lady was loaded."

"She wasn't drunk enough to be generous with her booze, and I never ask for a drink."

"She's a closet alcoholic," he explained. "Come on, I'll buy you a drink."

We once drove thirty miles after work, through a pouring rain in the back country of Tennessee for bacon and eggs—a waste of four hours sleep time. The host was drunk when we got there and passed out when we left.

Morgan was always very concerned about our health. He insisted on taking anyone ill or injured to a doctor right away. Once when we came into Chicago at four in the morning, I complained of a sore throat. After we had checked into a hotel, Morgan ordered me to bed and went all over downtown Chicago until he found a place to buy a remedy for it. There were many such attentive gestures to the sidemen. He would also give us bonuses for enduring special hardships and pay us extra for the tours.

Morgan was a critical boss on the job, but otherwise, he was just one of the guys. He had a marvelous sense of humor offstage. We arrived in Carlisle, Kentucky in midafternoon one day and found it deserted. There wasn't a soul on the streets. Nevertheless, through some mysterious spy system, the dance promoter heard that we were in town, and he came to let us into the joint. He had a boy with him, making the visible population of the town *two*. Morgan asked about hotel or motel accommodations and was told—not surprisingly—that there weren't any. "But there's a rooming house up the street," the kid said. "I'll run up and see if the old woman has any rooms for you." The kid was back in a few minutes. "She's out at Buzzard's Roost," he said, "and won't be back till about five."

"Buzzard's *Roost*!" Morgan said. "Where is that?"

"Out in the country a few miles," the kid said.

"Out in the *country*?! What the hell do you call this?"

We had never heard of Carlisle before, but to make things even, the folks there had never heard of the Russ Morgan band. We had to drive to Lexington for rooms that night.

Most of the dances we played were for couples, but some of the ballrooms in the big cities catered to singles. Some ballrooms had stag sections occupied mostly by spectator-listeners, not dancers, while others featured "stag night" once a week. There were quite a few stag women around, most of them older ladies out on a nostalgia binge. They had "known Russ Morgan personally" thirty years ago and wanted to hear his music again and to see his son.

Most of the men in the band were also up in years. Morgan knew full well that a bunch of kids wouldn't have been convincing when what people expected was the original Russ Morgan Orchestra. Even we older ones were suspect, but we received a little of the leftover adulation, anyway.

It was good to see that the sexual revolution had also reached into the ranks of the geriatric set, where it belongs. The elderly are more starved for romance than the young. I began to be more conscious of it one night in Dallas at the Wintergarden Ballroom. I was sitting at a table with some people I had met on a break—a man, his wife, and his mother. The mother was gushing over me a little, and she even made a few tentative verbal passes at me.

"My mother likes you," the man remarked, ostensibly joking. "Why don't you come home with us? I think she needs some attention." He nudged his wife and chuckled. "We won't watch."

I went along with the gag. "I'm not a closet lover," I said. "I'm an exhibitionist. No spectators, no performance."

23

THE TOURS WERE not all bad. After we would get physically numb and mentally rum-dum, we became travel-happy. We'd laugh over anything, whether it was funny or not. But in 1976 something happened that we couldn't laugh at.

By that time, Morgan had switched from vans to a bus. It was a converted motor home that wasn't designed for such travel, so something was always going wrong with it. After work on a job in Dyersburg, Tennessee, the bus wouldn't start. Some guests took us to our motel, and the next morning Morgan had the bus taken to a repair shop. We had to check out of the motel at noon and wait outside until about three o'clock when Morgan brought the bus back.

While we were waiting, I spent most of the time with Brodie Shroff. We sat on our suitcases and talked about our futures. We were both ready to retire. Brodie was sixty-two. He had been with Morgan about eight years, and he was tired of the band business. He was interested in antiques and had been collecting things on the tours, but this was going to be his last tour, he told me. He intended to find a little town that he liked, open an antiques store, and play once in a while just for kicks. He had looked at a couple of stores on this tour but hadn't yet decided where he wanted to settle. Maybe, he said, he would go to New Orleans for a few years first to play in a jazz band.

The next job was in a joint outside of Batchtown, Illinois. The little town is on a strip between the Mississippi and Ohio rivers, near the point where they converge. They use a ferryboat to cross the Mississippi there because the nearest bridge is forty-five miles upriver. We had often taken the ferry when we were playing there or when we passed through the area. This time, though, we arrived at 8:15—about fifteen minutes late. Since the ferry wouldn't be back for several hours, it looked as if we would miss the job.

Morgan called the joint's boss across the river to explain. The boss thought we would be able to make it across in motor-boats, and he arranged to have two of them pick us up. We sidemen didn't know about it until the boats arrived, and Morgan announced that we were to cross the river in them. I thought he must be kidding, but he and some of the men began loading the boats with the instruments and equipment. These were little flat-bottomed fishing boats, about sixteen feet long and four feet wide, with outboard motors. They had been designed to hold no more than five persons.

It was May; some of the men had put their topcoats on because it was getting chilly. It was already dark and the little settlement there supplied the only light to work by.

There were eleven of us, counting Morgan's fiancee, Bonnie Mock, who lived nearby and was going to the date with us. There had been lots of changes in personnel while I was with the band, but at that time our trumpet players were Vincent Shank, Dale "Brodie" Shroff, and Harlan "Hal" Hafner; Harold "Gus" Ehrmann, Arno Marsh, and I were on saxes; Theodore "Ted" Snyder was on bass; Russell "Russ" Black played piano; Edward "Eddie" Julian was the drummer; and Jack Morgan played trombone.

The boats took the instruments and equipment over first, accompanied by Morgan in one and Snyder in the other to unload them on the other side. Only the boat owned by the club's boss came back, though. The other belonged to a man who didn't want to make a second crossing because the river was pretty rough at that spot, and besides, he was late for dinner.

There were twelve of us, including the boatman, to make the trip in a boat built for five. Morgan wanted the man to make two trips, but the guy insisted that it was all right for all of us to go together. It wasn't.

We started off slow, and about forty yards out the driver gunned the motor. I was in the back of the boat, a three-seater, and suddenly from up front, I heard Eddie Julian shout, "Hey! We're going under!" Arno Marsh, who was sitting beside him, joined in the shouting. It was too dark to see well, but we felt the sudden rush of water on our feet. Morgan and Bonnie were in the seat in front of me and I remember Morgan's graphic shout of surprise only too well: "Hey! What the shit is *this?!*"

The boat simply dived under the surface. In a matter of seconds we were all in the river—fully dressed in our uniforms. Bonnie's foot was hung up in something in the boat, which was underwater by then. Morgan went down and got her foot loose, and he and Bonnie started swimming toward the shore. Shank, Hafner, Ehrmann, and I started for shore, too, but Marsh and Julian couldn't swim. They and Shroff, who was a few feet behind the boat, began shouting for help.

The boat had overturned, trapping some air that kept it afloat, so Black yelled to me when I had swum about thirty feet toward shore to come back, that the boat was floating. There was nothing to hold on to on the bottom of the boat, so Black shoved Julian and Marsh up far enough to reach over and hold onto the opposite edge. When I got back to the boat, he did the same for me. None of us could have made it without those boosts.

Snyder, the boatman, and Black were also hanging on to the boat. It began to sink on the side everyone was clinging to and to rise on the other. We were hanging on at an angle of about forty-five degrees. "There are too many of us," Black said. "You guys try to hang on. I'm going to try for shore." All of us were yelling to people that we could see in their yards onshore, but they couldn't hear us because someone was using a big gasoline-powered lawn mower. Of course, they couldn't see us either.

We were drifting downstream in the meantime, and we hit a few rough spots—the river has lots of little whirlpools along the shorelines. The boat was just perched there on one side and could have flipped over at any moment. It was a touchy situation for us, and we had no way of knowing if any of the others would make it to the shore.

Having been an Eagle Scout as a kid, I was a pretty good swimmer. I hadn't been swimming in many years and wasn't in good shape for it, but at least I knew what to do. Besides, I tend to remain calm in emergencies and feel a delayed effect later. So far, I had stayed afloat by treading water, swimming mostly upright, and keeping my head up. (I noticed later that I didn't even get my hair wet.) Julian and Marsh were panicky, but Snyder, although he was yelling to the people on shore, didn't panic. "Just hold on and be as still as you can!" I yelled. "You might tip us over! So far, we're safe!"

The tux shoes I was wearing were pretty heavy. I managed to toe one of them off while hanging on to the boat, with my legs still in the water, but I couldn't get the other one off with a bare foot. I wanted to lighten myself as much as possible in case I had to swim again, but I couldn't take anything else off while holding on to the boat. I was already panting, and my heart was racing, but I was determined to hold on as long as I could. The others were in the same kind of trouble. It's tiring even to hang on to something.

After twenty minutes, when the lawn mower finally stopped, and we saw people running around, we began to have some hope. A boat caught up with us about a hundred yards downstream. Hafner, dressed only in his briefs, was in the rescue boat holding flares. We learned later that he had taken off all his clothes in the water, which was quite a feat. He and the man with him, a settlement citizen, got us off the capsized boat and into the rescue boat.

The man wanted to save the other boat, so he fastened a rope to it. We started back upstream toward the settlement, but with all the weight and the other boat in tow we weren't making any headway. Then the plug came out of a repaired hole on the bottom of the rescue boat, and water began gushing in. "This one's going to sink too!" Snyder yelled to the driver. "Cut the goddamn boat loose and let's go!"

"Put your hand over the hole!" the driver yelled.

"I'm trying," Snyder said. "I can't hold it. Cut the boat loose!"

The man reluctantly cut the rope, and we started to make progress, reaching the landing just in time.

We in the boat didn't know if anybody besides Hafner had made it back. Finally, though, everybody was accounted for except Brodie Shroff. Ironically, Bonnie Mock had come upon Shroff's trumpet case floating down the river and had held on to it, using its buoyancy to help her to get to shore.

The Coast Guard came to search the river and the shore downstream. They found a package of my cigarettes and a little empty plastic bottle, which I had drained of vodka while waiting to board the boat, washed up on shore. That gave us some hope that Shroff, too, might have made it to shore with the drift. But the next day, his body was found a few miles downstream.

By strange coincidence only a few weeks before the boat accident, Warren Smith had drowned in California. I had gotten a letter from Thurman Teague telling me the details of Smitty's death, and because I knew they were friends—at one time Smitty had played in Shroff's little jazz band—I'd taken Shroff the letter to read. Later, I'd given him a Xerox copy of it. We had talked about Smitty's death again that day before leaving Dyersburg.

We were scheduled to play in South Bend, Indiana, the following night, so we left on the midnight ferry. Friends from all over that part of the country came to see us and give us their sympathy. All of the reports had been inaccurate, and people were anxious to hear what had actually happened, and to make sure that we were all right. We got a standing ovation, but a very sad one for us, when we set up to play.

I had not decided definitely when I would retire from the band—even after the disaster—although I knew it would be soon. Not wanting to cause Morgan any inconvenience, I left it up to him to decide. I played the Dunes for another four months, made another tour, and went back to the Dunes. As time went on, it became more saddening all the time to play the same jobs in the same towns with the ghost of my best friend on the bandstand. I became depressed and a little fearful of what might happen next, feeling that the law of averages would catch up to me sooner or later. I had survived quite a few near-fatal scrapes already.

After fifty-two years in the music business, I left the band in September, 1976, the last of the members of the 1970 band to leave. I am proud of a two-part letter I received from Jack Morgan after leaving. The first part was a friendly farewell; the second part, designed as a recommendation to future employers, was a favorable appraisal of my character and my services. He made a point to mention that this was the only written recommendation he had ever made. I showed it to Charlie Teagarden because he had been the one to recommend me to Morgan. "You ought to have that framed and hang it on the wall," Teagarden said.

Epilogue

RETIRING FROM THE Morgan band didn't mean that I was retiring from the music business altogether. I had no intention of "pissing on the fire and calling in the dogs," as Morgan put it in his letter. I couldn't quit cold turkey after all those years. All I wanted was a little hiatus between combat missions.

I had thought I would become nostalgic when I began writing this account, but nostalgia about music seems to be for the listeners, not the players. I found that I was looking at these incidents quite abstractly, as though they'd happened to someone else. Even though I hadn't thought much about any of these things since shortly after they occurred, I discovered when I began to concentrate on them that they were as vivid in my mind as if they had happened yesterday.

I only regret that I didn't have all the fun there was to be had. As much fun as there was, there still wasn't enough to go around. It's true that the music business is phony, but it's more fun than working. I have used the term *working* throughout this book merely to dignify the profession. Everybody knows we don't work; I've heard them all say it. We just get paid for having fun. We musicians are supposed to show enjoyment on the bandstand whether we feel it or not, but it is good, nonetheless, to have the chance to earn a living doing something that pleases you.

I long ago embraced the talmudic philosophy that man is held to account for all the permitted pleasures he failed to enjoy, so I intend to find whatever fun there is left. Maybe I will live long enough to capitalize on being old, as others have done. There is always something in the offing. It's even possible that noise will go out and music will come back someday, but as Pope wrote, "Blessed is he who expects nothing, for he shall never be disappointed."

Index